THE SUPREME COURT'S NEW WORKPLACE

The US Supreme Court has systematically eroded the rights of minority workers through subtle changes in procedural law. This accessible book identifies and describes how the Supreme Court's new procedural requirements create legal obstacles for civil-rights litigants, thereby undermining their substantive rights. Seiner takes the next step of providing a framework that practitioners can use to navigate these murky waters, allowing workers a better chance of prevailing with their claims. Seiner clearly illustrates how to effectively use his framework, applying the proposed model to one emerging sector – the on-demand industry. Many minority workers now face pervasive discrimination in an uncertain legal environment. This book will serve as a roadmap for successful workplace litigation and a valuable resource for civil-rights research. It will also spark a debate among scholars, lawyers, and others in the legal community over the use of procedure to alter substantive worker rights.

Joseph A. Seiner is Professor at the University of South Carolina School of Law. He was lead counsel in the US Courts of Appeals in employment-discrimination cases as an appellate attorney with the US Equal Employment Opportunity Commission in Washington, DC. Professor Seiner has been featured in a number of publications, including the *New York Times* and *Wall Street Journal*.

The Supreme Court's New Workplace

PROCEDURAL RULINGS AND SUBSTANTIVE WORKER RIGHTS IN THE UNITED STATES

JOSEPH A. SEINER

University of South Carolina

CAMBRIDGE
UNIVERSITY PRESS

CAMBRIDGE
UNIVERSITY PRESS

University Printing House, Cambridge CB2 8BS, United Kingdom

One Liberty Plaza, 20th Floor, New York, NY 10006, USA

477 Williamstown Road, Port Melbourne, VIC 3207, Australia

4843/24, 2nd Floor, Ansari Road, Daryaganj, Delhi – 110002, India

79 Anson Road, #06-04/06, Singapore 079906

Cambridge University Press is part of the University of Cambridge.

It furthers the University's mission by disseminating knowledge in the pursuit of education, learning, and research at the highest international levels of excellence.

www.cambridge.org
Information on this title: www.cambridge.org/9781316502808
DOI: 10.1017/9781316481141

First published 2017

Printed in the United States of America by Sheridan Books, Inc.

A catalogue record for this publication is available from the British Library.

Library of Congress Cataloging-in-Publication Data
Names: Seiner, Joseph A, author.
Title: The Supreme Court's new workplace: procedural rulings and substantive worker rights in the United States / Joseph A. Seiner.
Description: New York: Cambridge University Press, 2017. |
Includes bibliographical references and index.
Identifiers: LCCN 2017008237 | ISBN 9781107137998 (hardback) |
ISBN 9781316502808 (paperback)
Subjects: LCSH: Discrimination in employment – Law and legislation – United States. |
Discrimination in employment – Law and legislation – United States – Cases. |
Civil rights – United States. | Employee rights – United States. | Class actions
(Civil procedure) – United States. | Minorities – Employment – United States. |
United States. Supreme Court.
Classification: LCC KF3464.S457 2017 | DDC 344.7301/133–dc23
LC record available at https://lccn.loc.gov/2017008237

ISBN 978-1-107-13799-8 Hardback
ISBN 978-1-316-50280-8 Paperback

This book is dedicated to Alice Ann Seiner. Thanks for being such a loving, encouraging, and wonderful mother, and for always being there for me.

– J. A. S.

Contents

Illustrations

Tables

Preface

I love workplace law.

Early in my legal career I was struck by the impact procedural issues could have on employment claims. I saw first hand how few, if any, cases actually make it to trial. As an appellate attorney at the US Equal Employment Opportunity Commission, I began to fully understand how many companies would attempt to use procedural tactics to prevail in their cases, regardless of how strong the evidence of discrimination was in the matter against them. Procedure has always been something that has greatly interested me. The intersection between procedure and workplace law is one of undeniable significance.

Much of the literature and scholarship after Title VII of the Civil Rights Act of 1964 was enacted focused primarily on theory. Over time, however, theory has given way to procedure and now success in an employment-discrimination matter often turns on how adept attorneys are at maneuvering procedurally within a particular case. This trend has been mirrored in the federal courts, culminating in the last decade with numerous Supreme Court decisions on procedural questions that directly impact employment issues.

The Supreme Court, under the direction of Chief Justice John Roberts, has begun to chip away at the substantive protections offered to civil-rights victims and workplace litigants under the auspices of procedural rulings. Often dry, these cases frequently fail to attract public attention. Indeed, as discussed in this text, perhaps the most significant ruling undermining the substantive rights of civil-rights plaintiffs in years came in the context of an antitrust case. It thus likely went unnoticed by many civil-rights practitioners.

This book combines my passions for employment law and civil procedure by explaining how these Supreme Court procedural decisions have impacted worker rights. It is not enough to simply identify the problem. Rather, I also offer here a framework that litigants can successfully use to navigate the procedural minefield created by this case law. To help the practitioners and the courts I have put this framework in context rather than simply formulating an abstract theory that would be difficult to use in actual practice. Thus, I apply my proposed framework to one emerging area of the law – litigation by workers in the on-demand economy. Applying the theory to workers in the technology sector helps identify many of the advantages and shortcomings of the model offered here.

No approach is perfect. At the end of the day, only congressional intervention can completely remedy the existing problems facing the civil-rights community. In the meantime, however, this framework allows litigants to minimize the dangers of allowing many viable civil-rights claims to go unresolved.

It is impossible to write a comprehensive work on labor and employment law alone, and this text is no different in that regard, having benefited from the assistance of numerous individuals. I would like to thank a number of students at the University of South Carolina School of Law, including Megan Clemency, Elliot Condon, Chelsea Evans, Arden Lowndes, and Emily Rummel. The book also benefited from the helpful assistance of Inge Kutt Lewis. Finally, without the extraordinary efforts of Vanessa L. McQuinn, this book would not have been possible.

Those in the academic community were extraordinarily helpful in providing suggestions and insight into this topic. Earlier versions of this book were presented at the Duke University School of Law and the University of Indiana School of Law as part of symposia held at those schools. As this book is the culmination of research conducted throughout my career, I am indebted to all of those in the academic community who helped me to formulate my thoughts in this area. I offer special thanks to Suja Thomas, who has helped pave the way on scholarship related to the intersection of procedure and employment law. I would also like to acknowledge the superb co-authors of two of my works relied upon in this text, Benjamin Gutman and Benjamin Means. Finally, I would like to thank Dean Robert Wilcox at the University of South Carolina School of Law for his support in the development of this work and for all of the research assistance provided by the law school.

As an early note to this text, I would like to disclose that I directly worked as an attorney on a number of the cases discussed in this book while at the US Equal Employment Opportunity Commission (EEOC). The opinions expressed in this book in no way reflect the views of the EEOC or the US government. I would like to acknowledge the superb efforts of those at the EEOC who work so diligently to eradicate discrimination in the workplace.

This text naturally flows out of my previous research and scholarship, which examines the intersection of employment law and civil procedure. For certain topics and discussions, I refer the readers to a number of articles set forth here, on which this book relies:

Chapter 2, "Access to the Courts," draws heavily from the following articles: Joseph A. Seiner & Benjamin N. Gutman, "Does *Ricci* Herald a New

Disparate Impact?," *Boston University Law Review* 90 (2010): 2181; Joseph A. Seiner, "Plausibility Beyond the Complaint," *William & Mary Law Review* 53 (2012):987; Joseph A. Seiner, "After *Iqbal*," *Wake Forest Law Review* 45 (2010): 179; Joseph A. Seiner, "The Trouble with *Twombly*: A Proposed Pleading Standard for Employment Discrimination Cases," *University of Illinois Law Review* (2009): 1011; Joseph A. Seiner, "Pleading Disability," *Boston College Law Review* 51 (2010): 95; Joseph A. Seiner, "Plausibility & Disparate Impact," *Hastings Law Journal* 64 (2013): 287; Joseph A. Seiner, "Understanding the Unrest of France's Younger Workers: The Price of American Ambivalence," *Arizona State Law Journal* 38, no. 4 (2006): 1053.

Chapter 3, "Class Actions, Systemic Claims, and Arbitration," draws heavily from the following articles: Joseph A. Seiner, "Commonality and the Constitution: Applying *Wal-Mart* to State Court Cases," *Indiana Law Journal* 91 (2016): 455; Joseph A. Seiner, "The Issue Class," *Boston College Law Review* 56 (2015): 121; and Joseph A. Seiner, "Weathering *Wal-Mart*," *Notre Dame Law Review* 89 (2014): 1343.

Chapter 5, "Striking at Relief," draws heavily from the following articles: Joseph A. Seiner, "The Failure of Punitive Damages in Employment Discrimination Cases: A Call for Change," *William & Mary Law Review* 50 (2008): 735 and Joseph A. Seiner, "Punitive Damages, Due Process, and Employment Discrimination," *Iowa Law Review* 97 (2012): 473.

Chapter 6, "The On-Demand Economy Example," draws heavily from the following articles: Benjamin Means & Joseph A. Seiner, "Navigating the Uber Economy," 49 *University of California Davis Law Review* 49 (2016): 1511; Joseph A. Seiner, "Tailoring Class Actions to the On-Demand Economy," *Ohio State Law Journal* 78 (2017): 21.

I hope that the readers of this work enjoy contemplating and debating these issues as much as I have enjoyed putting this text together. Civil rights and civil procedure interact in a way that combines the technical precision of the law with the human element of workplace conflict. This intellectually stimulating topic will be one explored by the courts and academics for decades to come. My goal here is to further that important discussion.

Joseph A. Seiner
Columbia, South Carolina

Acknowledgments

The author gratefully acknowledges the permissions granted to reproduce the following materials:

- U2 Epigraph, Chapter 1, reprinted with permission from Hal Leonard Publishing.
- Leffler, Warren K. / Library of Congress Prints and Photographs Division. "Civil Rights March on Wash[ington], D.C.," August 28, 1963. Photograph. www.loc.gov/pictures/item/2013648832/.
- EEOC Charge Statistics Table, Chapter 1, reprinted from Joseph A. Seiner, *Employment Discrimination: Procedure Principles, and Practice* (2015), with permission from Wolters Kluwer.
- Flowchart, Chapter 1, reprinted from Joseph A. Seiner, *Employment Discrimination: Procedure Principles, and Practice* (2015), with permission from Wolters Kluwer.
- Types of Damages table, Chapter 1, reprinted from Joseph A. Seiner, *Employment Discrimination: Procedure Principles, and Practice* (2015), with permission from Wolters Kluwer.
- Chief Justice John Roberts' photo, Chapter 1, Wikimedia/Public Domain. https://commons.wikimedia.org/wiki/File:Official_roberts_CJ.jpg.
- John Ashcroft, Chapter 2, http://en.wikipedia.org/wiki/John_Ashcroft#media viewer/File:John_Ashcroft.jpg.
- Fire Fighters Gear photo, reprinted with permission from Liz West/Flickr. "Fire Fighter Gear," December 20, 2005. Photograph. www.flickr.com/photos/calliope/75703700/.
- Mat-Su NOW Walmart, Chapter 3, www.flickr.com/photos/walmartmovie/25552510/, reprinted with permission, Creative Commons license, creativecommons.org/licenses/by/2.0/.

- Types of Discrimination Charges table, Chapter 4, reprinted from Joseph A. Seiner, *Employment Discrimination: Procedure Principles, and Practice* (2015), with permission from Wolters Kluwer.
- Retaliation Claims Chart, Chapter 4, reprinted from Joseph A. Seiner, *Employment Discrimination: Procedure Principles, and Practice* (2015), with permission from Wolters Kluwer.
- National Archives at College Park, MD. "President George H. W. Bush Signs the Americans with Disabilities Act," July 26, 1990. Photograph. http://research.archives.gov/description/6037489#.

1

The Supreme Court, Employment Discrimination, and an Overview of Civil Rights

> Early morning, April 4
> Shot rings out in the Memphis sky
> Free at last, they took your life
> They could not take your Pride
>
> −U2 (*Pride*)

Half a century ago, the civil-rights community came together to fight pervasive discrimination. Dr. Martin Luther King, Jr., and others, helped bring equality in many areas of the law, including employment. These changes made the laws much more inclusive for minority groups across the country as workplace discrimination on the basis of race, color, sex, national origin, and religion became a federal violation.

The Supreme Court – and more precisely the Court under Chief Justice John Roberts – has walked many of these important advances back over the past several years, undermining the changes so many in the civil-rights community had fought for decades to achieve. Many of the decisions of the Roberts Court have gone largely undetected as they have turned on technical subtleties in the law, thus allowing the cases to fly largely under the radar. This text helps synthesize these cases in a meaningful way, bringing to light the subtle actions of the Supreme Court that have culminated in very substantive changes for workers.

THE CASE LAW

In *Wal-Mart* v. *Dukes*,[1] a million and a half women claimed that the nation's largest retailer had adopted a corporate policy of pay discrimination. These female employees of Wal-Mart maintained that the company had systematically acted on a company-wide basis to ensure that men were paid more and promoted at a faster pace. The proposed class action stole headlines across the country, and the massive case was poised to bring the discount giant to its knees. This would all change, however, when

1

FIGURE 1.1 Dr. Martin Luther King and Mathew Ahmann at the Civil Rights March on Washington, August 28, 1963.
Credit: Sherman, Rowland / US Information Agency / National Archives at College Park, MD.

the Supreme Court stepped in to reverse the appellate court's certification of the class action and to stop the systemic litigation in its tracks. The case was decided by a razor-thin majority, with the conservative Justices all aligned on the prevailing side.

Likewise, in *Ledbetter* v. *Goodyear*,[2] discussed in detail later in this chapter, the Court would act to suppress the rights of female workers in another high-profile claim involving pay and gender discrimination. In *Ledbetter*, the conservative Justices of the Court would change the rules of pay discrimination cases and make it far more diffi-cult for female workers to bring these claims. The case would alter the administrative guidelines for the timing of filing such suits, and abrogate the Court's previous – and more flexible – rules for bringing these claims. The case would subsequently take on a political dimension as the plaintiff, Lilly Ledbetter, became an advocate for women's rights in the following presidential election. In the first bill signed during his presi-dency, Barack Obama overturned the Supreme Court's decision in *Ledbetter*.

And, in *Ricci v. DeStefano*,[3] the Supreme Court would act to protect the rights of *white male* workers of a local municipality. In the case, these majority class members sued the New Haven, Connecticut, fire department, arguing that they were discriminated against on the basis of race when the city threw out the results of a test for promotion that it deemed to have an adverse impact against black workers. Reversing the decision of the lower court, the 5–4 conservative majority shifted the protections of discrimination law toward the majority class. The case would serve as a lightning rod during the confirmation hearings of Sonia Sotomayor, who had voted as part of the lower court to reject the claims of these white workers.

These high-profile decisions of the Supreme Court in recent years have thus caused confusion and discontent among those groups advocating for the rights of minority workers. Each decision has acted to strip minority groups of some of their protections and shifted control of the workplace more toward the employer and the majority class. Unfortunately, these decisions are not isolated events and represent only those instances where the Court was acting in a high-profile way to eviscerate the rights of minority workers. Several other decisions have gone largely undetected in the public eye and have further limited the discrimination protections of the workplace.

While *Wal-Mart*, *Ricci*, and *Ledbetter* are spectacular decisions that have gained widespread attention, the Roberts Court has also acted in a much more subtle and consistent way to limit the workplace rights of minority employees over the past ten years. This book addresses the seismic shift that has taken place in employment law over the last decade and explores the common thread that ties the Supreme Court's decisions together. When the Court's decisions are examined in a meaningful way, three primary trends emerge that suggest a dramatic shift on key procedural issues in employment-discrimination cases that all act together to limit the rights of minority workers.

These three procedural guideposts are all indicative of the paradigmatic shift in the law. Navigating these guideposts, this book explains how the Roberts Court has attempted to minimize worker rights by sidestepping major substantive issues and, instead, rejecting cases on more "technical" procedural grounds that are far less likely to capture the public's attention and imagination. This book does more than simply identify the problem, however. It also suggests workable solutions to allow civil-rights advocates the ability to better survive during this detrimental period. While the deck is stacked against workers on these issues, there are still opportunities available to help minimize the impact of the Court's decisions.

Broken down to its core, there are three overriding areas where the Court has acted to limit the protections of the workforce. The common theme of these holdings is the use of *procedural* – rather than *substantive* – mechanisms to limit worker rights. First, the Court has made it far more difficult in recent years to even bring a lawsuit. In *Bell Atlantic Corp.* v. *Twombly* and *Ashcroft* v. *Iqbal*, the Court has substantially raised the burden on plaintiffs for what is required to bring a viable lawsuit.[4] The lower courts have seized on the decisions and made it far more difficult for civil-rights litigants to pursue their claims. Attempts at congressional intervention have fallen flat, and employment-discrimination plaintiffs now face an uphill battle when pursuing these cases.

Similarly, the Supreme Court has acted to limit the ability of workplace plaintiffs to *aggregate* their claims. As seen in the *Wal-Mart* decision, the Court has intervened to block systemic employment claims and to require workers to bring their lawsuits on an individual level. Historically, class-action lawsuits have served a fundamental role in employment litigation – they have propelled widespread positive change in various industries that could not have been achieved on an individual level. These cases have provided a recovery for millions of workers who may not otherwise have brought a claim if they had been forced to act by themselves. These litigants are now left to pursue these cases on their own. And, after *Twombly* and *Iqbal*, it is far more difficult for these individual claims to even make it out of the starting gate.

Finally, even where employment-discrimination litigation is successful, the Supreme Court has stepped in to limit the relief available to workers. Thus, even where plaintiffs can successfully navigate the procedural hurdles put in place by the Court, the relief that they will attain is far less. In particular, the Court has acted to strike down the availability of punitive damages in these cases, and without this type of relief, there is far less incentive for workers to bring these claims in the first instance. The compensatory and punitive damages that seemed so robust when they were added to Title VII through statutory amendments have now become much more watered down and difficult to achieve. The statutory caps on these damages have remained static over the last two decades, and the impact of this form of relief has waned.

Thus, at each procedural turn in an employment-discrimination case – filing the claim itself, aggregating claims, and obtaining relief – the Court has put sizable hurdles in place to block civil-rights litigants from prevailing. This substantial shift in the law has taken place gradually over the past decade, and we are now faced with a landscape that greatly favors employers and the majority class in workplace disputes. The procedural hurdles are now present in other major areas of employment law, including claims of retaliation, and arbitrating claims before private judges. This book explains the subtleties of how the Supreme Court has acted to move the law toward employers in all of these areas. And, this text identifies the best ways for civil-rights litigants to survive during this era of uncertainty and adversity.

The Roberts Court has carefully manipulated the use of *procedural* mechanisms over the past decade to alter the *substance* of workplace claims. Indeed, no area of the law other than employment has seen this level of scrutiny and reconfiguration with respect to procedural issues. This book identifies and synthesizes these changes – and presents them in an easily accessible way. Though many of these cases have gone undetected over the last several years, the aggregate result of this body of case law is quite troubling. Before civil-rights advocates or Congress can act, however, the problem must be clearly understood. This book takes that first crucial step toward identifying the issue and addresses this paradigmatic shift in employment law head on. It seeks to spark a debate on how workplace litigants have been disadvantaged over the past decade. It is time for that debate to begin.

THE HIGHS AND LOWS OF EMPLOYMENT LAW

The theory of employment discrimination likely saw its heights in 1964 with the passage of Title VII of the Civil Rights Act. The statute was passed after much contentious debate, and was the direct result of years of concerted and concentrated efforts on behalf of the civil-rights community. Dr. Martin Luther King, and many others, fought hard for this legislative change in employment (as well as in many other areas of the law). While this book does not purport to provide a complete historical overview of the political wranglings behind the Civil Rights Act, it is worth highlighting the substantial and courageous efforts that directly lead to this important statute.

As the courts became more conservative in the 1980s, they would begin to cut back on the protections for workers found in Title VII. This was largely accomplished by the federal courts' narrow interpretation of the statute and its accompanying regulations. Congress would intervene in 1991 with several important amendments to Title VII. In particular, Congress codified unintentional discrimination claims, gave workers the right to a jury trial, and imposed compensatory and punitive damages on potential wrongdoers.

The year 1991 thus marked another high point for employees and the protections they were afforded against workplace discrimination. Again, however, the courts would turn more conservative with the addition of judges confirmed during the George W. Bush era. Indeed, over the last decade, the Supreme Court has issued a string of decisions that have cut at the core of the protections for minority workers. This text will explore these decisions in detail. For example, in *Vance v. Ball State*,[5] the Court defined the term "supervisor" very rigidly, limiting the ability of many workers to impute liability for discrimination to their company. And, in *University of Texas Southwestern Medical Center v. Nassar*,[6] the Supreme Court raised the bar for plaintiffs to establish causation in retaliation cases, again making it more difficult for workers to prevail on these claims. These cases, along with a host of other Supreme Court decisions, signaled a marked shift in the Court's approach to employment discrimination. An era of subtle maneuvering by the Court to strip workers of their rights has emerged. We thus find ourselves at another "low" point for workers and the civil-rights community, and litigants must now proceed with extreme caution when bringing an employment-related claim during the era of the Roberts Court.

This text lays the groundwork for explaining this marked shift in the law. It sets the stage by explaining how the Court's rigid interpretation of the federal employment statutes in recent years has impacted worker rights. It explains how the Court has consistently – over the past decade – chipped away at the protections of minority workers. Before delving into this topic, a brief overview of workplace antidiscrimination law can be helpful. This text is intended for both the casual and sophisticated reader, and an explanation of the mechanics of filing a workplace claim can be useful to those pursuing (or defending) claims in this area.

The Employment Protections of the Workplace

Perhaps the best known, and most frequently used, antidiscrimination law is Title VII of the Civil Rights Act of 1964, which provides numerous protections for workers. In particular, employees are protected under the statute from adverse actions by their employers on the basis of a protected characteristic. The statute expressly states that it is unlawful for an employer to "refuse to hire or discharge any individual, or otherwise to discriminate against any individual with respect to his compensation, terms, conditions, or privileges of employment, because of such individual's race, color, religion, sex, or national origin."[7] Title VII thus makes it an unlawful employment practice for employers to discriminate on one of these protected bases. The Age Discrimination in Employment Act (ADEA) – which was enacted three years later – operates in a similar manner to prohibit discrimination on the basis of one's age (those forty years of age or older). The Americans with Disabilities Act (ADA) adds additional protections for individuals in the workplace who have disabilities.

These federal statutes all work together to prohibit employers from taking an adverse action on the basis of several protected categories – race, color, religion, sex, national origin, age, and disability. There are other constitutional protections as well that make discrimination unlawful, giving workers equal protection under the law. And, numerous state and local laws add additional protections and often prohibit discrimination against workers on the basis of gender identity, appearance, and marital status.

The Equal Employment Opportunity Commission
and the Administrative Process

When a worker believes that she has been discriminated against by her employer, she must typically file a charge of discrimination with the Equal Employment

Opportunity Commission (EEOC). The EEOC is the federal agency charged with enforcing Title VII, the ADA, and the ADEA, among other statutes. An individual has 180 or 300 days to file a charge of discrimination, depending on the state (the vast majority of jurisdictions carry the longer 300-day window). For continuing violations, such as harassment, an individual must file the charge within 180/300 days of the last discriminatory event that has occurred.

When the EEOC receives a charge, it will typically triage it. "A" charges will be heavily pursued, "B" charges will be investigated more thoroughly, and "C" charges will often be rejected. After examining the charge, the Commission will either find cause or no-cause to believe that discrimination has occurred. For no-cause findings, individuals will be given a right-to-sue letter and will have ninety days to file a lawsuit in federal court. For those cases where the Commission finds cause (about 5 percent of the cases, though this number varies), it will attempt to settle the case through a process known as conciliation. If conciliation fails, the EEOC will either bring suit in the case itself, or issue a right-to-sue letter permitting the individual to bring a federal claim within ninety days.

When the EEOC was first created after the passage of Title VII, it had no independent litigation authority, and thus no real ability to enforce the statute. Congress subsequently amended the law, allowing the agency to bring suit on its own behalf against those that ran afoul of Title VII. The EEOC will typically bring between 200 and 400 lawsuits a year, though this number is also subject to variation. These raw litigation numbers may seem somewhat high, but in reality they represent an extremely small fraction of the charges that are filed in a given year, which fluctuate between 75,000 and 100,000 total charges. The data shown in Table 1.1 reflect the number of charges received by the EEOC in recent years. The spike in charges between 2008 and 2012 is likely the result of the great recession, when many workers found themselves suddenly unemployed.

Regardless of whether the EEOC or the individual files suit, the administrative process is complete at this stage of the proceedings and federal litigation may be initiated. The case will then be treated like any other civil claim in federal court, and will be subject to the same Federal Rules of Civil Procedure ("Federal Rules" or "Rules"), as well as the same discovery mechanisms.

The Civil Claim

When filing a civil claim of employment discrimination in federal court, the "rules" that apply are the same as they would be for other cases brought outside of the civil-rights context. The Federal Rules require that a plaintiff file a complaint showing entitlement to relief, and further provide litigants access to the rules of discovery. While the federal rules are generally applied to employment-discrimination claims in a manner

TABLE 1.1 *General Rise of EEOC Charges
in Recent Years*

Year	Charges
1997	80,680
1998	79,591
1999	77,444
2000	79,896
2001	80,840
2002	84,442
2003	81,293
2004	79,432
2005	75,428
2006	75,768
2007	82,792
2008	95,402
2009	93,277
2010	99,922
2011	99,947
2012	99,412
2013	93,727
2014	88,778
2015	89,385
2016	91,503

Source: EEOC, Charge Statistics FY 1997 through
FY 2016.

that would be similar to other civil cases, one nuance occurs with the requirement that workplace plaintiffs establish discriminatory intent in the case. By and large, the statutory language in this area mandates that an aggrieved party show that she was discriminated against *because of* a protected characteristic. This *because of* language has been widely interpreted as a requirement that the plaintiff show that the defendant acted with some type of discriminatory intent. Though a subset of important employment-discrimination cases exists for claims alleging unintentional discrimination, these cases are largely beyond the scope of this text, though this theory will be visited briefly later in this book with a discussion of the Court's decision in *Ricci* v. *DeStefano*.

If there is some type of direct, overt evidence of discrimination in a case, discriminatory intent is much easier to establish. Where an employer tells a worker that he is being fired because he "is black," he "is a Muslim," or because he "has a disability," showing discriminatory intent will be relatively straightforward. Though such evidence may have been possible to access decades ago when the statutes were first passed, today it is highly unusual to uncover this type of direct evidence of discrimination. Given that Title VII applies only to employers with fifteen or more employees, businesses of this size are typically sophisticated enough to steer clear of these openly discriminatory remarks in this day and age. There are some exceptions, of course, such as where a company or business attempts to maintain authenticity in its operations, or where safety concerns are implicated. These types of "Bona Fide Occupational Qualifications" are also beyond the scope of this work, but can become important distinctions in a very small subset of cases. For the most part, then, it is extremely rare to uncover direct, overt evidence of discrimination when litigating a workplace dispute.

Where there is no clear signal of discriminatory animus, the courts are typically left to infer such intent through circumstantial evidence. Years ago, the Supreme Court developed the test for these claims in perhaps the best known case of employment-discrimination law – *McDonnell Douglas Corp. v. Green.*[8] The *McDonnell Douglas* case held that, to give rise to an inference of discrimination, a plaintiff must show that she is in a protected class, that she is qualified, that she has suffered an adverse action, and that there is some other evidence of discrimination. Once this standard is met, the plaintiff has satisfied the *prima facie* case of discrimination, and the defendant (through a burden of production) must articulate a legitimate nondiscriminatory reason for its actions. The plaintiff – who maintains the burden of persuasion throughout the case – must then establish that the employer's stated reason is pretextual for true discrimination. The chart in Figure 1.2 helps illustrate how these elements are analyzed.

These elements of the *prima facie* case have – traditionally – been evaluated by the courts at the summary judgment stage of the litigation. Like other civil cases brought in federal court, only a handful of workplace cases are even argued before a jury, thus making summary judgment, and other procedural motions, a critical part of the case. In an employment-discrimination case, summary judgment typically occurs after discovery has already taken place (depositions, document exchange, etc.). At summary judgment, an employer must establish that *even if* all of the evidence is considered in the light most favorable to the plaintiff, no reasonable jury could find in the plaintiff's favor. This standard typically requires the employer to argue that even if we look at things in the employee's favor, at least one of the elements of the *prima facie* case has not been satisfied by the plaintiff.

This basic summary of the administrative process and the civil claim provides a starting point for understanding the mechanics of a typical employment-discrimination case, and thus, how the Supreme Court has used these mechanics to severely undercut core worker protections. As will be discussed later in this text, the Supreme

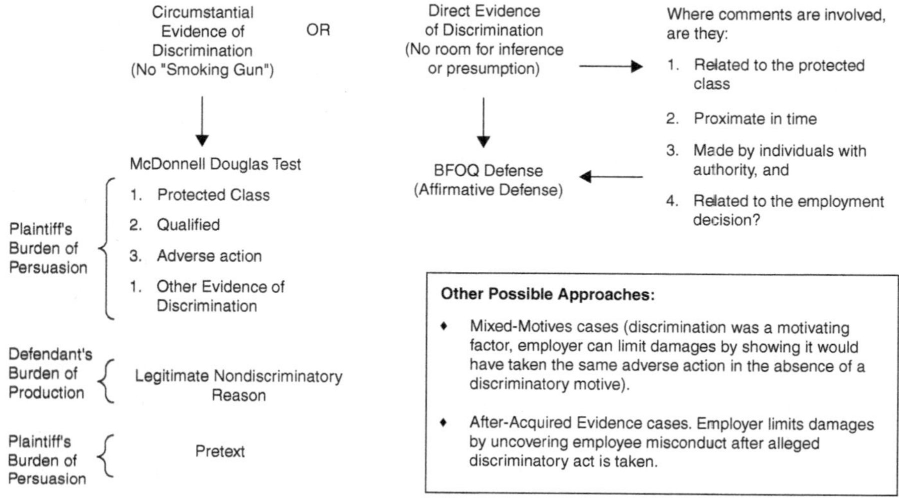

FIGURE 1.2 Intentional discrimination chart. Intentional discrimination claims play a substantial role in workplace litigation; this chart outlines how these claims are conceptualized.

Court's recent decisions have even accelerated when these *McDonnell Douglas* factors are evaluated to a much earlier stage of the proceedings. The Supreme Court's rulings in *Twombly* and *Iqbal* have raised the bar for the pleading standards in these cases and advanced the consideration of the *McDonnell Douglas* factors.[9] The *McDonnell Douglas* test has been the source of great consternation over the years, and has continually been reframed by the lower courts. Despite the widespread criticism of the test, it remains widely used in employment-discrimination cases.

There are many nuances in employment-discrimination law that are well beyond the scope of this book and that fill volumes of textbooks, treatises, and other research materials. The overview of employment-discrimination claims set forth here, however, provides a workable (though oversimplified) summary of how the vast majority of cases typically proceed. We now have a starting point and basic understanding of these claims, and can better explore and articulate the overwhelming impact that the Roberts Court has had in this area.

Relief in Discrimination Cases

In addition to the procedural mechanisms that distinguish employment-discrimination cases, the damages that are available to workplace claimants serve as an additional unique component of this area of the law. Trying to determine the appropriate relief in an employment-discrimination case can be difficult, and it is much more of an art than a science. Nonetheless, there are some basic guidelines that should be considered. And, as we will see in the following chapters, access to relief is one specific area where the Court has intervened in this field.

Generally speaking, successful plaintiffs suing under Title VII, the ADA, or the ADEA are entitled to back pay in the case. This form of relief represents damages from the date the discrimination occurred until the date of a finding of discrimination in the case. Second, the courts will often award front pay, which is a more equitable form of relief that represents damages from the date of judgment until some unspecified date in the future. Front pay represents the harm that occurs to victims of discrimination on an *ongoing* basis. Though reinstatement to a worker's former position is the preferred remedy to front pay, reinstatement is often impracticable given the level of hostility that can (and often does) exist between the parties in litigation. With both front pay and back pay, there is an expectation that the plaintiff will do her best to mitigate damages by securing other *similar* employment in an expeditious manner. Back pay, then, represents damages from the time of the discrimination to the date of judgment. Front pay represents damages from judgment to some unspecified date in the future. Both types of relief anticipate mitigation by the plaintiff. While reinstatement is preferred in all cases, it is frequently difficult to effectuate as a practical matter.

Cases brought under Title VII and the ADA also offer the possibility of compensatory and punitive damages. Compensatory damages reflect the emotional harm and suffering experienced by the plaintiff. Punitive damages are appropriate when the employer has acted with malice or reckless disregard toward the worker and the law. Typically, such damages will be awarded where the company is aware of its obligations under Title VII, but acts unlawfully in the face of this knowledge. Punitive and compensatory damages are capped under the statutes. For the largest employers (500 or more employees), plaintiffs can receive up to $300,000 in compensatory and punitive damages *combined*. This amount is reduced for smaller employers, and a sliding scale exists depending on the size of the company. Only those companies with fifteen or more employees are even covered by these statutes (the coverage requirement is slightly larger for the ADEA, which imposes a twenty-worker minimum).

Although punitive/compensatory relief is not available *at all* under the ADEA, liquidated damages are permitted. This form of relief represents a "doubling" of damages in the case. Statistically speaking, age claims represent some of the largest payouts in discrimination law. The higher salaries of workers at the end of their careers, combined with this doubling effect, often makes for much larger awards. Employers can avoid this "doubling" of damages if they can establish – through a burden of proof – that they have made good faith efforts to comply with the law.

TABLE 1.2 *Types of Damages*

Title VII Damages[a]	ADEA Damages
Back Pay ▪ Wages and Salary ○ Includes overtime, shift differentials, commissions, tips, cost-of-living increases, merit increases, and raises due to promotion ▪ Fringe Benefits ○ Includes vacation pay, pension and retirement benefits, stock options and bonus plans, savings plan contributions, cafeteria plan benefits, profit-sharing benefits, and medical and life insurance benefits ▪ Prejudgment Interest	**Back Pay** ▪ Wages and Salary ○ Includes overtime, shift differentials, commissions, tips, cost-of-living increases, merit increases, and raises due to promotion ▪ Fringe Benefits ○ Includes vacation pay, pension and retirement benefits, stock options and bonus plans, savings plan contributions, cafeteria plan benefits, profit-sharing benefits, and medical and life insurance benefits ▪ Prejudgment Interest
Front Pay (or Reinstatement) ▪ Front pay compensates for the future effects of discrimination when reinstatement would be an appropriate, but not feasible, remedy or for the estimated length period before the plaintiff could return to her former position	**Front Pay (or Reinstatement)** ▪ Front pay compensates for the future effects of discrimination when reinstatement would be an appropriate, but not feasible, remedy or for the estimated length period before the plaintiff could return to her former position
Compensatory and Punitive Damages ▪ Compensatory Damages: Awarded for future pecuniary losses, emotional pain, suffering, inconvenience, mental anguish, loss of enjoyment of life, and other nonpecuniary losses ▪ Punitive Damages: Awarded when defendant acts with malice or reckless regard	**Liquidated Damages** ▪ Available up to the amount of back pay for willful violations of the ADEA ▪ The ADEA allows damages only for pecuniary benefits connected to the job, but not compensatory damages for mental anguish, pain, suffering, humiliation, and loss of employment
Attorney's Fees ▪ Reasonable attorney's fees are available to the prevailing party	**Attorney's Fees** ▪ Reasonable attorney's fees are available to the prevailing party

[a] Barbara L. Johnson, *Types of Damages Available in Employment Cases*, www.americanbar.org/content/dam/aba/administrative/labor_law/meetings/2011/annualmeeting/004.authcheckdam.pdf, in Joseph A. Seiner, *Employment Discrimination: Procedure, Principles, and Practice* (New York: Wolters Kluwer, 2015), 584. Reprinted with permission from Wolters Kluwer.

Table 1.2 outlines and summarizes the different types of damages that can be pursued by plaintiffs in workplace cases. Evaluating the types of damages in an employment-discrimination case can be difficult. The table provides a useful summary of the relief that is available for these claims.

The Supreme Court has weighed in on the question of when punitive damages should be awarded in an employment-discrimination case. More recent decisions of the Court have directly impacted how such awards are evaluated, and will be explored in Chapter 4. Relief is a critical part of any case. Where the Court acts to restrict damages it limits the incentives available for aggrieved workers to avail themselves of the law in this area.

Systemic Litigation

One area that deserves special attention with respect to employment-discrimination law is systemic, or aggregate, litigation. This type of litigation occurs where multiple victims of discrimination bring suit as part of a single case. Employment-discrimination cases are particularly appropriate for these types of aggregate claims, as multiple individuals are often harmed in a workplace where discrimination is present. Specific policies or attitudes may pervade an entire workforce, harming many employees. And, overlapping personnel are often involved in harassing acts or other discriminatory actions.

Given their aggregate nature, these cases deserve careful consideration and are typically closely examined by the EEOC. Private plaintiffs must satisfy the requirements of the Federal Rules to aggregate their claims. The government, however, is not subject to these requirements. This text will address in much greater detail the importance of this distinction between governmental and private systemic claims. It will further discuss how the Supreme Court has elevated the bar for private plaintiffs trying to aggregate their claims. And, it will discuss how the Court has even affected private arbitration claims in this area. Finally, this text will explain the numerous approaches still available to plaintiffs seeking to proceed in an aggregate manner.

THE ROBERTS COURT AND ITS EFFECT ON PROCEDURE

This chapter has set forth the general, well-accepted guidelines for how to proceed administratively in an employment-discrimination case, when to file the claim in federal court, and what basic damages can be pursued in these matters. This basic understanding of the law is necessary to consider the scope of the impact that the Roberts Court has had on workplace claims. The Court has repeatedly acted through procedural maneuverings to substantially undermine the substantive rights of workers. In the chapters that follow, this text will examine the following areas,

FIGURE 1.3 Chief Justice John Roberts being confirmed on September 29, 2005. The Roberts Court has shaped the future of workplace litigation in the United States.
Credit: Photograph by Steve Petteway

exploring how recent Supreme Court precedent has undermined worker rights in each facet of the law:

- Limiting access to the courts through heightened pleading standards
- Restricting access to aggregate/collective rights under the procedural rules
- Diminishing the scope of retaliation suits
- Raising the bar for attaining punitive relief in civil-rights cases.

This text will consider each area in turn, and offer substantive solutions that plaintiffs can use to still effectively pursue workplace cases in the face of these Supreme Court decisions. Though the solutions offered here are a "patchwork" approach to resolving the problem, they nonetheless help civil-rights litigants to successfully navigate this complex area. Each chapter identifies the substantive area of the law narrowed by the Roberts Court and proposes a possible solution to the problem identified. The final chapter brings all of the proposed frameworks together in a single workable format, setting forth an overarching roadmap for workplace litigants to follow. This summary chapter further discusses how only congressional intervention can truly correct the damage done by the Roberts Court to civil-rights litigants and sets forth proposed legislation that could fix the existing problems.

In the chapters that follow, then, this text will look closely at how the Roberts Court has negatively impacted workplace cases through a narrow interpretation of pleading standards, aggregation of claims, retaliation, and relief. It will detail how each of these areas now presents enormous procedural difficulties for workers seeking to avail themselves of their workplace protections. Each chapter will explore ways for plaintiffs to litigate their claims in response to these decisions. This book will then provide context to the problem by examining an example of how the issues have emerged in one specific area of the economy – the technology sector. The text will conclude by offering a summary framework for litigating in areas where the Supreme Court has narrowed substantive worker rights, and will detail the type of congressional intervention needed to resolve these issues.

In essence, then, this text is more descriptive than it is normative – identifying the problem created by the Roberts Court for litigants and synthesizing these new procedural hurdles that are undermining substantive worker rights. The book then attempts to provide mechanisms for workers to use to help limit the impact of these Supreme Court cases. Through this framework, employment-discrimination claimants will be better able to understand the Supreme Court's actions, and to litigate successfully despite these decisions.

BUT WHY?

The ultimate question raised by this text is *why* the Roberts Court has acted to restrict worker rights. One can certainly speculate as to the reason. Perhaps it is the business-oriented ideology of many of the Justices. Or, perhaps there is an increased appetite on the bench to reduce the heavy workload of the lower courts by limiting the number of claims filed. Or, it could be that the Court believes that workplace cases are better suited for state or local judicial systems than the federal courts. It is even possible that the Supreme Court is unaware that it is using procedural mechanisms to undermine employee rights. Such a result seems unlikely, however, given the strong dissents often authored in these cases that will be explored in greater detail in the following chapters.

At the end of the day, there is simply no way to be certain of the Supreme Court's motivations with respect to workplace claims. There is no way to look into the hearts and minds of the Justices themselves. The best that we can do is to try to decipher the case law, and provide a detailed explanation of the Court's actions as well as the potential repercussions for workers. This text, then, does not judge the Court or engage in idle speculation as to the motivations of the Justices in this area. Rather, it seeks to synthesize an unidentified problem in a coherent way and provide specific solutions to these issues for workplace litigants. The Supreme Court has used procedure to disadvantage workers bringing substantive discrimination claims.

This book identifies the existence of this phenomenon. *Why* the Court has acted in this way, however, is well beyond the scope of this book.

CASE EXAMPLE: LEDBETTER

Before delving too far into civil-rights law and the workplace, it can be helpful to briefly explore one case where the Roberts Court has acted to limit employee rights, and how Congress intervened in the face of the procedural decision. *Ledbetter v. Goodyear Tire & Rubber Co., Inc.,*[10] a 5–4 Supreme Court decision, helps provide clear context to this discussion. In *Ledbetter,* the Supreme Court held that the continued effects of past discrimination do not toll the statute of limitations for filing a charge with the EEOC.[11] Petitioner Lilly Ledbetter filed a claim with the EEOC against Goodyear Tire & Rubber (Goodyear) when she discovered that she was being paid significantly less than her male colleagues based on a discriminatory performance review that she had received years earlier.[12]

A jury found for Ledbetter and awarded her back pay and damages. On appeal, Goodyear argued that all actions that took place more than 180 days prior to the filing of Ledbetter's EEOC charge were time-barred. The court of appeals agreed, holding that a Title VII pay discrimination claim could not be based on any pay decision made prior to the 180/300-day charge filing period. The Supreme Court granted *certiorari* to determine the proper application of the limitations period under Title VII.[13]

The Supreme Court rejected Ledbetter's argument that each paycheck, which unlawfully compensated Ledbetter less than her male counterparts, represented a separate act of discrimination. The Court instead held that any adverse effects resulting from past discrimination do not constitute a separate unlawful employment practice that would qualify as a new violation and restart the charge filing period. The Court thus found that Ledbetter's claim was time-barred because she was unable to establish discriminatory intent on the part of Goodyear *within* the charge filing window. In its decision, the majority emphasized the importance of strict adherence to procedural requirements in order to guarantee consistent administration of the law.[14]

In her dissent, Justice Ginsburg argued that the rule articulated by the majority ignored the fundamental characteristics of pay discrimination.[15] Because pay discrimination may occur in small increments, and employees often do not have access to comparative pay information, it may take a significant amount of time for victims of discrimination to become aware of their disparate income. Justice

Ginsburg further maintained that the EEOC charge filing period should distinguish between discrete, easily identifiable acts and events that are recurring and cumulative in nature. Finally, Justice Ginsburg noted that the majority's decision is incompatible with Title VII's broad, remedial purpose.[16]

The *Ledbetter* decision garnered national attention and headlines. The case became a major political issue as well, and Lilly Ledbetter spoke at the 2012 Democratic National Convention on the importance of women's pay issues and identifying sex discrimination.[17] The case was thus front-and-center in both the legal and cultural landscapes. Ultimately, the controversy swirling around this case led to congressional action. In the first bill signed into law during his presidency, Barack Obama enacted the Lilly Ledbetter Fair Pay Act of 2009.[18] This statute reverses the Supreme Court's holding in the case, and makes clear that *each* discriminatory paycheck signals a *new* act of discrimination by an employer. The law applies to Title VII, the ADA, and the ADEA.

In essence, then, the high-profile nature of the Supreme Court's overt decision undermining substantive worker rights through technical procedural reporting requirements led to congressional and presidential intervention. The other branches of government stepped in to restore workplace protections for employees that had been put in jeopardy by the Court.

Unfortunately, not all such cases are as high profile as the *Ledbetter* decision. In fact, many fly well under the radar. That is where this book comes in, as it attempts to identify the primary areas where the Supreme Court has acted through procedure to circumvent worker rights. As already noted, this text does not seek to speculate on the Court's motivations in this area. Rather, this book will describe the specific ways the Court has acted to undermine worker rights, examine the hurdles workers face in this area, and explore the ways that litigants can still prevail when alleging civil-rights claims. By bringing these issues to light, then, there is a greater prospect that individuals (and ultimately Congress) will act, as they did after the *Ledbetter* decision and controversy.

Litigants and legislatures must first fully understand the substantial hurdles in front of them before they can act, however. The battle to protect the civil rights of workers, which has been fought for so long and so hard, continues.

THE ROBERTS COURT AND THE MODERN ECONOMY

As noted, the primary purpose of this text is to identify the major areas where the Supreme Court has used procedural law to undermine substantive worker rights, and to provide a workable framework for litigants to use to successfully bring claims in this current environment. This text – in Chapter 6 – offers one concrete example of how the Court's decisions have directly impacted an emerging area of worker rights, exploring the impact of these cases on workers in the technology sector. The text will further explain how workers in this area may nonetheless successfully avail themselves of the law even in the face of these procedural hurdles.

The lower courts are still struggling with how to respond to technology-sector cases brought in the employment context. The Supreme Court's decisions raising the pleading bar and cutting off systemic claims have generated enormous controversy for the modern economy. Ultimately, the Supreme Court will have to take on these technology sector cases to help interpret how the law should be applied in this evolving area. Given the restrictive nature of how the Roberts Court has interpreted employment claims generally, litigants in the gig sector should be proactive in bolstering the amount of proof for these claims. Litigants will want to make certain that they have satisfied the heightened standards prior to bringing workplace suits in the modern economy. And, when seeking to aggregate their claims, workers must proceed cautiously to make certain that they have complied with Supreme Court case law.

The technology sector, then, puts the case law of the Roberts Court front-and-center and provides an excellent opportunity for this text to explain how the Court's decisions have negatively impacted this emerging economy. This chapter thus takes the theoretical discussion set forth in this text and makes it real, applying the frameworks to one high-profile segment of the economy. The text further shows how gig sector workers can still navigate the Court's procedural rules to successfully litigate their claims.

2

Access to the Courts and Enforcement

[W]hile it may be true that morality cannot be legislated, behavior can be regulated. It may be true that the law cannot change the heart but it can restrain the heartless.

– Martin Luther King, Address at Western
Michigan University, 1963, From Between Two Worlds[1]

The United States prides itself on maintaining vibrant antidiscrimination laws. As the introductory chapter addressed, Title VII, the ADA, the ADEA, and other laws led to sweeping reforms for workers beginning in the 1960s. For the first time, workers had a legal basis to bring a federal claim when they were discriminated against on a protected basis. During the early years of these statutes, thousands of federal discrimination claims were brought against employers both on individual and systemic levels. These claims yielded millions of dollars for the victims involved, created widespread public knowledge of the dangers that workplace prejudice can create, and resulted in reform at all corporate levels.

The key to the success of these laws, however, is that the United States actually enforces the statutes that it has enacted in this area. Other countries have also established aggressive antidiscrimination laws, but frequently fail to allow individuals the ability to avail themselves of those laws. Perhaps the best example of this is South Africa.[2] That country passed a comprehensive sexual harassment law in the face of overwhelming internal and external political pressures. The law was one of the most

This chapter draws heavily from the following articles: Joseph A. Seiner and Benjamin N. Gutman, "Does *Ricci* Herald a New Disparate Impact?," *Boston University Law Review* 90 (2010): 2181; Joseph A. Seiner, "Plausibility Beyond the Complaint," *William & Mary Law Review* 53 (2012): 987; Joseph A. Seiner, "After *Iqbal*," *Wake Forest Law Review* 45 (2010): 179; Joseph A. Seiner, "The Trouble with *Twombly*: A Proposed Pleading Standard for Employment Discrimination Cases," *University of Illinois Law Review* (2009): 1011; Joseph A. Seiner, "Pleading Disability," *Boston College Law Review* 51 (2010): 95; Joseph A. Seiner, "Plausibility & Disparate Impact," *Hastings Law Journal* 64 (2013): 287; Joseph A. Seiner, "Understanding the Unrest of France's Younger Workers: The Price of American Ambivalence," *Arizona State Law Journal* 38, no. 4 (2006): 1053.

FIGURE 2.1 Jury box. Very few workplace claims ever make it to a jury. Procedural issues have become an increasingly important part of understanding employment law.

expansive ever enacted. It adopted widespread prohibitions against this behavior and broadly defined the types of conduct that were being outlawed. These prohibitions were arguably more expansive than those on the books in the United States, and were certainly more clearly defined. At the end of the day, however, the law had no teeth. The country, which was unaccustomed to providing these types of protections, rarely enforced the law. Perhaps even more troubling, women who were victimized and subject to these statutory provisions refused to avail themselves of the law. It is difficult to tell whether this lack of enforcement was cultural in nature or was being advanced by officials in the country. Nonetheless, this example underscores the importance of enforcement. Simply having a law on the books is not enough.[3]

Enforcement questions extend beyond employment-discrimination laws, and often arise in this country in various other contexts. If tax laws are enacted but not followed in a particular administration, they will likely not be obeyed by many citizens. Older, outdated laws concerning sexual privacy are also not enforced; even some drug laws have gone by the wayside. We need look no further than the many examples provided in this country, then, to understand that a law must be enforced to have any real meaning. And it seems difficult to quibble with this basic premise.

The reason that the attitude toward discrimination in this country has changed over the last several decades has been the willingness of the government to adopt and enforce antidiscrimination laws. "[M]orality cannot be legislated," but "behaviour can be regulated."[4] This was certainly true in the 1960s, and it took a dramatic change in the law (as well as enforcement of those laws), to alter the way people perceived discrimination. These views did not change immediately, however, and there was firm opposition to Title VII of the Civil Rights Act of 1964, which itself received 130 negative votes in the US House of Representatives.[5] The years following the passage of the statute saw slow change in the public perception of this law. Many employers still continued to discriminate, and some courts were highly skeptical of claims brought by those who had suffered discrimination.

While one can certainly not say that discrimination has been eradicated, the present make-up of the US workforce, combined with the attitude of the general public and employers toward minority employees, has improved substantially. The EEOC still receives 80,000–90,000 charges of discrimination a year,[6] and finds cause in thousands of cases. Discrimination is still present in our society. In many ways, discrimination is now more subtle and subconscious in a large portion of these cases, and oftentimes, it is more difficult to detect. Nonetheless, when compared to the 1960s and 1970s, there can be little doubt that times and circumstances have improved. It is far better to work in today's environment, which is much more race conscious.

If enforcement of the laws begins to slip – if the laws are no longer vigorously enforced – I fear that we would see a slow return to some of the offensive discriminatory practices of the past. There would not be an immediate change in workplace culture. Instead, there would likely only be slight changes on the surface. Much like the decades it took to change the hearts and minds of prejudicial employers and workers after Title VII was passed, it would again take time to return to these more discriminatory practices. But those changes would come, and they would be inevitable. Throughout history there have been ebbs and flows in the tides of discrimination. During World War II, Japanese Americans suffered discrimination in internment camps and faced widespread skepticism and bias from the general public. More recently, the events of September 11, 2001 have led to overt and hidden bias against Muslim Americans, and the EEOC has seen a rise in such charges over time.[7] Thus, if the laws were no longer vigorously enforced, discrimination would inevitably again raise its ugly head over time. Where this discrimination would manifest itself is not completely clear, but it would undoubtedly occur.

Thus, while adoption of an adequate antidiscrimination law is an important first step, enforcement of that law is equally as important. Title VII was adopted with opposition, but its strong enforcement led to substantial changes in cultural, political, and economic environments over time. While there is little danger of those laws being reversed at present, the threat that those laws will no longer be strongly enforced exists.

The EEOC is charged with enforcing private sector employment-discrimination claims, but this government agency is too understaffed and too underfunded, and brings only between 200 and 400 claims in a given year.[8] Thus, the vast majority of claims are brought by public citizens, as the employment-discrimination statutes typically provide for a private right of enforcement. Because discrimination is now far more subtle and sophisticated than it was in the past, there is a greater need for workers to obtain information supporting allegations of discrimination during the discovery process. There is also a greater need to allow employees flexibility when navigating the complex legal landscape. Rather than providing this flexibility, however, the Supreme Court has taken a strong stance on rigidly interpreting procedural rules – allowing many who have been victimized by discrimination to fall through the cracks of the system.

THE SUPREME COURT AND PROCEDURE

In numerous cases over the past decade, the Supreme Court has interpreted procedural rules in a way that has negatively impacted civil-rights litigants. Procedure is the focal point of any federal case. Tinkering with procedure will always have a very real impact on substantive rights. The importance of procedural rules cannot be overstated. However, for lack of a better term, such rules are *boring*.

Not boring to civil procedural scholars or most law professors, but boring to the general public; these rules fail to capture the imagination of the average person walking down the street, or to grab the headlines of major newspapers. They often appear more technical in nature, and thus less controversial. As the Court is simply "following" (or interpreting) the Federal Rules, such cases also may appear less result-oriented. The Court is not attacking a particular policy stance or taking a political view on an issue; it is simply deciding a matter based on the rules of a system that has been intricately developed over time.

Procedural rules give the Court cover. Decisions based on these grounds are less transparent and typically less contentious in the public eye. But this can be quite deceptive. Procedural decisions can have a greater impact on the world around them than a ruling more firmly rooted in substantive grounds. When the Court changes the rules, or how those rules are interpreted, it is changing the game for all civil-rights advocates. It is making it more (or less) difficult to pursue these claims in the courts.

When a procedural decision limits access to the courts, it creates a potential danger that the employment-discrimination laws, which have been so carefully crafted over the years, will go unenforced. The discrimination laws themselves appear vibrant. They expressly prohibit discrimination on the basis of race, color, sex, national origin, religion, age, and disability. They further limit harassment and require equal treatment in the workplace. These laws have taken decades to refine, and Congress has revisited the specific provisions repeatedly over time. The laws arose during a period of racial turmoil in this country, and they now offer a promise of equality to all citizens in the workplace.

But this can all be undone through the use of procedure and a lack of enforcement of the laws. The last decade has seen the Supreme Court issue decision after decision that threatens to derail civil-rights litigation. The cases are not necessarily high profile in nature, but they nonetheless threaten a return to disparate treatment for workers. Collectively, these decisions paint a picture of a Court that has difficulty enforcing employment laws, and of a Court that largely desires a return to an earlier era. Just as the laws developed slowly, the return to this earlier time would be slow as well. But the course has already been set. Numerous procedural decisions have already begun to undermine the rights of workers. In the aggregate, these cases will limit access to the courts and lead to a lack of enforcement of employment protections.

This chapter examines the difficulty that civil-rights plaintiffs have faced in the last decade in accessing the judicial system. This chapter will focus heavily on the Supreme Court's controversial decisions in *Twombly* v. *Bell Atlantic* and *Ashcroft* v. *Iqbal*. Together, these decisions act to restrict the ability of all civil plaintiffs to access the courts. In particular, the Court's decisions raise the bar for the amount of information that must be included in the complaint, requiring litigants to plead a "plausible" claim. Because this standard is particularly amorphous, some of the lower courts have used this language to dismiss otherwise valid civil-rights claims.

The plausibility standard is particularly troublesome for employment-discrimination advocates. The cases are clear that to establish a plausible claim, the plaintiff must show the existence of discriminatory intent. This can be extraordinarily difficult at the early stages of the case, however, when there has been no discovery in the case. Employers are typically in possession of the documentation that would demonstrate discriminatory animus, and without access to this information, many litigants with legitimate claims will fall through the cracks. The federal courts have dockets that are overloaded with employment-discrimination cases, and many courts will use this plausibility standard as an opportunity to reject civil-rights cases and help clear their workload. Even where plaintiffs are successful in navigating the early dismissal stage of the proceedings, the courts have been increasingly reluctant to allow civil-rights cases to get before a jury. The courts have adopted particularly rigid standards for permitting a jury trial, and only a very small percentage of cases actually make it this far in the process. Where a case does proceed to trial, plaintiffs are extremely successful.

This chapter will conclude with a proposed procedural framework for litigating and analyzing employment-discrimination claims. This framework will help litigants to more closely examine whether they have enough information to proceed in a case and it will also allow the courts to more carefully examine these claims to determine whether the plausibility standard has been justified.

THE FEDERAL RULES OF CIVIL PROCEDURE

In federal litigation, the first document typically filed by a party is the complaint, which states the basis for the cause of action in the case. Frequently, the complaint is not overly detailed in nature and usually needs only to state the basic allegations of the case. The Federal Rules govern what a complaint must look like, and more broadly, these rules define how federal litigation must proceed.

The Federal Rules govern all federal litigation. They set the framework for how cases will proceed and outline the Rules for the entire process. Early in this nation's history, no such rules existed. Most claims were brought either in common law or equity, with equity cases requiring far more specificity as to the claim.[9] Over time, states began to integrate common law and equity cases into a unified system.[10] As these different state law systems were developed and tested, a preference began to emerge for more liberal pleading rules – those that did not require the plaintiff to provide too much specificity early in the case.[11] By 1938, the federal courts had developed the modern framework for procedural rules – the Federal Rules.[12] These Rules specifically rejected the formal code pleading approach to complaints requiring more details and specificity in the allegations. In its place, the Federal Rules adopted a "notice pleading" system, which required that a plaintiff give a defendant only basic notice of the details of a particular case to survive dismissal.[13] Under Rule 8(a)(2), the requirements for a plaintiff's complaint are basic and straightforward, "A pleading that states a claim for relief must contain ... a short and plain statement of the claim showing that the pleader is entitled to relief."

This "short and plain" requirement governed federal pleading for years. In an early Supreme Court decision interpreting the rule, *Conley* v. *Gibson*,[14] the Court would give plaintiffs tremendous leeway in filing a complaint. In that case, a group of railroad employees brought suit under the Railway Labor Act alleging that they were fired or demoted because of their race. The claim alleged that the workers' union offered no protections and failed to act in good faith when representing them against the company. Considering the sufficiency of this complaint, the Supreme Court famously concluded that "the accepted rule" requires that a complaint should not be rejected "unless it appears beyond doubt that the plaintiff can prove no set of facts in support of his claim which would entitle him to relief."[15] Applying this rule to the facts, the Court held that the allegations were sufficient to survive dismissal, and that the "simplified notice pleading" system would allow "liberal opportunity for discovery and other pretrial procedures" that would require the parties "to disclose more precisely the basis of both claim and defense."[16]

In *Conley*, the Court acknowledged that procedural rules could be used for mischief. The Court clarified early on that it would not tolerate using these Rules for gamesmanship, however, where "one misstep by counsel may be decisive to the outcome" of the case. Thus, the Court expressly rejected the idea of turning the procedural rules into a "game of skill." Rather, the Rules were there simply to require notice to the defendant of the basic allegations in the case. The rest could be sorted out later as part of discovery and trial proceedings. *Conley* is one of the best known and cited Supreme Court decisions of all time, with only a handful of cases being cited more often.[17] The decision would serve as the seminal case on notice pleading for decades to come.[18]

This liberal notice pleading standard has also been applied by the Supreme Court to employment-discrimination cases. In *Swierkiewicz v. Sorema N.A.*,[19] the Court would expressly consider this standard under the ADEA. In that case, a fifty-three-year-old insurance company employee alleged that he was demoted after spending almost six years at the level of senior vice president. The worker's position was filled by a younger employee with far less experience. The plaintiff was cut out of important business decisions, and subsequently suffered termination. Considering these allegations, the Supreme Court would expressly apply the liberal pleading standard from *Conley* to workplace claims. Referring back to this earlier decision, the Court emphasized Rule 8's requirement that only "a short and plain statement of the claim" is necessary at the early stages of the litigation.

The lower courts have similarly adopted liberal pleading standards, following the approach mandated by the Federal Rules. Indeed, in one well-known decision, Judge Easterbrook considered precisely what a plaintiff must allege to proceed in a Title VII case of discrimination.[20] The judge stated, " 'I was turned down for a job because of my race' is all a complaint has to say" to survive dismissal.[21] Again, the courts largely followed the notice pleading requirements set out in the procedural rules. Employment-discrimination cases, like all civil actions, followed this same basic approach. As long as the defendant had notice of the claim, the requirements had been satisfied.

The *Conley* standard, adopted in 1957, would dominate procedural decisions for the next fifty years. Then, the Supreme Court would dramatically change the pleading landscape, forever altering the access civil-rights litigants would have to the courts. In a seemingly innocuous case at the time, the Court would abrogate the *Conley* test, completely undoing the "any set of facts" standard. Though it was unclear at the time whether this analysis would extend beyond the antitrust context, the Court would subsequently extend its more rigid analysis to civil-rights claims. Each decision will be taken in turn for discussion in this chapter.

TWOMBLY AND *IQBAL*: LIMITED COURT ACCESS

Surprisingly, the two most devastating cases for employment plaintiffs in the last decade had absolutely nothing to do with employment. *Bell Atlantic v. Twombly*[22] and *Ashcroft v. Iqbal*[23] involved antitrust legislation and prisoners' rights, respectively. These cases put squarely at issue the most fundamental aspect of a federal court case – what the initial complaint must state to allow a litigant access to the courts.

Twombly

In *Twombly*, the Supreme Court considered a case involving the potential monopoly-like structure of regional telephone companies. The breakup of AT&T in 1984 led to a new structure in the communications industry. Incumbent Local Exchange Carriers (ILECs) still maintained regional monopolies after the breakup until Congress intervened in 1996. Under the new system, the ILECs were required to allow local communications companies to use their network, thus cutting into the monopoly-like structure. A class action was brought on behalf of all "subscribers of local telephone and/or high-speed Internet services" from 1996 to the date the complaint was filed in federal court. The complaint set forth various violations of the Sherman Act, which prohibits the "restraint of trade or commerce."[24] To support these allegations, the plaintiffs asserted that the ILECs engaged in a conspiracy to restrict trade and raise telephone and internet prices. The complaint maintained that these entities structured their activities to prohibit the emergence of local carriers. They further asserted that the ILECs had reached agreements to refrain from competing with one another.

In essence, then, the *Twombly* plaintiffs raised a massive class action on behalf of anyone who had paid for internet or phone services over the past decade. The class action maintained that local carriers conspired to prevent entry or competition in the marketplace. The lower court dismissed the allegations, maintaining that they failed to satisfy Rule 8. The court found the complaint too conclusory and lacking in factual support.[25] The appellate court reversed, relying on the "any set of facts" language from *Conley*.[26] This court found the defendant's argument that facts could not subsequently be uncovered to support the complaint to be unpersuasive.

The Supreme Court granted *certiorari*. In its decision, the Court expressly revisited its analysis of Rule 8(a)(2). The Court emphasized that the procedural rules require "more than labels and conclusions, and a formulaic recitation of the elements of a cause of action." In its now famous language, the Court mandated that plaintiffs allege a "plausible" basis for relief based on sufficient factual support. This plausibility standard, as it has come to be known, "simply calls for enough facts to raise a reasonable expectation that discovery will reveal evidence" sufficient to support the claim. The Court then contrasted this standard with *Conley*, and expressly abrogated the "no set of facts" language from that case. Indeed, it found that the *Conley* standard had been "puzzling the profession for 50 years" and that this standard had "earned its retirement." The Court was highly critical of *Conley*, noting that its language "is best forgotten as an incomplete, negative gloss on an accepted pleading standard."

The Court applied this new plausibility standard to the facts of the case, and found the complaint lacking. Specifically, there were insufficient facts in the complaint to support the conspiracy allegations brought under the Sherman Act. The Court also addressed the *Swierkiewicz* case, and found no inconsistencies between that ruling and the *Twombly* decision. The Court further noted that it was not adopting a new "heightened fact pleading of specifics," but rather requiring a claim to be "plausible on its face." The plaintiffs in this case had not "nudged their claims across the line from conceivable to plausible," and thus the allegations were insufficient.

The dissent in this case, written by Justice Stevens, emphasized the "dramatic departure from settled procedural law."[27] In particular, the dissent focused on the majority's abrogation of the well-established *Conley* standard. The dissent noted that prior decisions of the Court had cited *Conley* with approval more than a dozen times, and that approximately half of the states use a similar standard in their court systems. The dissent found the plausibility standard "irreconcilable" with Rule 8, as well as the *Swierkiewicz* decision. Justice Stevens further questioned whether the Court's new plausibility standard would be limited to antitrust cases, or whether it would extend to all civil litigation.

Iqbal

Litigants did not have to wait long for the answer to Justice Stevens' question about the scope of the *Twombly* decision. Many academics believed that *Twombly* was an isolated case meant to tackle only complex antitrust issues. After all, it was reasonable to require plaintiffs in a massive antitrust suit to do more than simply parrot the language of the statute in a complaint. By requiring more in these cases, defendants would be entitled to a better understanding of the claim and be less likely to find themselves forced into an unnecessary settlement.

In *Ashcroft* v. *Iqbal*,[28] the Court would expand upon the meaning of the plausibility standard, ultimately concluding that it would apply to all civil claims. In *Iqbal*, a Muslim citizen of Pakistan was arrested on immigration issues. Following the arrest, it was determined that he was "of high interest" to the investigation of the September 11, 2001 attacks on the United States. Iqbal was detained in a maximum security environment where he spent twenty-three hours a day in lockdown. Iqbal ultimately pled guilty to several criminal charges and returned to Pakistan after spending some time in prison. He filed a claim alleging constitutional violations while he was confined, and named numerous federal officials in his complaint including John

FIGURE 2.2 US Attorney General John Ashcroft speaks at a news conference on April 17, 2003, in Washington, DC In *Ashcroft* v. *Iqbal*, the Supreme Court made clear that the plausibility pleasing standard would apply to *all* civil claims.
Credit: Photograph by Stefan Zaklin/Getty Images.

Ashcroft and Robert Mueller. Iqbal asserted that the former attorney general and director of the FBI had "adopted an unconstitutional policy" that was related to an individual's race, religion, or national origin and resulted in unacceptable prison conditions. Iqbal thus maintained that the government had adopted (or condoned) a policy of treating detainees more harshly on the basis of their protected characteristics, running afoul of the First and Fifth Amendments to the Constitution.

The federal district court in the case denied the government's motion to dismiss, relying on the *Conley* "any set of facts" language. The *Twombly* decision was issued while an appeal in the *Iqbal* case was pending. The US Court of Appeals for the Second Circuit applied the new plausibility test to the *Iqbal* case, and concluded that there were sufficient factual allegations to allow the case to proceed. The Supreme Court again granted *certiorari*. In rendering its decision, the Supreme Court discussed that the Federal Rules mandate "more than an unadorned, the-defendant-unlawfully-harmed-me accusation."[29] There must be more than a "naked assertion" in the complaint, which is completely "devoid of further factual enhancement." In this case, the Court held that Iqbal had "not nudged" the allegations of discrimination "across the line from conceivable to plausible." The Court found the allegations far too conclusory, which "disentitles them to the presumption of truth."[30] The Court further found the nondiscriminatory explanation for the policies of the government – that it was looking into those "who had potential connections to those who committed terrorist acts" – was "more likely" than the allegations of the complaint. The Court found the allegations of discrimination without any factual support and thus insufficient to proceed.

In addition to finding that the factual allegations of the complaint did not state a plausible claim, the Court went on to address some of the legal arguments in the case. In particular, the Court expressly declined to limit the plausibility standard from *Twombly* to cases brought under the Sherman Act. Instead, the Court concluded that the *Twombly* standard should apply in "all civil actions," including "antitrust and discrimination suits alike." Thus, the *Iqbal* decision left little doubt that the plausibility standard would now be applicable to *all* federal civil cases. Moreover, the Supreme Court rejected the plaintiff's assertions that discriminatory intent in the case can be alleged "generally." Thus, the Court concluded that a complaint must assert more than simply that the defendant took an adverse action against an individual "on account of ... religion, race, and/or national origin." The Court demanded more – determining that conclusory statements such as these must be given some factual context. These "bare elements" in a complaint "fail[] to plead sufficient facts stated claim for purposeful and unlawful discrimination."[31]

The dissent, written by Justice Souter, was joined by Justices Stevens, Ginsburg, and Breyer.[32] These Justices believed that if taken as true, the allegations in the complaint demonstrated that the defendants were "aware of the discriminatory policy being implemented and deliberately indifferent to it." The dissent maintained that the complaint sufficiently linked Ashcroft and Mueller to the discriminatory practices, and therefore satisfied the plausibility standard. The Justices found "no principled basis for the majority's disregard" of these allegations.

Following *Iqbal* and *Twombly*, it is clear that in all cases something more than a conclusory statement is needed to proceed. Sufficient facts must be alleged to provide a plausible claim in the case. Intent cannot be alleged generally – specifics must be provided. Whether one agrees or disagrees with the Court's new standard, it leaves the state of the law remarkably unsettled. This uncertainty creates ambiguity in the process, and inconsistent results in individual cases. Indeed, the more amorphous standard can now be used by the courts to dismiss those cases with which they might disagree, or believe are cluttering its docket. The new plausibility standard is thus ill-defined, and fraught with problems.

THE *TWIQBAL* PROBLEM FOR WORKPLACE PLAINTIFFS

The plausibility standard is particularly troublesome for employment-discrimination plaintiffs. The standard requires a showing of intent without access to discovery. Intent is the key issue in any employment-discrimination case, but it can be almost impossible to establish without access to the defendant's witnesses or documents. As most discrimination cases are proven circumstantially, there is rarely a "smoking gun" establishing intentional bias. Plaintiffs have relied for years on discovery to help connect the dots in cases where discrimination is not overt or blatant.

Most discrimination in today's world takes place behind closed doors or even subconsciously by employers. Many studies have established that individuals are often unaware of the discrimination that they practice, or of their intrinsic bias against certain minority groups. Uncovering this type of discrimination can be difficult, if not impossible, if an employee is unable to access the documents, data, and other information in the employer's possession. This is not to say that plaintiffs should be allowed to go on a fishing expedition for discriminatory documents, but they should be permitted access to the more fundamental information needed in any case. The federal courts are able to control this type of discovery, and limit it when necessary. This type of careful case management can ensure that defendants are not being subjected to unfair or burdensome discovery in a case.

Access to the employer's documents is critically important in an employment-discrimination case, which presents a unique set of circumstances for plaintiffs. Unlike many other civil claims, without access to discovery, the plaintiff will often find it tremendously difficult to proceed. The employer will typically control the worker's personnel files, performance reviews, disciplinary records, and pay data. Similarly, the employer will have in its possession all of the same information related to the plaintiff's coworkers and supervisors. Discrimination by its very definition requires that the plaintiff show that she was treated differently from other employees. This can be almost impossible to establish without access to the records of other employees.

How can a women show that she was paid less than men without access to an employer's payroll records? How can a black worker demonstrate that white workers are statistically promoted at a faster rate without substantive documentation from the employer? Particular problems lie in the area of hiring discrimination, which is notoriously difficult to establish. An individual trying to show that she was not hired because of her race or sex faces a steep uphill battle. Applicants often fail to hear back from the employer or are rejected with little or no additional information. Such individuals would have a difficult time alleging a "plausible" hiring discrimination claim, as they would be relying initially on only speculation and conjecture.

Thus, the major hurdle for workers in surviving the dismissal stage of the proceedings is that the employer often controls much of the critical information that would support a discrimination claim. Without access to the information, many otherwise valid cases will be defeated early in the proceedings. By contrast, many other types of civil claims that arise outside of the workplace context do not have the "information" problem present in employment cases. In a typical negligence/car accident claim, for example, the plaintiff would have the same access to photos, police investigation reports, and insurance information as the defendant in the case. Or, in a medical malpractice case, the individual could often retrieve relevant medical information through other federal laws that could be used to establish the claim.[33] Workplace claims are far more difficult, however, as employees must carefully find a way to gather relevant documentation and claims in the employer's possession prior to bringing suit, and the employer will often stonewall once litigation is actually filed.

Another unfortunate reality for workplace plaintiffs is that it can be quite difficult to secure adequate representation in these cases. Attorneys know that the courts often disfavor the "clutter" that employment cases bring to their dockets. The potential payoff is not large in these cases. Claims brought under Title VII are capped and the larger punitive penalties are reserved only for the biggest employers. Because recovery is often tied directly to an employee's lost wages, lower paid workers do not stand to win much at trial – even where the discrimination is blatant. This creates a system where lower wage earners face additional barriers to the court system. Lawyers will be far less likely to take on a case for these workers because damages will be limited. Without adequate guidance from counsel, it can be almost impossible for a worker to prevail against an employer, who will be far more sophisticated in navigating the legal system. Though the government can step in to represent these workers, the truth is, it does so in only a handful of cases. Indeed, the EEOC typically brings only around 200 cases a year on behalf of aggrieved individuals, which is only a small fraction of the charges it receives annually.[34]

A final problem created by the plausibility standard is that the federal courts face an enormous backload of cases, and many of these are employment-related matters. Where courts are inclined to ease their caseload burden and dismiss these cases, the *Twombly/Iqbal* standard gives them an easy means of doing so. The standard is inherently amorphous, and it will take years to work out the ambiguity intrinsic to this new test. Indeed, the *Conley* "any set of facts" language was still being defined almost fifty years after its inception. The plausibility standard – which is far more ill-defined – will take equally long to interpret in the courts. Given this ambiguity, a court will rarely be second-guessed for dismissing an action that it deems not plausible on its face – even where the claim is otherwise viable.

For example, in *Mangum* v. *Town of Holly Springs*,[35] a federal district court considered a hostile work environment claim brought by a female city fire department employee. The employee alleged in her complaint that as a female firefighter, she was singled out because of her gender. More specifically, she was expressly told that others did not want to work with her because of her gender. She repeatedly complained about exposure to coarse and inappropriate language including use of the terms "mother f-ker," "c-ksucker," and "p-ssy." After one complaint about such language, the plaintiff was advised to "watch her back" and was subsequently exposed to enhanced vulgarities. This claim, despite being at the nascent complaint stage of the proceedings, presented a well-formulated cause of action. Indeed, it demonstrated all of the elements traditionally found in a hostile work environment claim. The action against her was expressly taken because of her gender in a traditionally all-male environment. The conduct was both severe and pervasive. The vulgar language and comments occurred frequently and even included threats to the plaintiff's safety. And the conduct only intensified after her complaints to management. Nonetheless, this case was dismissed by the district court using the *Twombly* standard. The district court acknowledged that while the environment may "perhaps" have been "unpleasant," the allegations failed to assert a hostile or abusive situation under the Supreme Court's new case law. Thus, there was no "plausible reading of [the] complaint" that would establish an actionable hostile work environment claim.

This type of result is startling. The *Mangum* case demonstrates that even with claims that clearly satisfy the pleading bar, the courts can use the plausibility standard to alleviate their dockets. The Supreme Court's new test is so subjective and malleable that it can easily be used to reject even strongly viable claims. This is not to say that such claims cannot be appealed, but this process is quite expensive, time-consuming, and risky. There are no more guarantees on appeal than there are in the initial case itself.

THE EMPIRICAL STUDIES

The *Mangum* case is only one example, and an argument can be made that the lower courts will occasionally issue bad decisions – regardless of the standard that is applied. Thus, a broader question that exists is the extent to which the plausibility standard is having an empirical impact on the dismissal rates across the field of employment-discrimination cases. Are courts – as a whole – now more likely to dismiss workplace claims using the Supreme Court's new standard? My early attempts to answer this question suggested that there was a small impact in Title VII cases as a whole, and a larger impact in disability cases. In a study performed shortly after the *Twombly* decision, my research showed that in cases involving discrimination on the basis of race, color, sex, national origin, and religion, there was "a higher percentage of decisions that grant a motion to dismiss in the Title VII context when the courts rely on the [] decision."[36] In analyzing cases brought under the ADA, I similarly found "a higher percentage of district court opinions granting motions to dismiss in the disability context in the year following the *Bell Atlantic* decision compared to the year prior."[37]

These studies, which were the first performed analyzing the specific impact of the plausibility standard on employment-discrimination cases specifically, create obvious concerns about issues of access to the courts. The problem, however, is that it is impossible to reach any firm conclusions from these types of studies, of which there are admitted shortcomings. Given the early nature of the plausibility standard, it can be almost impossible to construct a perfect analysis of the impact of the standard at this time. For example, the limitations of my analysis, which are detailed in my work, include a focus on published decisions. While this "reported case bias" would exist for both the pre- and post-*Twombly* cases, it does omit a number of decisions that went unpublished.[38] From the study, then, it is impossible to draw *conclusive* results from the numbers, regardless of how suggestive they are. Countless other studies have been performed after those I discuss here. These studies have tended to look at cases outside of the employment context, and have been performed at varying degrees of sophistication.[39] Most of the studies have been criticized at some level, as it is almost impossible to perform a perfect analysis in an area where many decisions evade detection by the courts, or to extrapolate from smaller samples. In his well-known piece, *The Twiqbal Puzzle and Empirical Study of Civil Procedure*, Stanford Law Professor David Engstrom highlights a number of the shortcomings of the *Twombly/Iqbal* studies, discussing the inherent difficulty with performing these types of analyses. While I disagree with Professor Engstrom's fundamental conclusions regarding the value of these analyses,[40] he is undoubtedly correct that many studies will suffer from some degree of flaw – no such analysis can be perfect at this time.

A more reliable determination of the access to justice problem created by the plausibility standard is far more time consuming and exhaustive than an empirical review – and involves an actual assessment of the facts of the thousands of cases analyzed under this standard. As part of the research for my empirical studies, I closely examined the way in which the courts were applying the standard. While this analysis is undoubtedly subjective, the anecdotal results were convincing. The lower courts are clearly using the standard to reject otherwise valid cases from proceeding. While, as noted earlier, it can be difficult to establish this fact on an across-the-board empirical level, there can be little doubt that in specific individual cases the plausibility standard is blocking valid cases from proceeding in the federal courts.

One clear example of this involves the overwhelming allegations of sexual harassment that were rejected by one federal court in the *Mangum* case discussed earlier.

In another case decided shortly after *Twombly*, *Urbanski v. Tech Data*,[41] an employee brought a race discrimination claim against the company for which she worked. The worker in the case alleged that she was black, that she had applied for a job at the company for which she was qualified, that she was rejected, and that the employer either hired someone outside the protected class or continued to solicit applications. Rigidly applying the *Twombly* standard, the district court rejected this complaint, finding that the plaintiff had failed to plead facts showing that she was *"more* qualified than her comparators." While such facts are not necessary to establish a *prima facie* case of discrimination, the court concluded that "claims of a general *prima facie* case do not suffice to show that [the plaintiff] is entitled to relief."[42] This decision flies in the face of the *Swierkiewicz* decision discussed earlier, which held that a plaintiff need *not* plead a *prima facie* case of discrimination. The district court, using the plausibility standard, thus elevated the pleading bar for employment cases.

In a related case, *Williams v. Ford Motor Co.*,[43] another federal district court rejected the allegations in a race discrimination suit. This complaint alleged that the company "followed a policy and practice of discrimination against Plaintiff" because he was black. The complaint further detailed the statute that was violated (Title VII), and included unlawful termination on a specified date as the specific adverse action that was taken. Again, the federal district court found the complaint "insufficient to 'raise a right to relief above the speculative level.'"[44] Though the allegations identified the protected race that was in question (black worker), the adverse action that occurred (fired), the date of the act, and a causal link, this was still insufficient to be permitted to proceed.

Although not a statistically significant sample, the *Mangum*, *Urbanski*, and *Williams* cases clearly show early specific examples of situations where the courts were using the plausibility standard in an overly aggressive manner. These cases all specified express details about the facts involved with the discrimination, yet each case was rejected by the lower court. The subjectivity and ambiguity of the plausibility standard allowed these courts to do so within months of the *Twombly* decision being issued. As the courts grow even more sophisticated in this regard, they can easily rely on the standard to disregard those cases that they are disinclined to consider, even where those claims are otherwise valid and should be permitted to proceed.

The lack of a definitive, clear standard for motions to dismiss under Rule 8 will thus wreak havoc for employment-discrimination plaintiffs. Courts will be free to use this plausibility test to clear those cases from its docket with which it is disinterested. The appellate courts have done little to help clarify the standards either. For example, in one case, *EEOC v. Concentra Health Services, Inc.*,[45] the Seventh Circuit Court of Appeals found that *Twombly* had abrogated substantive amounts of its prior pleading jurisprudence. At the same time, the court stated that it was "doubtful" whether the plausibility standard "changed the level of detail required by notice pleading." Thus, the decision seemingly raises the bar for employment-discrimination claims while expressly stating that this is not what is being done. These mixed signals only muddy the waters further, leaving the lower courts wide discretion with how to proceed with individual claims. The struggle that all courts face in this regard is not surprising, as the Supreme Court upended five decades of well-established pleading precedent and replaced it with a highly amorphous standard for which it provided little guidance. It can come as little surprise to the Supreme Court – or anyone else – that some of the lower courts would take this opportunity to rebuke civil-rights claims.

THE *SWIERKIEWICZ* DEBATE

One question *Twombly* and *Iqbal* implicitly raise is whether *Swierkiewicz* remains a good law. As noted earlier, *Swierkiewicz* stands for the proposition that a plaintiff need not plead a *prima facie* case of discrimination under Title VII to survive dismissal. Can this holding withstand the plausibility test created by the Court? While this remains an open question, I believe that the holding of *Swierkiewicz* remains intact.[46] Part of the concern over the continued viability of the case is that the opinion cites to *Conley* three times and permits "conclusory allegations of discrimination" in Title VII cases.[47] *Twombly* and *Iqbal* abrogate *Conley*, and expressly reject any type of allegations based on "mere conclusory statements."

Nonetheless, in the face of these concerns, the *Twombly* Court expressly explained how it was distinguishing the decision from *Swierkiewicz*. Had the Court wanted to, it could have expressly overruled the decision. Instead, the Court went out of its way to explain how its holding was in accord with the earlier case. Indeed, citing to *Swierkiewicz* with approval, the Court stated that it was *not* "requir[ing a] heightened fact pleading of specifics," explaining how the Title VII case would comport with the plausibility test.[48] The *Twombly* Court thus appeared concerned about reconciling its decision with *Swierkiewicz*. The *Iqbal* Court, however, did not cite *Swierkiewicz* at all. While *Swierkiewicz* must now be considered in the broader context of the plausibility standard, it does appear to still be good law with respect to Title VII claims. Until the Court expressly abrogates the decision, it should be relied upon in employment-discrimination cases. Plaintiffs should not be required to plead a *prima facie* case to be permitted to proceed.

My reading of *Twombly*, *Iqbal*, and the plausibility standard suggests that *Swierkiewicz* remains intact. However, this proposition is not without its critics. Indeed, scholars have called into question the continued viability of the case.[49] The appellate courts are already struggling with how much weight to give the decision. For example, the Ninth Circuit Court of Appeals concluded that the Supreme Court had "reaffirmed the holding of *Swierkiewicz* ... for Title VII employment discrimination"[50] cases. By contrast, the Third Circuit held "because *Conley* has been specifically repudiated by both *Twombly* and *Iqbal*, so too has *Swierkiewicz*, at least insofar as it concerns pleading requirements and relies on *Conley*."[51]

This disagreement among scholars and the courts will only lead to more uncertainty and ambiguity as plaintiffs attempt to formulate their complaints. In my view, *Swierkiewicz* is good law, and should be interpreted as such until the Supreme Court expressly states otherwise. *Swierkiewicz* provides structure and substantial guidance to plaintiffs attempting to plead an employment-discrimination case. If the case were overturned, it would lead to years – even decades – of confusion over what must be alleged in a Title VII complaint. I cannot imagine that this is the result that the Supreme Court intended to achieve. And if this was its intent, it would assuredly have been more overt in clarifying the reach of its decision.

THE GOOSE AND THE GANDER

One fascinating aspect of the *Twombly/Iqbal* plausibility test is the applicability of the standard to defendants. More specifically, the first document typically filed in a federal civil case is the federal complaint. As noted earlier, the complaint must satisfy Rule 8(a) by including "a short and plain statement of the claim showing that the pleader is entitled to relief." The defendant will often respond by answering that complaint. Within this answer, the defendant usually includes what are known as "affirmative defenses." The Federal Rules also govern those affirmative defenses. Under Rule 8(c) the defendant must "affirmatively state any avoidance or affirmative defense" in its pleading response. The question thus arises as to whether this affirmative defense raised by the defendant would need to satisfy the "plausibility standard." More simply put, is what is good for the goose good for the gander – will we hold defendants to the same standard that we hold plaintiffs?

Like most legal questions following *Twombly/Iqbal*, the answer is unclear, and there are two divergent views on the issue. The first view concludes that the plausibility standard was articulated by the Supreme Court in the context of the complaint, and it should therefore be so limited.[52] This view relies on the argument that the Court decided the cases expressly under Rule 8(a), and failed to mention affirmative defenses or Rule 8(c) anywhere in the opinions. Similarly, there is an identifiable difference between Rules 8(a) and 8(c). The Rule for complaints requires a "showing that the pleader is entitled to relief." By contrast, Rule 8(c) requires only that the defendant "affirmatively state" its defense. Arguably, then, a "showing" creates a higher threshold than a "statement," lending credence to the theory that the Court would apply the higher plausibility standard only to the plaintiff's complaint.

In addition, from a policy/practical standpoint, defendants already have an enhanced incentive to provide detailed information in the response about the affirmative defense. If the defense is not adequately identified and set forth in the response, a court can bar it from being raised later in the case. This provides an incentive for defendants to exhaustively support their position. This incentive simply does not exist for plaintiffs, who might actually benefit from providing less clarity in the complaint. For policy reasons, then, the plausibility standard makes much more sense as a sword to force plaintiffs to provide clarity in the complaint. Defendants are already likely, as a practical matter, to make certain that their defenses are well-supported.

Finally, there is an additional practical consideration here – the timelines for filing a complaint and a response. Plaintiffs can often have months (or even years) from the time the charge of discrimination is submitted until the federal complaint is filed. This gives them a sufficient amount of time to gather facts, interview witnesses, and seek documentation. They also may benefit from any information the employer might provide to the federal government, as well as any documentation uncovered by an EEOC investigation. By contrast, under Rule 12(a), defendants have only twenty-one days from the time the complaint is filed to issue a response. Given the substantial time constraints imposed on defendants under the Rules, it may seem unfair to expect them to provide a detailed defense so early in the process. This limited timeframe would comport with the Rule's requirement that only a "statement" of the defense is required in the response.

A more compelling argument, however, is that the plausibility standard would apply to *both* a plaintiff's complaint and a defendant's affirmative defense. The Rule 8(c) requirement that a defendant "affirmatively *state* any avoidance or affirmative defense" in its response is directly analogous to the plaintiff's requirement under Rule 8(a)(2) of providing a "short and plain *statement* of the claim." The Court's reasoning in both *Iqbal* and *Twombly* seems firmly grounded in the requirement of what type of "short and plain statement" must be provided to the opposing side to satisfy the rule. The Court did not emphasize any of the language that would distinguish the two requirements of Rules 8(a) and 8(c). Thus, in its parsing of the language in the Federal Rules, the Court's plausibility standard would appear to apply to *all* pleadings in a case, not simply the plaintiff's complaint.

In addition, much of the Court's reasoning for adopting the plausibility standard is based on more practical considerations. These same policy rationales would apply to the affirmative defense. The Supreme Court appeared concerned with the high cost of discovery, as well as adequate notice being provided to the opposing side. These same basic considerations would apply equally to both plaintiffs and defendants. A plaintiff can approach discovery with a more streamlined approach if it has been given sufficient explanation of the defenses in the case. Inadequate notice would only result in additional discovery being required to uncover the specific nature of the defenses that are being asserted. Thus, substantial judicial resources can be saved by imposing the same plausibility requirement on defendants that already exists for plaintiffs.

Further policy considerations also support this approach and the twenty-one-day time constraint discussed for responding to the complaint, in many ways, may be a red herring. The defendant will often readily have the information at its disposal necessary to provide sufficient detail to state a plausible affirmative defense. For example, one of the most common affirmative defenses – the assertion that the plaintiff has failed to file a claim within the statute of limitations – would not require any substantial investigation on the part of the plaintiff. By contrast, the plaintiff is typically faced with the daunting task of providing sufficient facts to establish that the defendant was operating with discriminatory intent.[53] Much of the evidence that would prove this fact would be in the defendant's possession, making it far more difficult for a plaintiff to state such a claim early in the proceedings prior to any discovery. Thus, the defendant should – at least by comparison – easily have access to the information that would allow it to respond adequately to a complaint. And, where the information cannot be readily obtained by the defendant, the courts can (and should) allow amended pleadings pursuant to Rule 15. This would permit defendants to include a new defense when it was identified later during the course of discovery.

Prior to the adoption of the plausibility test, the courts have tended to apply the same standard to both the motion to dismiss a complaint under Rule 12(b)(6) and a motion to strike an affirmative defense under Rule 12(f). For example, one federal court determined that "the standard by which 12(f) and 12(b)(6) motions are evaluated are mirror images."[54] Most other courts have made similar determinations, evaluating the two motions under the same standard.[55] As the same standard was applied to motions to dismiss and motions to strike an affirmative defense prior to *Twombly* and *Iqbal*, there can be little justification for treating the two differently now.

Nonetheless, there has already been substantial disagreement in the lower courts.[56] A number of these courts have limited the plausibility standard to the complaint, not extending it to the defendant's pleadings. These courts have emphasized the time limitations for defendants in responding to the complaint and have highlighted the differential in language between Rules 8(a) and 8(c).[57] The majority of courts, however, appear to be applying the plausibility standard more broadly, expecting the same factual support for an affirmative defense as would be found in a complaint. These courts have found that it is more "even handed" to apply the standard to both parties, which will have sufficient information to proceed more clearly into discovery.[58] Similarly, these courts maintain that a contrary reading "sets the pleading bar far too low"[59] for defendants and hold that "a wholly conclusory affirmative defense is not sufficient."[60]

The disagreement in the lower courts reflects the irony over this issue. Much of the judiciary would restrict access to plaintiffs in seeking relief for civil-rights violations. These courts would require the plaintiffs to find evidence of discriminatory intent without the use of the federal procedural mechanism of discovery. Many of these same courts, however, would require far less of the defendants when responding to these complaints. These courts would permit a more cursory statement of the defense to stand, and would allow defendants to explore the contours of the defense within the scope of discovery. The existing bias in the courts toward the defendant (and employer) may serve to limit the effect of many of the civil-rights laws. While these laws are vibrant on their face, they become meaningless when plaintiffs are not permitted to proceed with their claims.

Twombly and *Iqbal* have failed to capture the public's attention or to make national headlines. These decisions, however, have done much to alter the rights of civil-rights plaintiffs across the country. Without the ability to vindicate themselves of employment law violations, the procedural rules have now been set up to make it increasingly difficult for workers to even play the game.

SURVIVING THE PLAUSIBILITY STANDARD: PLAINTIFFS

This is not to say that the plausibility standard will completely eviscerate civil-rights claims. Indeed, many employment-discrimination claims have still been allowed to proceed to discovery. The deck is now simply stacked against plaintiffs, and unsophisticated parties can easily find their otherwise valid claims rejected by the courts. The key, then, is not to be unsophisticated when it comes to the *Twombly/ Iqbal* standard. Indeed, in all civil-rights cases, plaintiffs should be extraordinarily cautious (even somewhat paranoid) when pleading their claims. The subjective, ambiguous pleading standard created by the Supreme Court has made it easy for those courts inclined against civil-rights claims to clear their docket of these cases. Plaintiffs must proceed carefully, and insulate their claims from dismissal (and enhance their chances on appeal where a claim has been improperly dismissed by the district court).

Before filing a complaint, plaintiffs should always: (1) understand the plausibility standard and how it has been applied in the particular jurisdiction where the case will arise; (2) make themselves familiar with the plausibility rulings of the particular judge assigned to the matter (if known in advance of filing the complaint); (3) be knowledgeable in how to articulate enough factual matter to support the claim and standard in the jurisdiction; and (4) always err (at least at this early stage in the development of the law) on the side of "overpleading" facts to help survive dismissal.

This may sound easier said than done. After all, with such a subjective standard, it is difficult for a plaintiff to ever know when she has crossed the line from "conceivable" to "plausible." Fortunately, the Supreme Court has also given plaintiffs a clear standard to apply in employment-discrimination pleadings. The *Swierkiewicz* decision discussed earlier provides employment-discrimination plaintiffs with a "safe harbor"[61] for pleading these claims. *Swierkiewicz* stands for the basic proposition that a plaintiff need not plead a *prima facie* case of discrimination to survive a motion to dismiss under Rule 12(b)(6).[62] This basic premise was confirmed by the Supreme Court in its *Twombly* decision as well.[63] The corollary to this premise is that where a plaintiff does plead a *prima facie* case of discrimination, she will be insulated from dismissal. While there can obviously be very limited exceptions to this corollary, as a general rule, where a *prima facie* case is pled, it should survive dismissal.

Discussing this general rule, I have developed a framework that all employment-discrimination plaintiffs can follow when pleading a case under Title VII. By following this framework, plaintiffs can avoid the trap that has been set under the *Twombly/Iqbal* standard and assure that a claim will satisfy the plausibility standard. While not all claims will neatly fit under this framework, the vast majority of cases will fall in line with the standard established here. In short, after *Twombly* and *Iqbal*, plaintiffs should assure that their claims provide factual information supporting:

1. The victim of the alleged discrimination;
2. The approximate time that the discrimination occurred;
3. The protected characteristic at issue;
4. The qualifications of the victim for the position;
5. The nature of the discrimination suffered;
6. Other evidence of discrimination (that others outside the protected class were treated better, statistical data, discriminatory comments, etc.); and
7. That the discrimination by the employer was *because of* the plaintiff's protected characteristic.[64]

Where a plaintiff is able to establish all of these facts, she should be permitted to proceed with the case and survive dismissal. While straightforward, this test identifies the factual component of all of the major issues in a typical employment-discrimination case. It states who has suffered the adverse employment act; whether the act occurred on the basis of race, color, sex, national origin, or religion; what precise adverse action was involved and when it occurred; and provides a causal link. This information is actually more than what is required by *Swierkiewicz* and the *prima facie* case. Providing this information should insulate plaintiffs from having their claims dismissed.

To provide an example of what can be alleged in a case of discrimination, consider the following basic facts pled in a hypothetical complaint of a victim of race discrimination: "On May 9, 2017, I was demoted by my employer because I am black despite having performed satisfactory work for ten years in my prior position. A less qualified white employee was promoted to my prior position."

These basic factual statements should be enough to proceed in the matter, as they provide the primary components of the *prima facie* case: they include the protected category at issue (black worker), the basis for the plaintiff's qualifications (ten years of satisfactory work), the adverse action that was suffered (demotion), and other evidence of discrimination (white worker treated better). In addition to providing the basic facts of the *prima facie* case, the statements also identify the victim of discrimination ("I" or the signatory to the complaint), the timing of the discrimination (May 9, 2017), and the causal link ("demoted ... because I am black"). Despite being a very short, plain statement, there can be little doubt that it provides enough information to survive dismissal. Indeed, it sets forth all of the information required of the *McDonnell Douglas* test, as well as other details of the case.

Surviving dismissal should not be difficult in an employment-discrimination case. The problem arises not from the length of the complaint – which, as seen above, can often be quite short – but rather from particular omissions that are made. If a plaintiff fails to identify one of the critical seven factors identified here, she opens herself up to a dismissal motion. This is true regardless of how much specificity is identified in the other factors. Thus, for example, a ten-page complaint identifying the nature of the discrimination at issue might be lacking if it does not provide some "other evidence" of discrimination – such as how similarly situated employees outside of the protected class are treated differently from the plaintiff. Plaintiffs should thus use this framework as a checklist of sorts to ensure that they have provided all of the relevant information in the complaint.

This is not to say that the courts should dismiss a case where this information is not provided. Indeed, I have previously argued that far less is required for a plaintiff to proceed.[65] However, by providing this information, plaintiffs have exceeded the mandates of *Swierkiewicz* and the *prima facie* case. There can be little doubt that plaintiffs who provide this basic core information in the complaint should survive dismissal. Similarly, plaintiffs may want to include additional information in the complaint that helps paint the picture of the discrimination involved. This should not be necessary under the requirements of the law, but is advisable where plaintiffs have the facts to do so. In the current environment, where there is a tendency by the courts to use the plausibility standard as a sword, plaintiffs should err on the side of including *more* facts than necessary to help protect their claims.

The safe harbor created by the seven-part framework set forth here should not distract the courts or litigants from the true purpose of the *prima facie* case. The Supreme Court has repeatedly emphasized that the *McDonnell Douglas* test was not meant to provide an onerous burden for plaintiffs.[66] Rather, it was simply meant to weed out those cases that were – on their face – not properly before the court. Where a plaintiff is not even qualified for a position, or cannot articulate what adverse action was suffered, the case clearly should not be permitted to go forward. But where these basic facts are provided, and the framework has been satisfied, a Title VII claim should not be dismissed. While plausibility will take years to define in the employment-discrimination context, there can be little doubt that pleading a *prima facie* case provides plaintiffs with some protections. And where the seven elements of the proposed standard are properly identified in the complaint, it would be erroneous to reject the plaintiff's claim.

If there is disagreement on the framework that I have provided, it will likely come from the causal link requirement. I argue here that simply stating that a plaintiff has been demoted *because of* her race is enough to state a claim. The other circumstances provided in the complaint (that a white worker was treated better) help further substantiate causation in the case. Nonetheless, some courts might require more. Specifically, courts rigidly applying the plausibility standard might look for some further evidence that the employer has intended to discriminate. Based on *Swierkiewicz*, *McDonnell Douglas*, and other Supreme Court cases, this view would seem inconsistent with what the Court has required in the past. However, plaintiffs should be wary of this type of additional requirement on intent. And, if the plaintiff does have this type of evidence in its possession at the time of filing the complaint, it should certainly be pled.

Another possible disagreement with my standard would be that it requires *too much* of the plaintiff. After all, in a pre-*Twombly* decision, Judge Easterbrook famously stated, "'I was turned down for a job because of my race' is all a complaint has to say" to survive dismissal.[67] This statement includes far less information than the framework set forth earlier. I agree with Judge Easterbrook that the statement he provides should be sufficient to proceed in a Title VII case. My seven-part framework set forth here is intended to protect those plaintiffs in cases where the judge does not take as lenient of a view on the dismissal standard as Judge Easterbrook. The framework is meant to provide a safe harbor, *not* a minimum pleading standard.

One final consideration – already addressed earlier – is the viability of the *Swierkiewicz* decision after *Twombly* and *Iqbal*. If the courts ultimately reject that case, it will add more confusion on the question of what an employment-discrimination plaintiff must allege in the complaint. My view, however, is that *Swierkiewicz* will remain intact as demonstrated by the *Twombly* Court's approval of the case and the other considerations noted earlier. Regardless, a plaintiff who pleads the seven-part framework outlined above should still plead enough facts to establish a plausible claim.

THE PLAUSIBILITY STANDARD, A GOLD MINE FOR DEFENDANTS

The seven-part framework set forth here was obviously developed to help protect plaintiffs and civil-rights litigants. However, it also highlights the opportunity that defendants have been given in recent years to pursue dismissal at a far earlier stage of the proceedings. From the defense perspective, it now makes far more sense to challenge a plaintiff's pleadings under Rule 12(b)(6) if any weaknesses can be readily identified. As Professor Suja Thomas has opined, the motion to dismiss is now the new motion for summary judgment.[68] In prior years, moving for the dismissal of an employment-discrimination case at the complaint stage of the pleadings was often an exercise in futility that would simply drive up the legal fees of both parties. After the Supreme Court pleading decisions, however, employers should seriously evaluate the validity of the case at this earlier point in the litigation to advocate for their clients zealously.

Thus, defendants can similarly use the seven-part framework identified here to test for any weaknesses in a plaintiff's case. If a particular fact has not been pled, the employer should ask whether the failure of the plaintiff to do so undercuts the plausibility of the case. If all of these facts have been pled, defendants should be more cautious in bringing such a motion, as it will likely fail.

SURVIVING THE PLAUSIBILITY STANDARD: DEFENDANTS

The seven-part framework addressed earlier tells only part of the story. This framework provides a safe harbor for plaintiffs attempting to allege an employment-discrimination claim. As noted earlier, however, there is a substantial question as to whether the plausibility test also applies to a defendant's affirmative defense. Though not all of the lower courts have required defendants to plead a plausible affirmative defense, many of the lower courts to reach the question have done so. And there is no indication that the Supreme Court will address this question any time soon.

Thus, unless defendants are certain that the court where the claim has been filed does not require a plausible statement of the affirmative defense, employers – just like plaintiffs – should be cautious when proceeding with their claims. This issue goes beyond employment-discrimination cases and would similarly apply to all civil claims. Defendants are often put in a difficult situation when responding to these claims, as they must assert their defense within twenty-one days under the Federal Rules.[69] This does not give them much time to gather the necessary information to issue an adequate response. Nonetheless, in the employment setting, employers will usually have the information necessary to respond to the complaint.

Just like plaintiffs, during this uncertain period in the jurisprudence, employers will want to *overplead* their affirmative defense to assure that it will not fall victim to the plausibility standard. The possible defenses that an employer can raise in a particular case are countless, and it is thus difficult to articulate a framework that would capture all of these scenarios and lead to a plausible defense. Nonetheless, there are some obvious generalities that can be made. The employer must make sure that it is providing the employee with enough information about the defense to give sufficient notice and allow the opposing side to gather further details during discovery. In this way, employers must make certain to provide the legal basis for the defense, as well as the basic facts that make it applicable to the particular case.

In many instances, this might be extraordinarily straightforward. For example, where the defendant believes that the plaintiff's claim is barred by the statute of limitations, only a very basic claim is needed. Under Title VII, the statement would simply state that the plaintiff failed to file a charge within 300 days, or failed to file the complaint within 90 days of receiving the right-to-sue letter. This information would provide sufficient notice to the plaintiff of the contours of the defense. To increase the plausibility of such a defense, the employer might also want to include specific dates and times to show how the plaintiff failed to comply.

In other contexts, pleading a plausible affirmative defense might be more difficult. In one of the more common defenses raised in the employment context – the *Faragher-Ellerth* defense to sexual harassment claims – more specificity is needed than in the more typical affirmative defense pleadings. In these cases, employers often attempt to evade liability for harassment claims by arguing that they (1) adopted and properly maintained an antiharassment policy and complaint procedure;[70] and (2) the plaintiff did not make a complaint under the policy, and this failure was unreasonable.[71] Although there are many ways in which the defense can be asserted, these two elements demonstrate one of the most common articulations. In this scenario, then, more detailed information would be needed to state a plausible affirmative defense than is more commonly required. The employer would be required to state facts that show the existence of the policy, as well as demonstrating that the policy was effective and well-maintained. Similarly, the employer would need to state that the employee did not adequately complain under this procedure and that the plaintiff's failure to do so was unreasonable. The defense could be bolstered by including some of the basic components of the policy, indicating that there were multiple avenues of complaint, and stating that all employees were trained on the policy on a regular basis. Obviously, the specifics of the pleading would depend highly on the exact nature of the case, and the type of employer involved.

The specificity with which a plausible affirmative defense must be pled will thus depend largely on the nature of the defense itself. As seen earlier, a simple statute of limitations defense will be straightforward. A more complex sexual harassment claim may require a far more detailed response. The employer must carefully evaluate each situation to ensure that it has included enough facts in its response to adequately articulate a plausible affirmative defense. Just like plaintiffs, defendants should be wary of falling into the trap of stating a defense that is too conclusory and not supported by sufficient factual detail. Failure to adequately state the defense runs the risk of waiving the defense in the case. Defendants are thus best advised to err on the side of including enough details to justify the defense, rather than simply parroting the statutory language. As more cases are decided on these grounds, it will become clear exactly how much detail will be required of defendants. As of now, this issue is just as unclear – if not more so – than the question of what is required of the plaintiff's complaint.

CONGRESSIONAL INTERVENTION

The *Twombly* and *Iqbal* cases sent a shockwave through the academic and legal community. Though not high-profile decisions, the cases were quickly seen as having a negative impact on many plaintiff-side groups. Civil-rights plaintiffs were particularly seen as suffering the most from the decisions.[72] As noted, many attempts to empirically quantify the impact of the cases were performed, with varying results. Attempts at congressional intervention were also made, and bills were proposed in committees of both the US House of Representatives and the US Senate.[73] Both governing bodies held hearings on the issue and a tremendous amount of oral and written testimony was generated. Many agreed that the cases would be devastating for civil-rights plaintiffs. However, the bills ultimately went nowhere and the holdings of the decisions are still intact.

The dry, procedural nature of the cases may likely be to blame for the lack of success of any legislative intervention. The cases turned on technical points of law, and the decisions did not draw major headlines. There was little political push to overturn these decisions, which did not capture the public's attention.

CONCLUDING THOUGHTS ON PLAUSIBILITY

The irony of the *Twombly* and *Iqbal* decisions is that, in my view, they have done far more to undo civil-rights litigation than any other case in decades. And this has all occurred largely under the radar. The decisions change the fundamental ability of plaintiffs to bring civil-rights claims. Individuals now face a steep uphill battle to even gain access to the judicial system. The courts are now far better able to reject those cases that are deemed to simply be cluttering their dockets, regardless of the viability of the claims. Congressional intervention is needed, but has not occurred. Unsophisticated or *pro se* litigants will have tremendous difficulty adequately pleading their cases. Even seasoned attorneys will continue to grapple with the meaning of "plausibility." The seven-part test set forth here will help all litigants to evaluate the quality of the pleadings. This test allows plaintiffs to put their best foot forward in the litigation and helps them to better navigate the difficult judicial process.

The proposed framework offers a number of benefits to the litigants, and should be considered in all employment-based litigation. Perhaps the most obvious advantage of the framework is its transparency and simplicity. The model proposed here allows the parties to quickly and easily assess the merits of the case and identify any potential shortcomings. The framework is straightforward and helps readily identify the primary elements of any employment-discrimination case. In the face of a plausibility standard mired with ambiguity and confusion, the proposed test would bring much-needed clarity to a vague area of the law.

The framework is multifunctional and can be used by all parties involved, including the courts. Plaintiffs can use the proposed test in a number of ways. Most importantly, it can be used to ensure that the pleadings in the case are complete and state a plausible claim. However, plaintiffs can also use the test earlier in the process – when evaluating whether to bring the initial claim. Thus, the test will save enormous judicial resources by preventing the litigation of claims that fail to satisfy the legal standards. Defendants can use the test to identify potential shortcomings in a plaintiff's case as well, and to move for dismissal where such weaknesses are found (keeping in mind, however, that the test does not create a minimum pleading standard). Finally, the judiciary can similarly use the framework to help evaluate potential claims and further define the plausibility standard in employment-discrimination cases. The proposed model can thus help some courts to resist the temptation that might exist to dismiss an otherwise valid discrimination claim by using the plausibility test to adopt a heightened pleading standard. The uniformity brought by the test would clarify an uncertain area for everyone involved with civil-rights cases.

The framework will also help save judicial resources. The uniformity brought by the proposed model will lead to more streamlined pleadings and prevent plaintiffs from filing cumbersome complaints. Plaintiffs will also be less likely to bring frivolous claims in the first place, and all parties will be more likely to settle cases where the standard implicated is more transparent. More certainty in the process unquestionably leads to reduced litigation costs and a greater potential for settlement.[74]

While the proposed model has a number of very practical benefits, it also makes a valuable contribution to the law. Most notably, it adds to the rigorous debate over how to define plausibility. While this contribution is limited to one area of jurisprudence – employment-discrimination claims – this field is one that is most in need of clarity. Applying the plausibility standard to civil-rights matters is fraught with problems, and a more definitive framework provides some certainty to an otherwise ambiguous area. The test helps separate out those claims that are merely "conceivable" from those that are plausible, and in doing so sheds light on this problematic area.

SUMMARY JUDGMENT: THE MORE TRADITIONAL WAY TO BLOCK CIVIL-RIGHTS CASES

The motion to dismiss has now become a valuable tool in the arsenal of employers to block civil-rights claims from advancing. What makes this tool particularly attractive is that it can be used at the inception of the litigation. No documents need be turned over and no depositions need to be taken. It is an extraordinarily cost-effective way of handling litigation for employers. Without doubt, the plausibility standard will be an enormous hurdle for plaintiffs trying to access the courts to bring civil-rights claims.

The truth is, however, that even before *Twombly* and *Iqbal*, few cases were making it to trial.[75] They were proceeding past the complaint and discovery phase of the litigation, but were being rejected at summary judgment.[76] Even before the plausibility standard, then, the courts have been hostile toward employment litigation. This hostility simply came later in the process.

In an employment-discrimination case, a defendant's motion for summary judgment typically occurs after discovery has concluded. At this stage of the proceedings, the defendant argues that, even if the facts that have been uncovered are viewed in the light most favorable to the plaintiff, there is not enough evidence to allow the claim to go forward. This is a judicial determination, and thus, if the judge agrees with the defendant's position, that judge will take the case out of the hands of the jury. The summary judgment motion was not typically used as often in the early days of Title VII.[77] It has now become routine, however, and a defense attorney who fails to raise the motion could even be sanctioned for malpractice depending on the facts of the particular case.

This is likely the result of three Supreme Court decisions that dramatically altered the litigation landscape and invited the courts – rather than juries – to resolve many disputes before them. Known as the *Celotex* trilogy, the Supreme Court's decisions in *Anderson v. Liberty Lobby, Inc.*,[78] *Celotex Corp. v. Catrett*,[79] and *Matsushita Electric Industrial Co. v. Zenith Radio Corp.*,[80] all widely resulted in additional claims being resolved through Rule 56. While the *Celotex* trilogy has been widely criticized by many academics,[81] it has had a particularly negative impact in the employment-discrimination area for civil-rights litigants.[82]

Professor Arthur Miller – the leading scholar on procedural law issues – has correctly summarized the widespread impact of these decisions:

> On a practical level, the three decisions collectively forge a new, stronger role for the motion. *Matsushita* requires that the moving party's evidence be sufficient to render the plaintiff's claim implausible. *Anderson* allows the trial court to enter judgment if the evidence produced by the plaintiff is not sufficient, under the applicable standard of proof, to convince the judge that a reasonable jury could return a verdict in his favor. And *Celotex* has made it easier to shift the burden of adducing support for the nonmovant's legal position on a Rule 56 motion and effectively obliges the plaintiff to come forward, on the defendant's motion, with her case before trial. Stated differently, *Celotex* has made it easier to make the motion, and *Anderson* and *Matsushita* have increased the chances that it will be granted.[83]

It is impossible to quantify how many claims are thrown out on summary judgment and how many cases actually make it to trial in the workplace context. In one of the better known studies on this question, which was conducted by Kevin Clermont and Stewart Schwab, the authors were able to conclude that only 3.7 percent of employment cases go to trial.[84] This is a remarkably low number and signals just how difficult it is to carefully navigate the litigation process. What is equally revealing is the success rate of those workplace claims that are put before a jury. One study determined that employment plaintiffs prevailed in approximately 60 percent of cases that made it that far in the litigation.[85] And, the average recovery for the worker in those cases was in the low six figures.[86]

This begs the question, then, that if employment-discrimination plaintiffs are highly successful when their claims are put before a jury of their peers, why is the judicial system so reticent to allow these cases to make it that far in the process? How many claims are being thrown out of the process that would otherwise result in a favorable verdict if evaluated by a jury? One current federal judge, Mark Bennett, has lamented on the difficulty all litigants have had getting before a jury and sees this as a dramatic paradigm shift in recent years.[87] From Judge Bennett's eloquent essay on the subject:

> [S]ummary judgment motions were filed far less frequently in [the early] days, and were rarely granted. Back then, I read the advance sheets for every reported employment discrimination case in federal court, and seldom did I read a decision granting summary judgment on facts that troubled me. Many circuits had a clearly stated preference against summary judgment in employment discrimination cases, especially disparate treatment cases, because they almost always turn on delicate factual nuances of intent ... As employment discrimination cases worked their way through the [courts] in the 1990s and beyond, the principles that summary judgment was

"disfavored" or should be used "sparingly" were ignored far more often than they were followed by both the district courts and the Eighth Circuit Court of Appeals. The federal reporters are filled with hundreds – if not thousands – of employment discrimination cases where, despite the fact that these principles were the existing law of the circuit, courts swiftly granted summary judgment.[88]

Judge Bennett has beautifully summarized the recent trend in this area. Summary judgment has been and continues to be an effective way of evaluating the validity of cases in the employment-discrimination area after discovery has already taken place. Other areas of the law may not necessarily have such a mechanism in place. Thus, the rigid pleading standards of *Iqbal* and *Twombly* may make far more sense in contexts other than those claims that arise from the workplace. Summary judgment is already an effective way of assuring that only the most viable cases find their way to a jury. Indeed, many have exhaustively written on the topic of how summary judgment itself is far too rigid of a standard in unnecessarily preventing otherwise viable cases to proceed to court.[89]

With summary judgment providing this unique filtering function in employment-discrimination cases, there is simply no need to duplicate this function at an earlier dismissal stage of the litigation. *Twombly* and *Iqbal*, therefore, make little sense in the employment setting, particularly where it is so difficult for plaintiffs to allege evidence of discriminatory intent without access to the discovery process. Nonetheless, as we see in numerous cases already, the practical effect of *Twombly* and *Iqbal* may be to move up this "filtering mechanism" in employment-discrimination cases from summary judgment to the motion to dismiss.[90]

RICCI AND ACCESS TO JUSTICE ISSUES

One important recent case, *Ricci v. DeStefano*,[91] addresses a more nuanced access to justice issue. The case is extraordinarily complex, but is worth analyzing here because of the way the Roberts Court reached out to protect the interests of the *majority* group in workplace claims. A more detailed analysis of the case follows.

In 2003, the City of New Haven, Connecticut, administered a test to 118 of its firefighters for possible promotions to lieutenant and captain positions within the department.[92] The city planned to use the test to determine who would be eligible for promotions for the next two years, and many candidates studied extensively for the exam "at considerable personal and financial cost."[93]

The city hired a consulting group, at a cost of $100,000, to help prepare and administer the tests.[94] The consultants selected by the city specialized in promotional tests administered to public-safety officials, and the group performed an extensive analysis to make certain that the exam would measure the knowledge and skills

FIGURE 2.3 Firefighter's gear. The Supreme Court's opinion in *Ricci* v. *DeStefano*, which involved a group of firefighters at the New Haven, Connecticut, fire department, remains a controversial decision that played a significant role in Justice Sonia Sotomayor's confirmation hearings.
Credit: Photograph by Liz West

necessary for the vacant positions. As part of this process, the group observed the daily tasks of the officers and conducted interviews with those in the department. Minority firefighters were "oversampled" as part of this analytical process to make certain that the test ultimately developed would not be biased against minority candidates. Based on this information and other departmental sources such as training manuals and departmental procedures, the consulting group developed a multiple-choice exam and a separate oral test.

To grade the oral examinations, the group selected thirty assessors, all of whom held a higher rank than the positions that were being filled. Two-thirds of these assessors were minorities, and all of these individuals received several hours of training on how to evaluate candidate responses. The candidates sat for the test at the end of 2003, and the results revealed that a disproportionate number of white exam-takers had passed the exam:

Seventy-seven candidates completed the lieutenant examination – 43 whites, 19 blacks, and 15 Hispanics. Of those, 34 candidates passed – 25 whites, 6 blacks, and 3

Hispanics … [T]he top 10 candidates were eligible for an immediate promotion to lieutenant. All 10 were white …

Forty-one candidates completed the captain examination – 25 whites, 8 blacks, and 8 Hispanics. Of those, 22 candidates passed – 16 whites, 3 blacks, and 3 Hispanics … [Nine] candidates were eligible for an immediate promotion to captain – 7 whites and 2 Hispanics.[95]

Though city officials questioned whether these results suggested that the examination was discriminatory, the consulting group maintained that the test was valid and that the poor performance of minority candidates "was likely due to various external factors."[96] The consulting group also indicated that these results were consistent with other departmental tests. At hearings on whether to certify the results, the New Haven Civil Service Board heard from firefighters who argued strenuously on both sides of the issue. The leader of the consulting-group team that had prepared the examination explained how the test was job-related and "facially neutral."[97] The Board also heard from an industrial psychologist who expressed concerns about the methodology of the examination but concluded that the test was "reasonably good."[98] A retired minority fire captain from another state further indicated that the test questions were job-related. And a university professor told the Board that the results were consistent with testing in other areas.

At the final Board meeting on the issue, New Haven's city counsel nonetheless argued that the results should *not* be certified because of the city's potential liability under Title VII of the Civil Rights Act of 1964.[99] The counsel expressed concern over the "severe adverse impacts" that resulted from the written test. The chief administrative officer, who appeared on behalf of New Haven's mayor, also argued that the test should be discarded because the results "created a situation in which black and Hispanic candidates were disproportionately excluded from opportunity."[100] At the end of the meeting, the Board was deadlocked in a vote on whether to certify the test results, meaning that they would not be certified.

A group of white firefighters and one Hispanic firefighter who passed the test sued the city, alleging violations of the Equal Protection Clause of the Fourteenth Amendment, Title VII, and other statutory provisions. The district court entered summary judgment for the city, concluding that the city's "motivation to avoid making promotions based on a test with a racially disparate impact … does not, as a matter of law, constitute discriminatory intent under Title VII."[101] The Second Circuit affirmed in a short *per curiam* opinion, and the Supreme Court granted *certiorari*.

In a 5–4 vote the Supreme Court reversed and entered judgment for the plaintiff firefighters.[102] Writing for the majority, Justice Kennedy recounted the plaintiffs' argument that by failing to certify the test results, the city "discriminated against them in violation of Title VII's *disparate-treatment* provision."[103] In contrast, the city maintained that its refusal to certify the examination results did not violate the statute because "the tests appear[ed] to violate Title VII's *disparate impact* provisions."[104] The Supreme Court therefore saw its task as resolving this apparent conflict between the disparate-treatment and disparate-impact provisions of the statute.

The Court began its analysis by making it clear that the city's decision to discard the test "would violate the disparate-treatment prohibition of Title VII absent some valid defense."[105] Even though the city's actions may have been "well intentioned" and "benevolent," the decision was still made on the basis of race in violation of Title VII, as the examination was discarded "because the higher scoring candidates were white." The city's "express, race-based decisionmaking violates Title VII's command that employers cannot take adverse employment actions because of an individual's race." Thus, the Court determined that the city would be liable under Title VII unless an employer's attempt to avoid a disparate-impact suit creates a defense that would "excuse[] what otherwise would be prohibited" conduct.[106]

In considering the contours of such a defense, the Court adopted a "strong-basis-in-evidence standard" for Title VII claims "to resolve any conflict between the disparate-treatment and disparate impact provisions."[107] Thus, an employer may "engage in intentional discrimination for the asserted purpose of avoiding or remedying an unintentional disparate impact" only if the employer has "a strong basis in evidence to believe it will be subject to disparate-impact liability if it fails to take the race-conscious, discriminatory action."[108] Applying this standard, the Court concluded that the statistical disparity reflected in the test results failed to create a strong basis in evidence justifying the city's belief that it would have been liable for disparate impact if it had certified these results. Even with this statistical disparity, the city would still have been able to avoid liability if it could have demonstrated that the tests were job-related and consistent with business necessity. If the city had satisfied this job-related standard, minority firefighters challenging the test would not have been able to prevail unless they established that "there existed an equally valid, less-discriminatory alternative that served the City's needs but that the City refused to adopt."[109]

Given the extensive measures taken by the consulting group in creating and administering the tests – and taking into account the statements of the witnesses who appeared before the Civil Service Board – the Court found no factual dispute as to whether the tests were job-related and consistent with business necessity. Indeed, the majority concluded that the city had "turned a blind eye to evidence that supported the exams' validity."[110] Thus, the city had not shown a strong basis in evidence for its belief that the tests were not job-related and consistent with business necessity.[111] Similarly, the Court failed to find a strong basis in evidence for a less discriminatory alternative to the testing procedures used by the city. In this regard, the city's failure to implement another selection procedure immediately may have proven fatal to this part of its case, because its inaction suggested that an equally effective alternative was not readily at hand. Taking all of these facts into account, the Court held that the city's attempt to "create a genuine issue of fact based on a few stray (and contradictory) statements in the record" failed to rise to the strong-basis-in-evidence standard.

In sum, the Court found "no evidence – let alone the required strong basis in evidence – that the tests were flawed because they were not job-related or because other equally valid and less discriminatory tests were available to the City."[112] The Court emphasized that "[f]ear of litigation alone cannot justify an employer's reliance on race to the detriment of individuals who passed the examinations and qualified for promotions."[113] The process used by the city in developing and administering the tests was "open and fair," and the city had been careful to craft a neutral exam and had encouraged "broad racial participation."[114] The Court thus concluded that the city's refusal to certify the examination results violated Title VII's disparate-treatment provisions, and determined that summary judgment should have been entered for the firefighters.

Justice Scalia, concurring in full in the Court's opinion, addressed the equal protection issue that the majority avoided.[115] Justice Scalia questioned the constitutional validity of the disparate-impact provisions of Title VII, noting that if the government cannot discriminate against an individual because of race, "then surely [the government] is also prohibited from enacting laws mandating that third parties – e.g., employers, whether private, State, or municipal – discriminate on the basis of race."[116] In Justice Scalia's view, disparate impact puts "a racial thumb on the scales," frequently forcing companies "to evaluate the racial outcomes of their policies."[117] Though acknowledging that the issue need not be resolved in this case, he opined that "it behooves us to begin thinking about how – and on what terms – to make peace between" disparate impact and equal protection.[118]

Writing for the dissent, Justice Ginsburg (joined by Justices Stevens, Souter, and Breyer) argued that the majority's holding "ignores substantial evidence of multiple flaws in the tests New Haven used," and noted that other cities have utilized better examinations that resulted in smaller racial disparities.[119] The dissent also noted that the majority had failed to paint a complete picture of the situation in New Haven, highlighting the racial disparity in the composition of the city's firefighters that had persisted for years (and that the majority's opinion had omitted). The dissent accused the majority of breaking a long-standing promise of civil-rights law "that groups long denied equal opportunity would not be held back by tests 'fair in form, but discriminatory in operation.'"[120]

As the dissent's vehemence reflects, *Ricci* represents a significant development in disparate-treatment doctrine that may profoundly influence that area of the law, especially the so-called reverse-discrimination lawsuits alleging a bias in favor of minorities. Other scholarship has focused on this aspect of the decision, including potential limitations on the Court's analysis and its implications for traditional Title VII (as opposed to reverse-discrimination) cases.[121]

Ricci will also have a strong influence on the future of disparate-impact law. The Court's extended analysis of the evidence on job-relatedness and alternatives is likely to affect how lower courts approach those issues in other cases.[122] Justice Scalia's concurrence also raises questions about the constitutionality of Title VII's prohibition on disparate impact. Other scholarship is examining these constitutional questions and what they may signal about the future of the entire disparate-impact framework.[123] All of these issues merit further exploration.

For purposes of this text, however, we see an example of how the Roberts Court seems to go out of its way to preserve "reverse discrimination" claims. To be fair, it is somewhat of a stretch to call *Ricci* a purely "procedural" decision. Its implications for access to justice issues are directly implicated by this text, however, as seen in much greater detail earlier. The precise meaning and impact of the decision will be explored for years. The tenor of the case, though, is clear – the Court is reaching out to protect the interests of the majority group while the interests of minority workers remain at risk. As noted in the previous chapter, this text does not seek to examine the motivations of the Roberts Court on civil-rights issues. Nonetheless, the *Ricci* case does provide an important signal as to where the Court is heading on these issues.

CONCLUSION

For years, the federal courts have been restricting the ability of employment-discrimination plaintiffs to bring their claims before a jury. Summary judgment has served to weed out a vast amount of employment-discrimination litigation that was purportedly not properly before the courts. The Roberts Court – through its decisions in *Iqbal* and *Twombly* – has now moved this filtering process to the earlier stages of the litigation. This dramatic change in the law has received enormous attention in the academic literature, but has gone largely unnoticed in the public eye. The model offered here for employment-discrimination plaintiffs filing a complaint will help assure that plaintiffs properly plead their claims. Though the Federal Rules have changed and the deck is now stacked against civil-rights plaintiffs, cautious litigation in this area can help assure that these individuals will not make any procedural missteps. Similarly, as set forth in this chapter, defendants must also be cautious when responding to the allegations against them. While this area of the law is now far more confusing for all litigants, a cautious and prepared approach to pleading can help avoid potential traps and permit the case to advance in the proceedings. As *Ricci* demonstrates, the Court is also more receptive to claims from the majority group. In the face of this environment, minority plaintiffs must be extraordinarily careful when litigating their claims. This text provides a framework to ensure that these plaintiffs properly set forth their allegations.

3

Class Actions, Systemic Claims, and Arbitration

If you're part of a group of employees working for a major US corporation with a gripe about unfair treatment, your collective voices were potentially muffled [after the US Supreme Court's 2011 decision in *Wal-Mart Stores, Inc. v. Dukes*].

– NBC News report, following the *Wal-Mart* decision[1]

The Supreme Court's decision in *Wal-Mart v. Dukes,* heralded last term as a game-changer in employment class actions, has lived up to the hype.

–Reuters News report, following the *Wal-Mart* decision[2]

Workers have recently faced extraordinary challenges when attempting to act collectively in the workplace. This chapter will explore the procedural requirements that the Court has imposed in these collective cases, highlighting the increased scrutiny on the commonality standard found in the *Wal-Mart* decision. The Court's hesitation in permitting class-action claims has broken down largely along ideological lines, and the more conservative members of the Court have resisted these cases. This trend against systemic litigation has extended beyond the use of formal litigation, and the Supreme Court has recently also restricted the ability of workers to aggregate their claims in the arbitration setting. In *AT&T Mobility v. Concepcion,* the Court severely curbed the ability of workers to bring class-action type claims before private judges.

This chapter thus identifies how the Supreme Court's recent case law has restricted the ability of workers to pursue class-action claims. The chapter further identifies the best way for employees to proceed in light of these decisions. Specifically, this chapter encourages more governmental intervention in systemic cases, as the EEOC and

This chapter draws heavily from the following articles: Joseph A. Seiner, "Commonality and the Constitution: Applying *Wal-Mart* to State Court Cases," *Indiana Law Journal* 91 (2016): 455; Joseph A. Seiner, "The Issue Class," *Boston College Law Review* 56 (2015): 121; and Joseph A. Seiner, "Weathering *Wal-Mart*," *Notre Dame Law Review* 89 (2014): 1343.

56

Department of Justice are not subject to the Court's new requirements. The chapter further explores how more narrow class-action cases can evade the Court's heightened scrutiny. The chapter further advocates for civil-rights groups to "take the Supreme Court at its word" and orchestrate a broad-based strategy of overwhelming employers through the extensive filing of individual claims. This type of strategy has worked in the past, as civil-rights groups have successfully coordinated efforts at identifying new causes of action. Finally, this chapter concludes with the possibility of "cabining *Wal-Mart*," by arguing in the courts that the decision is limited to only a handful of massive-type systemic claims. The *Wal-Mart* decision was unique in that it involved more than a million potential class members. A strong argument can be made, then, that the limitations the Supreme Court identified in this case apply only to this type of massive litigation.

Class-action claims have enjoyed a long history of helping to prevent discrimination in employment. From the time of the early *Teamsters* decision – which recognized broad-based social discrimination in the workplace – systemic claims have served as an important threat to employers and encouraged the prevention of workplace bias. Systemic claims make headlines and frequently result in large dollar verdicts against the employer. This type of litigation thus helps educate the public on the topic of discrimination, deters employers from wrongful conduct, and punishes those who run afoul of the law. By applying more rigid standards to class-action cases, then, the Court has procedurally limited the ability of many workers to aggregate their claims. This, in turn, severely undercuts the goals Congress set out in Title VII, and limits the rights of many minority workers.

BASICS OF THE CLASS CLAIM

When litigating a class claim in federal court, there are a number of basic considerations that should be reviewed. Class cases are essentially aggregated claims brought on behalf of a substantial number of aggrieved workers. Class actions make it easier for the parties involved to litigate the case, and smaller dollar cases can be combined into larger claims. These cases also lighten the load of the courts, as they combine hundreds or thousands of claims into a single action.

When the Federal Rules were developed and refined, the value of the class claim was specifically identified.[3] Class-action litigation now proceeds under Rule 23. Class claims must satisfy all of the requirements of Rule 23(a) as well as one of the categories of Rule 23(b). Rule 23(a) requires that a class-action claim satisfy the following requirements: numerosity, commonality, typicality, and adequacy of representation.

All class claims must be sufficient in their size. Numerosity varies by the particular jurisdiction, but all courts require some minimum number of class members. Although this number can vary, most courts permit cases involving more than forty claims to proceed. Similarly, the claims alleged must involve common issues. If the issues at stake are too varied, the courts will not permit the claims to be aggregated under the Rules. There must also be sufficient "typicality," and the cases must be typical of one another under the Rules. Finally, those attorneys chosen to represent the plaintiffs in the case must be competent to do so – the representation must be adequate for the aggregation of the claims to be allowed.

If a class-action case satisfies these different requirements, the courts will look to whether one of the three different ways of certifying the case has been satisfied under Rule 23(b). Rule 23(b)(1) allows a class if there is a risk of "inconsistent or varying adjudications ... that would be dispositive of the interests of the other members not parties to the individual adjudications or would substantially impair ... their interests." A class claim brought under Rule 23(b)(2) is allowed where the litigants would primarily be seeking injunctive-type relief. Claims under Rule 23(b)(3) proceed where "questions of law or fact common to class members predominate [and the] class action is superior to other available methods" of litigation.[4]

Determining whether these complex standards are satisfied is often a difficult process, and the courts have identified varying standards for systemic litigation under these rules. It is thus a very jurisdiction-specific area of the law, and it is not uncommon for plaintiffs to "forum shop"[5] when bringing these types of claims. In the employment-discrimination context, the Supreme Court has long recognized the importance of systemic litigation in helping to deter discrimination and carry out the goals of Title VII. In *International Brotherhood of Teamsters* v. *United States*, for example, the Supreme Court recognized early on that an employer can be liable for class-wide discrimination where it "regularly and purposefully" treats minorities in an adverse manner. The Court found that where the facts show "a pattern or practice of ... disparate treatment" that is "racially premised," this type of claim can be pursued. The Court in *Teamsters* also identified the important role of statistical evidence when pursuing systemic discrimination cases, which is often a critical component in class-action claims.[6]

GOVERNMENTAL SYSTEMIC LITIGATION

Private litigants pursuing class-action, employment-discrimination claims must satisfy the elements of Rule 23. Thus, the claims must be sufficiently numerous, have adequate commonality, be typical of one another, and adequately represent those involved. Governmental entities, such as the EEOC, also enforce Title VII, as discussed in Chapter 1. These governmental agencies, however, are not subject to Rule 23. Indeed, the Supreme Court has clearly held that "Rule 23 is not applicable to an enforcement action brought by the [Commission] in its own name and pursuant to its authority ... to prevent unlawful employment practices."[7] There are, of course, certain prerequisites that governmental agencies must meet prior to filing a systemic claim. For example, the agency must file a discrimination charge, give notice to the employer, perform an investigation that results in a discriminatory finding, and an attempt to amicably resolve the matter. After satisfying these requirements, the EEOC is able to proceed with a systemic claim against the employer. It need not bring a claim on behalf of a certain number of workers, or satisfy the other elements of commonality or typicality. The government, then, is free to bring systemic litigation in an employment-discrimination case without being subjected to the typical Rule 23 requirements imposed on private litigants.

THE IMPORTANCE OF SYSTEMIC LITIGATION FOR WORKPLACE CLAIMS

The importance of class-action litigation in employment matters cannot be over-stated. Many individual acts of discrimination often go unnoticed. The maximum penalty for even the largest employers for a single act of discrimination is $300,000, plus potential back pay and attorneys' fees. While this type of judgment can be significant, it is not likely to substantially deter Fortune 500 companies or make headlines. Class-action litigation, however, serves multiple important functions in the working environment. Employers who are sued on behalf of numerous employees and face multimillion dollar judgments quickly take notice of the workplace climate and immediately make changes to provide a better environment.

Large class-action judgments also educate the general public, providing notice that employment discrimination will not be tolerated in the workplace. These cases often make headlines, thus informing other companies of the importance of maintaining a discrimination-free environment. And, while some might disagree, class actions also serve a punitive role, providing retribution to employers that have run afoul of the statutory prohibitions against employment discrimination in a systemic manner. These actions also allow workers with smaller monetary claims, who might not otherwise have been able to obtain representation, participation in broader systemic litigation, and access to their statutory rights. As already noted, class claims serve a vital function for the court system itself. These claims help aggregate hundreds or thousands of individual cases, thus streamlining litigation and reducing the workload of the federal court system.

In the years following the passage of Title VII, the Court recognized the importance of these claims to the enforcement of the statute. Over the past decade, the Supreme Court has – through more subtle procedural maneuvering – acted to substantially curb the opportunities for plaintiffs to pursue systemic claims in private cases. While the motivations of the Court are not entirely clear, there has been tremendous concern in the business community that class claims – whether appropriately brought or not – can force a company to settle regardless of the merits of the case. Thus, the mere prospect of defending against this type of litigation – even where the claims are meritless – has raised numerous concerns about the equity of these types of cases. Whether the Supreme Court has acted in response to these concerns is unclear. What is transparent, however, is that the past decade has seen a concerted attack on any attempt of workers to aggregate their claims.

WAL-MART: THE PRACTICAL END OF CLASS CLAIMS IN THE WORKPLACE?

Perhaps the most high-profile instance of the Court acting to disrupt systemic claims under Title VII came in 2011 with the decision in *Wal-Mart Stores, Inc. v. Dukes.* While many of the Court's recent procedural decisions that have undermined worker rights have flown largely under the radar, the *Dukes* decision stands as a strong exception. The case garnered high-profile attention, drawing media focus from around the world.

The public interest in the case was not surprising, as it involved "one of the most expansive class actions ever," brought against the nation's largest retailer.[8] In *Dukes*, a narrowly divided Supreme Court considered whether a proposed class case involving approximately one and a half million aggrieved women should be certified by the Court. The plaintiffs in the case maintained, under Title VII, that they had been inappropriately treated in pay and promotion matters at the company. They sought injunctive and declaratory relief in the case, as well as back pay. The Court would directly take on the issue of whether this mammoth Title VII class action should be certified.

Wal-Mart operates its business by giving its individual store managers substantial discretion in making pay and promotion decisions, which are often subjective in nature. The plaintiffs in the case maintained that the local managers had used their discretion in adversely affecting women and created a disparate impact against this protected group. The plaintiffs further maintained that Wal-Mart, as a corporate entity, was aware of this disparate treatment, but did nothing to intervene – thus creating an intentional discrimination claim. The plaintiffs alleged a "corporate culture" at Wal-Mart that promoted discriminatory bias against females. This effect may have even been subconscious, but it permeated the entire corporate entity. According to the plaintiffs, all women at the company were affected by this bias, thus allowing a class action on behalf of female employees of Wal-Mart across the country (Figure 3.1).[9]

The district court largely agreed with the plaintiffs in this case, and certified the class. An en banc court of appeals had trouble reaching a common resolution to the question. The majority sided with the plaintiffs' arguments that there was sufficient commonality in the case to certify the class. It further found sufficient typicality in the case to allow it to proceed.

FIGURE 3.1 The National Women's Law Center holds a rally in front of the Supreme Court to "stand with the women of Wal-Mart and demand fair pay for women" as the Court hears the Wal-Mart sex discrimination case on Tuesday morning, March 29, 2011. The Supreme Court's decision in *Wal-Mart* provided guidance on how the Court views the commonality standard in class-action cases brought in the workplace context. Credit: Photograph by Bill Clark/Roll Call

The Supreme Court would take on this issue, resolving the dispute in a way that dramatically altered the aggregate rights of all civil-rights plaintiffs. Of the four requirements of Rule 23(a) discussed, the Court would focus its analysis in the case on the applicability of *commonality* under procedural law. Essentially, the Court would examine whether the 1.5 million claims alleged by the plaintiffs were sufficiently common to one another to justify class certification.

To show commonality, the Court required that the plaintiffs find some "common contention" in their claims, that is "of such a nature that it is capable of class-wide resolution." This requires "that determination of its truth or falsity will resolve an issue that is central to the validity of each one of the claims in one stroke."[10] The Court emphasized that "[d]issimilarities within the proposed class are what have the potential to impede the generation of common answers." By defining the class action in this way, the Court concluded that the plaintiffs had fallen short of establishing the facts necessary for the certification of their claim:

> Here respondents wish to sue about literally millions of employment decisions at once. Without some glue holding the alleged reasons for all those decisions together, it will be impossible to say that examination of all the class members' claims for relief will produce a common answer to the crucial question why was I disfavored.[11]

The Court further noted that for certification to be appropriate, the company would be required to establish – through "significant proof" – that it had "operated under a general policy of discrimination." The Court found no such policy in this case, rejecting the plaintiffs' statistical and social framework evidence. Though Wal-Mart did have a common policy of allowing local managers to make promotion and pay determinations, the plaintiffs had insufficient proof that there was "a common mode of exercising discretion that pervades the entire company." The plaintiffs in this case were thus unable to provide a common policy that "ties all their 1.5 million claims together." Quoting the lower court's dissenting opinion, the Court concluded that class certification was inappropriate in this case, as the individuals in the purported class:

> held a multitude of different jobs, at different levels of Wal-Mart's hierarchy, for variable lengths of time, in 3,400 stores, sprinkled across 50 states, with a kaleidoscope of supervisors (male and female), subject to a variety of regional policies that all differed … Some thrived while others did poorly. They have little in common but their sex and this lawsuit.[12]

The Supreme Court thus held that under the Federal Rules, the plaintiffs' claims could not be certified. The Court thus rejected the federal appellate court's decision, which had allowed the cases to be aggregated. This is not to say that any individual claim of the 1.5 million prospective plaintiffs was invalid; but these cases must be brought separately against the company rather than on a class basis.

The dissent, authored by Justice Ginsburg and joined by Justices Sotomayor, Breyer, and Kagan, created a divisive 5–4 split in the case – vigorously challenging the majority's definition of "commonality," noting that this approach "disqualifies the class at the starting gate."[13] The dissent argued that there need not be complete commonality in the case as to all questions or facts, and that even a 'single" common question should be sufficient to "satisfy the commonality requirement." The Court emphasized that while women worked over two-thirds of the hourly jobs at the company, management is comprised of almost two-thirds men. And, the statistics in the case demonstrate that females at Wal-Mart "are paid less than men in every region [and] that the salary gap widens over time even for men and women hired into the same jobs at the same time." The "tap on the shoulder" approach at the company for promotion gives supervisors wide discretion in choosing managerial employees. The dissent further detailed how pay rules do have some uniformity across the retailer's stores, and discussed the "corporate culture" that exists at the company.

The dissent thus maintained that there was enough evidence to establish that "gender bias suffused Wal-Mart's company culture,"[14] and that the claims shared sufficient commonality in this regard. The dissent pointed to numerous discriminatory comments made by management in this regard, which bolster the statistical evidence presented in the case. That statistical evidence, which included expert regression analysis, was (according to the district court) enough to give rise to an "inference of discrimination." The dissent took issue with the majority's failure to give any "credence to the key dispute common to the class: whether Wal-Mart's discretionary pay and promotion policies are discriminatory."[15] As the dissent summarized its argument:

> Wal-Mart's delegation of discretion over pay and promotions is a policy uniform throughout all stores. The very nature of discretion is that people will exercise it in various ways ... The Court errs in importing a 'dissimilarities' notion ... into the Rule 23(a) commonality inquiry.[16]

The strongly worded dissent demonstrates the importance of this issue and the difficulty plaintiffs will have aggregating future cases.

WHAT *WAL-MART* REALLY MEANS

Many have weighed in on the meaning of the *Wal-Mart* decision for employment plaintiffs, and the overall view has been that the decision presents substantial problems for plaintiffs – thus undermining civil rights. The academic scholarship has been quite harsh on the case. One view is that "the Court did more than pull the procedural rug out from under the decade-long lawsuit; it called into question the future of systemic disparate treatment law."[17] Yet another well-known scholar stated that "*Wal-Mart* v. *Dukes* opens up a third dimension to the ongoing judicial enfeeblement of employment discrimination law."[18] And a third preeminent scholar argued that the decision "is likely to make certification of a nationwide class far more difficult."[19] The list goes on, but it is clear that those looking closely at the issue see one less weapon – the class action – available to many employment-discrimination plaintiffs.[20] Why the gloomy outlook on this case for workers? It is difficult to refute the overwhelming voice of the critics. The *Wal-Mart* case, as the dissent vigorously points out, presented substantial statistical and anecdotal evidence of a corporate-wide policy of gender discrimination. The case included numerous discriminatory comments made by management-level employees, and an alarming statistical disparity of the pay gap between male and female workers. If such a case, which was meticulously litigated by the plaintiffs, cannot even make it out of the "starting gate," the future is certainly not bright for other employment plaintiffs attempting to aggregate their claims.

Wal-Mart signals a new procedural barrier for the employment discrimination class claim: commonality. As noted by the dissent, this barrier was much lower in prior systemic litigation. But it will now be a focus for the federal courts as they attempt to sort out which workplace claims should be certified. There can be little doubt, then, that the critics (and dissenting Justices) are right. The bar has been raised – again through a procedural mechanism – and the standard for bringing employment-discrimination claims is far more difficult. The importance of these claims in educating the public, punishing employers for discriminatory acts, and assuring that a broader range of victims are compensated has already been explored. *Wal-Mart* undermines these objectives, and the case is a strong blow to civil-rights advocates everywhere.

Concepcion: *Limited Aggregation for Arbitration Claims*

Wal-Mart was the second recent Supreme Court opinion to limit the complex litigation rights of workers, as the Court had decided *AT&T Mobility LLC* v. *Concepcion* less than two months earlier.[21] In *Concepcion*, the Supreme Court held that the Federal Arbitration Act preempted California law, thus restricting the ability of individuals in the case to pursue complex arbitration claims.[22] In its decision, the Court expressed significant concerns over class-wide arbitration, noting that it "requires procedural formality" and "makes the process slower, more costly, and more likely to generate procedural morass." Though *Concepcion* arose in the context of a consumer dispute, its implications for workplace litigants are substantial, as many employers require that employees arbitrate workplace-discrimination claims. While the intricacies of *Concepcion* are beyond the scope of this chapter, the case demonstrates the further difficulty plaintiffs now face when attempting to address systemic workplace discrimination.

Hope After *Wal-Mart*?

Simply agreeing with the critics of *Wal-Mart* to date does very little to add to the ongoing discussion. There is hope after *Wal-Mart*, however, for plaintiffs seeking to bring systemic litigation. This text will outline several tactical approaches that plaintiffs can still use to help counter the procedural blow dealt to plaintiffs in this case. These approaches help provide a patchwork solution to the problems created by the Supreme Court in *Wal-Mart*. Although only congressional intervention can completely remedy the impact of the decision, there are nonetheless still ways for plaintiffs to successfully proceed after *Wal-Mart*. Each approach should be considered by the civil-rights community with respect to the aggregation of claims.

The Governmental Approach

There is one certain response to the *Wal-Mart* case that would still help vindicate the rights of victimized workers: the EEOC, which is not subject to the decision, must bring more systemic litigation. As already discussed here, governmental agencies like the EEOC need not comply with Rule 23. Thus, these groups – primarily the EEOC and Department of Justice (in claims involving state or municipal employees) – are free to bring aggregate claims without being subjected to the heightened commonality standard created by the Court. It is a loophole of sorts and allows the government to vindicate the rights of workers without satisfying this particular standard.

In systemic ligation brought by the government, the Supreme Court has made clear that "Rule 23 is not applicable to an enforcement action brought by the [Commission] in its own name and pursuant to its authority ... to prevent unlawful employment practices."[23] There are, of course, certain basic requirements that must be met in filing these cases, as discussed earlier. Simply put, the EEOC must file a charge, give the employer notice, conduct an investigation that reveals reason to find cause of discrimination, and enter into conciliation attempts with the employer. These requirements are far less stringent than those imposed under Rule 23, with commonality of claims being noticeably absent. The EEOC, then, could help fill the gap of class-action cases that will likely be created by the *Wal-Mart* decision by focusing its litigation efforts more on systemic claims.

The EEOC is in a particularly unique position to pursue a more vibrant approach to pattern or practice claims. Indeed, all individuals seeking to bring an employment discrimination cause of action must file a charge of discrimination with the agency. This gives the EEOC the chance to review and investigate somewhere around 80,000 and 90,000 charges each year. The agency can be quite selective in determining which pattern or practice claims to bring and seek out those claims that have the most potential. Thus, the agency truly gets a global picture of which discrimination claims are available to bring in any given year. If the Commission were to adopt a policy of aggressively monitoring these charges for pattern or practice claims, it could help fill the role currently played by private litigants. Not subject to the same procedural requirements, the EEOC could vindicate the rights of workers that might not now satisfy the heightened *Wal-Mart* standard. The agency currently considers the presence of systemic discrimination when determining whether to file a case. The approach offered here would simply heighten these current practices and more aggressively pursue instances of systemic litigation that private litigants might not be able to bring.

This governmental approach to the problem created by the *Wal-Mart* decision has several practical advantages. Aggregate litigation can achieve a number of results not possible with individual claims. First, the Commission can sometimes recover for those individuals who may not have filed a timely charge. Indeed, the EEOC maintains that it can seek relief for those it does not identify until discovery.[24] This view is not without controversy, but it definitely demonstrates the more flexible nature of these types of pattern or practice claims. Second, the Commission is able to specifically seek monetary relief in these types of systemic claims; after *Wal-Mart*, this may be more difficult for individual litigants. Finally, if the government is successful in establishing a pattern or practice of discrimination, it obtains a substantial procedural benefit in the case. Where such discrimination is sufficiently alleged, the burden of proof switches from the EEOC to the defendant. Thus, the company has the burden of establishing that it is *not* liable for specific instances of discriminatory conduct. This is considerably different from the typical case of individual discrimination, where the plaintiff maintains the burden of proof throughout the litigation.

The governmental approach is not without its limitations, however. Historically, the EEOC has been an underfunded agency. Thus, the government would likely lack the resources necessary to adequately fill the role previously played by the private plaintiffs' bar in pursuing class-action suits. And, if the EEOC were to focus its efforts more keenly on systemic discrimination, it would come at the cost of not pursuing as many cases of individual employment wrongs. Cases of individual workplace discrimination also play a critical role in Title VII litigation, and backing away from some of these cases would certainly undermine the EEOC's enforcement efforts. The bottom-line problem would thus be resources. As an underfunded agency, the EEOC could choose to pursue more class-action cases, but it would come at a significant cost.

Similarly, there are substantial differences between EEOC pattern-or-practice litigation and suits brought by the private plaintiffs' bar. Most notably, the EEOC represents the government rather than the individual victims involved. While the interests of the two groups often align, there are sometimes substantial differences in the goals of litigation between the victims and the government. In particular, there may often be a divergence in the type of relief the two groups view as appropriate in a particular case. Of course, individual plaintiffs would be free to seek their own counsel to intervene in these matters to protect their rights.

Finally, there may be some remaining questions as to whether the *Wal-Mart* decision limits or restructures what a governmental pattern-or-practice case would look like. It is possible that the strict commonality requirement adopted by the *Wal-Mart* Court will also be applied to EEOC pattern-or-practice claims. It is equally possible that the courts will limit the type of relief the government can seek in these types of actions. These possible limitations seem unlikely, however. *Wal-Mart* was decided specifically under Rule 23. And the Court was clear that the contours of that Rule were driving its decision. However, the Supreme Court has held that the EEOC is *not* subject to Rule 23, and the *Wal-Mart* decision would thus be largely inapplicable to governmental actions. Notably, the EEOC has already taken the position that *Wal-Mart* does not impact its authority to pursue systemic discrimination claims.[25] Nonetheless, it is difficult to forecast how the lower courts will interpret *Wal-Mart* in the context of pattern-or-practice cases.

In sum, the governmental approach is appealing. It offers a class-action-like mechanism to fill much of the gap left by *Wal-Mart*. It allows the government to seek both monetary and injunctive relief for employment-discrimination victims, even where a timely charge has not been filed. And, there are notable procedural benefits to this type of litigation. However, it is far from a perfect solution. The government simply lacks the resources necessary to completely take over all systemic claims. And there may be some question as to whether *Wal-Mart* itself undermines the EEOC's ability to bring pattern-or-practice claims.

Procedural Responses

In addition to the governmental approach, there are also many procedural vehicles available to plaintiffs that could help navigate the *Wal-Mart* decision. These procedural responses help address the shortcomings of individual litigation where the employer's discrimination is pervasive and widespread. These procedural responses would thus tend to focus on the similarity in issues between the various victims of employment discrimination and help find ways of streamlining this litigation before the courts. Though there are numerous ways to approach systemic discrimination from a procedural perspective, using collateral estoppel, consolidating cases, and cabining *Wal-Mart* deserve particular attention.

OFFENSIVE USE OF COLLATERAL ESTOPPEL One currently overlooked response to the *Wal-Mart* decision would be for plaintiffs to more aggressively use collateral estoppel as part of their litigation strategy. This procedural mechanism could be considered where victims face similar issues or fact-patterns arising from a single employer. The classic definition of collateral estoppel provides that it "bars the relitigation of issues actually adjudicated, and essential to the judgment, in a prior litigation between the same parties."[26] Also known as issue preclusion, it is commonly stated that collateral estoppel requires more than that "some question of fact or law in a later suit was relevant to a prior adjudication between the parties."[27] Instead, "the contested issue must have been litigated and necessary to the judgment earlier rendered."[28]

Collateral estoppel thus serves to prevent important issues from being retried in subsequent litigation. The Supreme Court has clarified that "mutuality of parties" is not necessary for claims of issue preclusion. Thus, a plaintiff need not have been directly involved in prior litigation with the defendant to avail itself of this doctrine. Offensive non-mutual collateral estoppel thus allows plaintiffs to prevent the defendant from relitigating questions that have already been resolved, even where a different plaintiff was involved in the earlier case. There are obvious concerns in the application of this doctrine, which is why the Supreme Court was clear that the lower courts would have "broad discretion" in how (and whether) it is utilized. The touchstone in this regard is the question of fairness. Offensive nonmutual collateral estoppel should be used only "on a case-by-case basis depending on whether the prerequisites of a full and fair opportunity to litigate the issue in the prior action and fairness are present."[29]

In deciding whether the lower courts should permit the offensive use of issue preclusion, the Supreme Court outlined four different factors to consider. These factors all work to ensure fairness in the application of the doctrine:

> First, the [plaintiff] "probably could not have joined [the prior] action." Second, the seriousness of the case and the possibility of subsequent claims by private parties gave the defendants substantial incentive to contest the first action. Third, the decision in the [prior] action did not contradict any previous decision. Finally, no new procedural advantages likely to produce a different result had accrued to the defendants in the second action.[30]

Simply put, then, a plaintiff may use collateral estoppel where they could not have joined the prior case, where the prior case was of substantial significance to the defendant, where there is no conflict between the prior decision and other holdings, and where different procedural issues are not involved in the new case. These elements must all be weighed by the district court, which should be given significant deference to its decision.

The offensive use of collateral estoppel would provide an important procedural mechanism for plaintiffs to fill the *Wal-Mart* gap in employment-discrimination cases. It is not uncommon for an employer to discriminate against multiple individuals. And where this discrimination occurs at a single employment site, there are likely to be many of the same issues, facts, and policies involved in the case.

Take, for example, a typical hostile-environment case where a male supervisor harasses several female workers. In this type of case, there may not be enough individuals involved to certify a class action, or the claims may not have sufficient commonality. Nonetheless, the potential claims would likely share several important issues and facts, such as whether the employer had an effective employment policy in place, whether the alleged harasser was acting as a supervisor under the law of the particular jurisdiction, or whether the employer had knowledge that any harassment had occurred. Where established in one case, these facts need not be relitigated in subsequent actions. By resolving common issues only once, future cases would be streamlined, thus leading to significant judicial economies. Collateral estoppel could therefore significantly help reduce the role of burdensome litigation in these types of cases.

It is not unusual for an employer to be sued by multiple plaintiffs, and where common facts or policies are involved in the litigation, there would be little reason for a court to resolve these issues more than a single time. By permitting the plaintiffs to estop the issues from being raised in subsequent litigation, the courts would go a long way toward filling the *Wal-Mart* gap.

One key element of the offensive use of collateral estoppel is that it is permitted only where the issue arose in a serious case where the employer had "substantial incentive to contest the ... action."[31] Thus, before an employer can be estopped from contesting an issue, it must have seriously litigated the issue in something other than a minor action. In the context of employment discrimination, this likely would not be a difficult element for most plaintiffs to establish, as the employer will have substantial incentive to vigorously defend all allegations of discrimination brought in federal court. An employer is likely to take all such cases, and the corresponding issues therein, very seriously. Nonetheless, issues that are simply incidental to the initial litigation, or issues raised in minor cases (such as frivolous claims brought by pro se plaintiffs), will not be dispositive against the employer in other matters.

This solution is not perfect, and the offensive use of collateral estoppel falls far short of providing the benefits of a true class-action claim. Unlike collateral estoppel cases, not all parties to a class action would need to have filed timely charges of discrimination. Thus, class-action claims would allow more plaintiffs to bring suit than would the use of the procedural mechanism suggested here. Similarly, class-action claims will often put more dollars at stake as part of the initial suit, which forces defendants to seriously consider settling the claims. Though collateral estoppel may have some negative effects on portions of an employer's subsequent cases, it would not have the same potential financial impact on an employer as these class cases. Rather, the damages would likely be fewer and spread out over time. Finally, and perhaps most importantly, class actions have the benefit of substantially streamlining the litigation on the issue of liability. Though collateral estoppel offers the potential for significant judicial economies by resolving certain issues before the court, it falls far short of the economies offered under Rule 23. This is particularly true as the ultimate question – the issue of liability – must still be tried in every case.

In sum, the offensive use of collateral estoppel cannot take the place of the class action in employment-discrimination cases. Nonetheless, this procedural mechanism would help fill the *Wal-Mart* gap by avoiding the relitigation of issues that had already been resolved. Combined with other procedural tools offered here, issue preclusion offers several benefits to the traditional single employee–employer litigation often brought in the federal courts. Collateral estoppel has not been seriously explored in the academic literature as a means of streamlining employment-discrimination claims. In light of *Wal-Mart*, the use of issue preclusion must be considered as a way of avoiding the needless relitigation of issues that have already been resolved.

CONSOLIDATION   Other procedural mechanisms may also help fill the *Wal-Mart* gap created for systemic litigation. Similar to the use of collateral estoppel, judges may also streamline employment-discrimination claims with common issues through the *consolidation* of cases against the same employer, which is allowed under Rule 42(a). Consolidation is effective "as a matter of convenience and economy in judicial administration" where "separate actions present[] a common issue of law or fact."[32] Again, substantial deference is given to the district court's decision as to whether to consolidate the matters.[33] Unlike collateral estoppel, where an issue is resolved in an earlier case for subsequent litigation, consolidation allows important issues to be resolved *at the same time*. Thus, consolidation offers the benefit of allowing an issue to be resolved as part of a single proceeding.

Consolidation can take two primary forms. First, where there is a "common question of law or fact," a judge can "join for hearing or trial any or all matters at issue in the actions."[34] Second, the judge can simply "consolidate the actions."[35] Under the Federal Rules, the court thus has substantial discretion in how to organize the consolidation of a case or issue.

By trying multiple claims or issues through a single trial, the courts are able to simplify the litigation. Witnesses are required to testify only once, and the court and parties are subject to a single suit on a particular issue. Similarly, one trial is likely to be resolved much more quickly and inexpensively than multiple proceedings. And, there is less risk that the trier-of-fact will resolve the disputes differently, which would lead to a potential inconsistency of judgments. Where the individual allegations differ from one another, the court can still bifurcate the proceedings to resolve these specific issues.

In determining whether to consolidate the claims, the court should weigh these potential benefits against "the specific risks of prejudice and possible confusion" in merging the matters.[36] Thus, the benefits involved should be considered against the chance that the parties may be harmed through consolidation, or that expanding the scope of the trial will ultimately confuse the trier-of-fact. From a more practical standpoint, it may also be difficult to identify or isolate the specific issues or claims that can be decided jointly. The courts must be cautious in crafting how the consolidation will occur.

Like the offensive use of collateral estoppel, the consolidation of cases offers a procedural mechanism that is particularly attractive in the employment-discrimination context. As the policies, managers, facts, and issues often overlap in workplace disputes, merging separate claims can be an effective and efficient way of managing a court's trial docket. As discussed, harassment provides a useful example of these potential efficiencies. Where two (or more) individuals allege to have been victimized by the same harasser over a similar period of time, the two claims will likely involve the presentation of many of the same witnesses and policies. Whether the company has implemented an effective antiharassment policy, whether the harasser involved was a management-level employee, and how the employer responded to any complaints are all issues that could be resolved as part of a single trial. This type of consolidation would thus streamline the cases and prevent the needless multiplication of litigation. Common issues could thus be resolved in a unified manner, and the proceedings could then be bifurcated as necessary to determine issues that are unique to the individual cases.

Again, however, the benefits must be weighed against any potential prejudice against the parties. Such prejudice might arise against the employer, for example, as multiple victims will be alleging the same type of discrimination against the company. An employer will look far less sympathetic in the eyes of the trier-of-fact where numerous litigants have come forward with allegations of discrimination. In addition, harassment claims are often fact-specific, and the experiences of one victim may be completely different from those of another. There may be certain instances, then, where consolidation simply does not make sense in the employment context.

The consolidation of cases or issues thus provides another procedural tool that would help fill the *Wal-Mart* gap in employment-discrimination cases. Again, this procedural mechanism cannot completely replace Rule 23. The class action offers numerous additional benefits to the simple consolidation of cases. Namely, consolidation does not typically anticipate the mass litigation of claims across the country involving multiple claimants in numerous jurisdictions. Rule 23 is much better suited for these types of claims. And, the administrative requirements (such as filing timely discrimination charges) will likely be more relaxed in the class setting. Similarly, the actual identification of the victims involved is much less stringent in the class-action context. Finally, this procedural tool is not as powerful a weapon for plaintiffs, who would likely be able to command higher settlements through the threat of systemic litigation.

Despite these drawbacks, the consolidation of cases or issues is another way to streamline discrimination claims. And, it offers many of the same economies of scale available to class-action litigants.

CABINING WAL-MART   In addition to the offensive use of collateral estoppel and consolidation, a third procedural response to *Wal-Mart* would be for the courts and parties to limit the reach of the decision. In this regard, *Wal-Mart* can be seen as a very unique class-action case, involving the single largest workplace suit brought against the country's biggest private employer.

The courts may not want to extrapolate the principles of *Wal-Mart* beyond the facts of the decision itself. There are likely to be few, if any, employment cases as broad as *Wal-Mart*, which involved over a million individuals. As the Court itself recognized, it was "one of the most expansive class actions ever." Quite simply, then, it is possible that the *Wal-Mart* decision may only apply to *Wal-Mart*, or to the handful of other corporations that might be seen as similarly situated. By *cabining Wal-Mart*, the lower courts would thus limit the scope of the case, and apply the tenets of the Supreme Court's decision to only the largest cases brought against the biggest employers.

Given the massive size of Wal-Mart as an employer and the sheer magnitude of the class action brought against the company, it can be easy to understand the Supreme Court's reluctance in allowing the class action to go forward. Though the opinion is far from a model of clarity on the application of the rules of class certification, there is a fair concern over how this type of enormous systemic class would actually proceed. Trying a class case on behalf of more than a million individuals would be a difficult, if not impossible, undertaking for the lower court. And it is extremely difficult to imagine what that case would even look like or how it would be structured. Such a daunting claim would leave the company with little choice but to settle the action.

Putting aside both the reasoning and accuracy of the decision, the reluctance of the Court to certify the class is thus easily understood. What is less clear, however, is how far the principles from the decision should extend. Given the way in which the decision is framed, it seems a fair reading of the case to limit the holding to only the largest claims brought against the biggest employers. In this way, the Court created the *Wal-Mart* rule – a tenet that requires a strict interpretation of commonality for *massive* employment-discrimination claims.

The decision is replete with instances where the Court expressed concern over the magnitude of the case that had been brought. The Court repeatedly notes the size of the class and employer, and emphasizes that the "respondents wish to sue about literally millions of employment decisions at once." Given the enormity of the case, the Court appeared reluctant to find the "glue" that would bind the claims together, thus making it "impossible to say" that there is a commonality of the actions. In the Court's view, there was simply no "specific employment practice" to tie the "1.5 million claims together."

The Court's repeated emphasis of the size of the class and the employer cannot be overstated. For the sake of brevity, this chapter will not go through each instance. However, a few illustrative examples will help clarify the importance that the Court places on these elements of the case. As the Court provides,

In a company of Wal-Mart's size and geographical scope, it is quite unbelievable that all managers would exercise their discretion in a common way without some common direction ...

[W]hen the claim is that a company operates under a general policy of discrimination, a few anecdotes selected from literally millions of employment decisions proves nothing at all ...

[The class members] held a multitude of different jobs, at different levels of Wal-Mart's hierarchy, for variable lengths of time, in 3,400 stores, sprinkled across 50 states, with a kaleidoscope of supervisors (male and female), subject to a variety of regional policies that all differed ... Some thrived while others did poorly. They have little in common but their sex and this lawsuit.[37]

The size of Wal-Mart and of the action against it are thus the threads that hold the decision together. Where a massive claim has been brought against this type of employer, there must be more than "a few anecdotes" of discrimination. In this type of instance, the Court seems to be asking for the smoking-gun memorandum instructing its managers to discriminate. With no memorandum forthcoming, there are simply too many differences between the individual stores and plaintiffs. There is thus no commonality and the class claim cannot proceed.

The *Wal-Mart* rule created by the Court thus provides that where a massive claim has been brought against a massive employer, the plaintiff will have a heightened burden of proof in establishing commonality. Or, at a minimum, the courts will examine the commonality requirement much more closely. But what the decision omits is any discussion of the vast majority of class-action cases that look nothing like *Wal-Mart* at all. The Court notes that this is one of the largest systemic claims "ever,"[38] yet it fails to instruct us on how to analyze a lesser claim involving a smaller defendant with fewer allegations of discrimination. This is likely because the decision was really intended only to apply to the *Wal-Mart* situation itself.

Given the heavy reliance of the opinion on the size of Wal-Mart and the putative class, then, this chapter proposes that the Court's opinion should be limited to the fact pattern before it. *Wal-Mart* should be cabined and restricted to its facts. The problems of litigating this type of class action are obvious, and the Court's reluctance to certify is easily understood. The problems in litigating a less massive class action are not as notable, and have been routinely undertaken by the courts.

If the *Wal-Mart* decision could be cabined, it would have obvious procedural benefits for plaintiffs. By limiting *Wal-Mart* in this way, the decision would have little or no impact on the legal landscape. The vast majority of class cases are much smaller in size and scope than *Wal-Mart*, and the decision would be inapplicable to these claims. Plaintiffs in other cases would thus be free to seek certification of their claims without a heightened inquiry of commonality. Rather, the courts would examine this question as they had done in the past. This would preserve all of the benefits of class claims that the critics of *Wal-Mart* argue have been destroyed. Most notably, the ability to bring a systemic claim against an employer with relaxed administrative requirements would remain intact. And, the ability to deter the employer from discriminating under even the threat of such a class-action claim would still endure. By restoring these benefits, the *Wal-Mart* gap would be filled.

Limiting the *Wal-Mart* decision might have some unintended consequences, however. If only large employers are ultimately protected by the decision, it could encourage companies and industry to consolidate in an effort to thwart this type of systemic litigation. It is unclear how realistic a possibility this would be. Nonetheless, the temptation of firms to insulate themselves from class litigation would serve as a powerful incentive for these companies to consider merging to increase their size. Moreover, to the extent that *Wal-Mart* can be seen as favorable legal precedent, limiting the decision would undo much of the positive impact of the case. Though this chapter takes no express view on the validity of the decision, a strong argument can be made that *Wal-Mart* advances class-action law. And some may view the decision as providing much-needed guidance on the interpretation of commonality under the Federal Rules. Though there is obvious room for debate on these questions, restricting *Wal-Mart* to mega-suits would certainly also limit any positive benefits of the decision.

As a procedural mechanism, cabining *Wal-Mart* may not be a practicable solution. The counterargument is straightforward – *Wal-Mart* is not only about massive lawsuits and applies to *all* employers. The Court's repeated reliance on the size of the employer and class seem to belie this argument, but it will ultimately be a matter for the lower courts to decide how broadly to apply the decision. In the end, the *Wal-Mart* rule proposed by this chapter is well supported by the Court's own logic, and offers an additional way around the decision for victimized employees. The procedural strategy of cabining *Wal-Mart* should be advanced by plaintiffs, and seriously considered by the courts. This strategy offers another way to fill the *Wal-Mart* gap.

TAKING *WAL-MART* AT ITS WORD An additional procedural approach to addressing *Wal-Mart* runs contrary to the previously discussed strategy of cabining the decision. This approach would be to simply take *Wal-Mart* at its word, and apply the decision broadly to all employment-discrimination cases.

By taking *Wal-Mart* at its word, plaintiffs that might otherwise pursue class-action claims would instead file suit individually against the employer. This could mean that employers who would typically be subject to a single class-action claim may now be facing hundreds or even thousands of individual actions. In *Wal-Mart*, for example, the class certified by the lower courts included more than a million individual claims. *Wal-Mart* does not prevent these plaintiffs from filing suit against their employer individually. If anything, the decision expressly encourages it. A lack of commonality between the claims suggests that each claim should be examined individually.

Rather than attempting to find a way around *Wal-Mart*, then, plaintiffs can simply embrace it. By filing thousands of individual cases against an employer, the company may ultimately become overwhelmed and completely bogged down by the litigation. Instead of defending against one suit, companies will find themselves litigating individual cases across the country. This strategy could put employers in the situation of being careful for what they wished for, as *Wal-Mart* may not be the answer to their litigation problems. This is particularly true where the voluminous individual litigation would result in inconsistent judgments against the employer.

From a procedural perspective, this strategy would involve massive organization by plaintiffs' attorneys. As each individual case would require careful adherence to the administrative requirements of Title VII, the prospective plaintiffs would want to make certain that they have exhausted these requirements. A careful analysis of which suits to bring initially – and in what jurisdiction – would also be critical to the overall success of this strategy. Certainly plaintiffs would want to bring the most egregious discrimination cases first in jurisdictions that are particularly sympathetic to these types of claims. Success in the initial cases in a mass individual litigation setting would increase the likelihood of settlement of the later cases. By taking the decision at its word, plaintiffs could thus exploit – rather than fill – the *Wal-Mart* gap and use it as a sword against employers that have discriminated against their workforce.

This type of organization would be extremely difficult for plaintiffs to structure. However, successful organization of these claims could have an enormous payoff, both financially and through the attainment of injunctive relief against those that run astray of civil-rights rules and regulations. It would not be the first time that civil plaintiffs have taken part in an orchestrated nationwide litigation strategy. Civil-rights and employment-discrimination plaintiffs have a well-known history of organizing around common causes and vindicating individual rights.

The strategy of forgoing class-action litigation and pursuing mass individual litigation against employers could be enormously burdensome for defendants. The companies would be required to bear the burden of the defense in each specific case that is brought. And, in those cases in which the defendant loses the claim, the plaintiff can seek attorneys' fees as part of the recovery. Defendants would lose all of the efficiencies and economies of scale that come with class-action suits.[39] Instead of a single case that could be quickly settled, employers may now be scrambling to defend individual claims brought throughout the country. Of course, employers may ultimately prevail in the individual cases and not face some of the potential damages that would otherwise be incurred. The attorneys' fees alone in these cases, however, would be an enormous cost to employers – even where the company ulti-mately prevails in the suit.

Needless to say, this strategy comes at a cost for plaintiffs. While some employ-ment-discrimination victims may benefit and have the opportunity to present their claims in court, other prospective plaintiffs may fall through the cracks of the litiga-tion. In this regard, some individuals may not file a timely charge of discrimination, or may fail to file suit in a timely manner. Other victims may be unaware of their rights and not file a charge at all. Still others may not feel comfortable with the pros-pect of individual litigation in the federal courts against their employer and decide not to pursue their rights. Further, many cases that might have only a marginal value associated with them may not ultimately be pursued. Thus, individual litigation cannot achieve many of the same benefits as class-action lawsuits. Such suits offer safety in numbers, relaxed administrative requirements, streamlined costs, efficien-cies, and discovery, which can help identify potential victims. Class-action claims, where settled, also offer a recovery for all victims. In individual litigation, many victims of discrimination may ultimately lose their case through procedural pitfalls, poor lawyering, or an unsympathetic jury.

Similarly, this strategy comes at an immense cost to the entire judicial system. By encouraging mass individual litigation, the *Wal-Mart* decision may end up increas-ing the workload of the federal courts. *Wal-Mart* itself offers a valuable lesson in this regard. The decision involves more than a million potential victims of discrimi-nation. If even a tenth of these individuals decided to pursue individual litigation instead of bringing a class claim, the courts would be burdened with more than a hundred thousand additional cases. The efficiencies of Rule 23 would be lost. This multiplier effect could thus overwhelm the courts. Employment-discrimina-tion cases already make up a substantial portion of the federal court docket. *Wal-Mart* may only increase the number of individual cases that the federal courts must address. And, while many class-action suits are ultimately settled, the sheer volume of individual cases would ensure that some of these claims result in a trial.

Taking *Wal-Mart* at its word may thus be an effective procedural strategy for plain-tiffs. Rather than pursuing class claims, employment-discrimination victims may carefully organize and bring individual suits. For the reasons noted, however, the strategy is not without its risks or costs. This multiplication of litigation could ulti-mately prove overwhelming for both defendants and the courts. Rather than filling the "*Wal-Mart* gap," this strategy uses it to the advantage of discrimination victims. But it comes with a price.

THE ISSUE CLASS A final procedural response to *Wal-Mart* involves an often over-looked rule – issue class certification. The Federal Rules allow a group of plaintiffs to certify certain issues common among them, even when the putative class itself has not been certified. Specifically, Rule 23(c)(4) provides that "[w]hen appropriate, an action may be brought or maintained as a class action with respect to particular issues."[40] Even when a class has not been permitted to proceed under Rule 23(b), then, litigants can still certify particular issues common to a class under Rule 23(c)(4).[41] This Rule thus allows a court to "treat common things in common and to distinguish the distinguishable."[42]

Issue class certification offers many of the traditional benefits of class certification under Rule 23(b). Most notably, the issue class provides trial judges enormous flexibility when managing a systemic case of workplace harm. Although class claims are different, Rule 23(c)(4) allows the judge to separate specific common questions in the case and resolve other issues individually. The judge can thereby tailor the certified issues to the facts of the specific case, thus leading to more efficient litigation. In this way, issue class certification also results in more streamlined proceedings. Courts can resolve claims that touch on a common issue a single time, while allowing the remaining issues in the case to be litigated separately.

Issue class certification is especially useful in class-action, employment-discrimination cases, particularly after *Wal-Mart*. This is because workplace class-action claims often present the two criteria often required for issue class certification: (1) systemic litigation involving a common set of facts; and (2) varying degrees of harm among the individual plaintiffs.[43] Indeed, a survey of the case law and literature in this area reveals that three common factors are often involved in the outcome of workplace litigation: common corporate policies, common personnel, and common company practices. Specifically, because employer policies affecting an employee's terms, conditions, and privileges of employment are often uniform across a business, these cases will frequently present a common set of facts for numerous plaintiffs. Moreover, because the managers, supervisors, and executive officers are the same at a particular company, there are often similar issues when these same "players" are involved in the wrongdoing. Finally, workplaces typically involve common practices – informal procedures or rules that are often more of an issue of corporate culture than written policy. Cases of discrimination frequently implicate these common company practices.[44]

Yet, despite their similarities, employment-discrimination claims also vary substantially from one another. Damages, for example, differ broadly among discrimination claims. That is, even when workplace claims arise from similar facts, the relief available to plaintiffs varies tremendously across workers. This is true because employees will often have different rates of pay and different positions at the company. Discrimination results in different degrees and kinds of psychological and emotional harm for individual workers. Therefore, each employee's specific damages must be determined on a case-by-case basis.

Given these similarities and differences, workplace claims are often ripe for issue class certification under Rule 23(c)(4). Because they inherently vary, discrimination claims will not always be suitable for traditional class treatment under Rule 23(b), as the *Wal-Mart* case clearly demonstrates. As these systemic cases often will arise from the same set of facts and involve the same polices, practices, and personnel, there will frequently be common issues that can be separated out and certified as an issue class. By resolving these common issues on a class basis, courts can handle the litigation much more efficiently.

Revised Relief

The governmental and procedural responses to *Wal-Mart* set forth earlier are effective ways of addressing the potential negative effects of the decision. A final way of filling the "*Wal-Mart* gap" would be to take a renewed look at the relief available in employment-discrimination cases. In light of *Wal-Mart*, the time has come to specifically reanalyze the effectiveness of punitive relief under Title VII, and for plaintiffs to more aggressively seek exemplary damages. Punitive damages serve many of the same goals as class-action litigation. To the extent that the Supreme Court has weakened the role of systemic litigation, the role of punitive damages in employment-discrimination cases should be enhanced. Of the potential plaintiff responses to *Wal-Mart* discussed here, this approach is admittedly the least practical to implement. But it is worth exploring as it offers substantial potential benefits to employment-discrimination victims.

I have previously explored the viability of punitive (or exemplary) damages in employment-discrimination cases, and have explained how this form of relief falls far short of providing an effective remedy for plaintiffs.[45] From both an empirical and anecdotal perspective, punitive damages do not live up to the threat that they purport to be for Title VII litigation. The goals of punitive damages are oft stated, and include deterrence, retribution, and education.[46] The goals of exemplary damages in the employment-discrimination setting are not as clear, but focus on deterrence and compensation to the victim. The Supreme Court has recently emphasized that, in a more general sense, "the consensus today is that punitives are aimed not at compensation but principally at retribution and deterring harmful conduct."[47]

Class-action, employment-discrimination litigation serves many of the same functions as punitive damages for workplace claimants. Even the threat of class claims succeeds in deterring discriminatory conduct. Employers are fully aware of the potential for mass litigation, as well as the enormous awards and attorney fees that are associated with these lawsuits. Though many employers strictly comply with Title VII for altruistic reasons, others likely do so to avoid embroiling themselves in systemic disputes.[48] Similarly, class claims can be seen as a form of retribution, and they certainly punish those employers that discriminate. Though punishment is not necessarily a goal of Title VII, the multimillion dollar verdicts and settlements often associated with systemic litigation can be seen as a way to penalize those employers that run afoul of civil-rights legislation.

Class-action claims also educate the public and employers more generally. These mass claims often make headlines, and thus serve the goal of informing the public about employment-discrimination laws. Finally, systemic litigation also helps to compensate individual victims of workplace abuse. As noted, many individuals who suffer from employment discrimination may be unable or afraid to pursue their claims. The class action offers a mechanism for these victims to receive a recovery for their injuries, often through a broad settlement of all claims.

Class-action litigation thus serves the same broad functions as punitive damages for employment-discrimination plaintiffs. Systemic cases serve to compensate victims, educate the public, punish employers that violate the law, and deter others from discriminating. By potentially eroding the benefits of class claims, *Wal-Mart* leaves many of the goals of Title VII unfulfilled. The decision largely undermines the ability of plaintiffs to bring systemic discrimination claims, thus making the benefits of these actions unavailable to many victims. This is where punitive damages can step in, and help fill the *Wal-Mart* gap.

As punitive damages serve many of the same functions as class-action claims, the courts and litigants could use this form of relief to fill the void left by the *Wal-Mart* decision. Thus, plaintiffs should be more aggressive in pleading for punitive relief, and the courts should more actively entertain this type of claim. In the employment-discrimination context, punitive damages are generally appropriate where a managerial agent – acting with knowledge of the law – violates Title VII. The employer also has the opportunity to demonstrate that it was acting in good faith to avoid liability for punitive damages.

The government and civil-rights groups should actively seek out those cases to prosecute that meet this standard. Though egregiousness is not a necessary element to attain punitive relief, those cases with a particularly unsympathetic employer are likely to yield higher exemplary damages. Thus, where possible, plaintiffs should prosecute those claims with egregious fact patterns where the employer had knowledge that it was acting contrary to the tenets of Title VII. As already discussed, the EEOC is in the best position to select these cases, as it has the opportunity to initially review the claims before a lawsuit is ever filed. Victims of discrimination must file a charge with the government prior to bringing suit, giving the EEOC the unique opportunity to select and pursue those claims that are most likely to yield punitive damages. To the extent *Wal-Mart* applies primarily to larger employers, this also affords the government the opportunity to focus on claims against bigger companies. And, under the sliding scale provided by Title VII, larger employers are potentially subject to higher punitive damage awards.

Similarly, the courts should be particularly sympathetic to claims for punitive relief against employers. Though the judiciary is obviously bound by the legal standards outlined in Title VII and set forth by the Supreme Court for exemplary relief, the lower courts should not apply these standards too rigidly as they have done in the past. The issue of punitive damages is largely a jury question, and the courts should err on the side of allowing the trier-of-fact to resolve the matter. Research has shown that punitive damages have had little impact in Title VII litigation. If a more vibrant exemplary damage scheme can be effectuated, it would substantially help to fill the *Wal-Mart* gap.

Moreover, in light of *Wal-Mart*, the time has come to revisit the role of punitive damages in employment-discrimination cases more broadly. Punitive and compensatory relief is currently capped in Title VII cases to a maximum combined amount of $300,000 for the largest employers.[49] And these caps are substantially lower for smaller companies. These amounts have remained static since punitive and compensatory damages were added to Title VII as part of the Civil Rights Act of 1991. Given the impact of inflation over the last two decades, punitive relief is a far less effective weapon than it was when the amendments were originally passed. Indeed, it would take over $500,000 in today's economy to have the same impact as a $300,000 award when the caps originally went into effect.

For punitive damages to be an effective substitute for class-action claims, these caps must either be raised substantially or completely eliminated. A single $300,000 award is not likely to grab the attention of a Fortune 500 company. However, a multimillion dollar award likely would, and it would thus serve as a powerful incentive to deter future abusive conduct. Similarly, large punitive awards would also attract substantial media attention and help inform the public of the risks associated with overt discrimination. Heightened awards will also compensate those victims whose lives have been so negatively affected by the unlawful conduct of large corporations. Finally, large punitive awards will punish – in a meaningful way – those employers that discriminate with full knowledge of the illegality of their actions.

The current caps prevent any of these traditional goals of punitive damages from being effectively carried out. If the caps were eliminated, it would go a long way toward reinstating the purpose of Title VII litigation. This would, however, leave obvious concerns over juries awarding inappropriate awards that would exceed what is warranted by the facts of the case. In these circumstances, the courts could reduce the amount of the award through remittitur. Like in many other areas of the law, then, the courts would police the individual jury verdicts for excessiveness. Indeed, this is already done in Title VII litigation, where awards are often reduced by the courts. The only difference would be that the courts would have more discretion in determining the appropriate amount of the award, which could be in excess of $300,000 if the caps were eliminated. Similarly, the Supreme Court has emphasized that punitive awards must comply with due process constrains and has expressed a concern over runaway jury awards. The federal courts have the expertise and experience necessary to monitor these awards and make sure that they are within acceptable levels.

This is certainly not the first time that this proposal has been made, and others have already persuasively argued for eliminating the existing caps. My previous scholarship has even suggested that punitive damages be replaced with liquidated relief, and that the courts should reformulate the way they approach exemplary damages. Indeed, legislation has even been proposed that would accomplish the goal of abolishing the statutory caps. This chapter admittedly does not offer a novel idea in this regard. However, it does reengage this debate in light of the controversial *Wal-Mart* decision. In addition, it explains how a more vibrant approach to exemplary relief can help fill the gap left by *Wal-Mart*, thus helping to vindicate victims of employment discrimination. This decision will serve as a landmark – and potential low point – for civil-rights litigants for years to come. This text thus revisits the punitive relief debate at a critical juncture in civil-rights litigation. In the absence of class-action employment discrimination, punitive damages must take on a greater role.

Thus, in light of the Supreme Court's recent decision, this chapter advocates that plaintiffs and the government more actively pursue punitive relief, that the courts more willingly entertain these claims, and that the current limits on relief be eliminated. I acknowledge that this is a broad proposal. Asking for the courts to be more sympathetic to claims for exemplary damages is a substantial request, and one that may go disregarded. Civil-rights advocates must be careful in the cases that they select – and how they present the evidence – to help achieve the goals outlined here. Similarly, asking for congressional intervention to lift the caps is not easily done, and revising legislation is difficult to accomplish. Nonetheless, the time to act is now. *Wal-Mart* is just one of several recent Supreme Court decisions undermining the protections afforded to workplace litigants. Reevaluating punitive relief – either through more aggressive litigation or legislation – can help civil-rights protections from being eroded further.

IMPLICATIONS OF THE PROPOSED APPROACH

In *Wal-Mart*, the Supreme Court weakened the class-action mechanism for civil-rights litigants, undermining an important tool for Title VII plaintiffs. The benefits of identifying creative responses to *Wal-Mart* cannot be understated. The governmental approach, procedural response, and revised relief all offer promising approaches to this decision. This section briefly summarizes those benefits, and situates this argument within the scope of the broader academic scholarship.

If the government, which is not subject to Rule 23, were to take a more active role in pursuing systemic discrimination claims, it would result in a number of clearly identifiable benefits. In particular, the EEOC can often recover for victims who have not filed a timely charge or have not been identified at the time the complaint is filed. The EEOC can also seek both monetary relief and injunctive relief for victims of company-wide discrimination. Nonetheless, the government may lack the resources necessary to fill the role previously performed by the private plaintiff's bar. And, while the EEOC often acts for the benefit of victims, its interests are not always completely aligned with those of the individual claimants.

Similarly, the procedural responses discussed here offer an additional way to address *Wal-Mart*. The offensive use of collateral estoppel and the consolidation of cases could help streamline mass-employment litigation and result in substantial judicial efficiencies. These procedural tools both simplify employment matters by reducing the amount of litigation necessary in these cases. These mechanisms are particularly attractive for employment disputes, which often involve the same policies, managers, and facts. However, these approaches also have their drawbacks. Specifically, the administrative requirements are not as relaxed as they are in the class-action setting, and these mechanisms are not as powerful a weapon as cases brought under Rule 23.

Plaintiffs may also attempt to minimize the impact of *Wal-Mart* by limiting the reach of the decision. A strong argument can be made that the decision should apply only to the largest cases brought against the biggest employers. Cabining *Wal-Mart* would substantially reduce the impact of the decision on the legal landscape. Few class claims are as big as the one brought against *Wal-Mart*, and no private company is larger. This solution may be difficult to implement, however, as the courts may be reluctant to limit the decision to massive lawsuits and may apply it more broadly to all employers. A counterstrategy would be to take *Wal-Mart* at its word and pursue mass individual litigation against employers. This could overwhelm companies with voluminous litigation and force them to settle many individual disputes. This strategy would also present its own challenges – most specifically finding ways to organize and structure the litigation. And, issue-class certification offers yet an additional procedural tool that can help litigants to navigate the difficulties created by the *Wal-Mart* decision.

Finally, given the similarity in goals between punitive damages and class-action relief, the time has come to revisit exemplary relief in employment cases. A more vibrant and effective damages structure as part of Title VII would help attain the goals previously accomplished through systemic litigation – deterrence, retribution, and education. Such change is extraordinarily difficult to achieve, and the courts and legislature may be reluctant to revitalize the relief available to victims of discrimination. However, the idea must be pursued given the importance of replacing the protections previously afforded by systemic litigation.

As these responses all reflect, no solution is perfect, and each has its own drawbacks. The class action served as a powerful weapon for civil-rights plaintiffs and acted as a strong deterrent for employer discrimination. No one tool can take its place. Identifying other means of addressing *Wal-Mart* will be critical for Title VII plaintiffs, as well as carefully critiquing any alternative approaches to systemic litigation. This text does not purport to be exhaustive – it only attempts to move the discussion away from the difficulties of *Wal-Mart* and toward a solution.

As noted throughout this text, there is a wealth of superb scholarship already addressing *Wal-Mart*, and this chapter attempts to situate itself within that literature. In her excellent article, Professor Melissa Hart does a superb job of identifying the problems created by the Court's decision.[50] Professor Hart notes that it is "essential to consider other solutions" that would help address the dilemma created by *Wal-Mart*.[51] She briefly outlines some suggestions, noting that the EEOC could become more active in pursuing systemic litigation. Professor Hart also notes different procedural mechanisms that could be used, specifically identifying different provisions of the Federal Rules. Finally, she raises the possibility of attempting to correct the decision through some type of "legislative fix."[52] Professor Hart's work superbly identifies the issues created by *Wal-Mart*, and acknowledges the need to move the debate toward a remedy. This book attempts to pick up where Professor Hart left off by offering additional solutions and carefully critiquing possible responses to the decision.

Similarly, Professor Suzette Malveaux performed an early and helpful analysis of the decision.[53] She noted the problems inherent with *Wal-Mart*, highlighting "the potential to cut short a number of employment discrimination class actions premised on the theory of excessive subjectivity as a discriminatory policy." Professor Malveaux's work did go further, however, and also began to consider possible ways through the decision. She correctly observed that the actual impact of *Wal-Mart* could be limited, as "cases the size of *Dukes* are rare," and "[s]maller classes are bound to be more successful."[54] Professor Malveaux also explored additional ways that plaintiffs could pursue class actions. Thus, while she correctly noted that *Wal-Mart* has "tipped the balance in favor of powerful employers over everyday workers,"[55] Professor Malveaux also began to identify different ways that plaintiffs may approach the decision. This book expands upon that very early analysis, carefully offering different approaches to the decision and considering ways to fill the void left after *Wal-Mart*.

In sum, the early academic literature does an excellent job of highlighting the difficulties that plaintiffs will face when addressing systemic employment discrimination. Some of this work also identifies the need to find a solution to the problems created by *Wal-Mart*. The governmental approach, procedural response, and revised relief proposed here attempt to offer such a solution. Each approach has its own challenges, however, and plaintiffs must carefully consider both the benefits and drawbacks before pursuing a particular approach. Other alternatives surely exist; hopefully, others will identify additional ways to address the problems created by the decision.

CONCLUSION

Wal-Mart created an enormous challenge for victims of systemic discrimination. The class action is a critical tool in the arsenal of plaintiffs for fighting workplace abuse. Nonetheless, there are numerous ways of addressing mass litigation that go beyond the strict constraints of Rule 23. The EEOC should take a more active role in pursuing complex discrimination claims. Plaintiffs must also consider different procedural mechanisms that are still available to address company-wide abuse. And the issue of the sufficiency of punitive relief in Title VII cases should be revisited. These solutions are not a complete fix, but each approach offers promise and potential benefits for discrimination victims. The Court's decision should be denounced, but it should not go ignored. Plaintiffs must act quickly to find ways to fill the void left after the *Wal-Mart* decision.

A FINAL NOTE: *WAL-MART* AS A CONSTITUTIONAL FLOOR?

The Supreme Court's *Wal-Mart* decision was expressly decided on the basis of Rule 23. The decision undoubtedly helps define what commonality means under the Federal Rules. However, there is nothing in the case that specifically states that the decision was intended to apply any more broadly than this. Nonetheless, the tenor of the decision itself could be logically extended beyond the confines of the procedural provisions it discusses. Indeed, it is entirely plausible to read the decision as one that creates a constitutional floor for all systemic claims. In this way, *Wal-Mart* can be read as imposing a rigid definition of commonality on all class-action plaintiffs – *regardless of whether those litigants bring their claims in federal or state court.*

The defense bar has already latched on to this possible interpretation of *Wal-Mart*. Some defendants have even raised this possible defense to class-action claims brought in state court. Unfortunately, this argument has not yet been adequately explored by the litigants. This is likely because the theory is still in its infancy, and it implicates complex rules of constitutional interpretation.

The constitutional implications of Rule 23 have been explored by numerous Supreme Court decisions. In perhaps the earliest and best-known case on this issue, the Court addressed the due process implications of class-action litigation in

Hansberry v. *Lee*.[56] In *Hansberry*, the Court noted its "deep-rooted historic tradition that everyone should have his own day in court." This principle is in direct conflict with systemic litigation, where some individuals may be bound by a decision to which they were not formal parties. The conflicting principles of having one's day in court and encouraging complex litigation that can save enormous judicial resources can create difficulty for the presiding judge.[57] Nonetheless, the Supreme Court concluded that this type of complex litigation can still satisfy the due process requirements. In an eloquently written decision, the Court reasoned that:

> there is scope within the framework of the Constitution for holding in appropriate cases a judgment rendered in a class suit is *res judicata* as to members of the class who are not formal parties to the suit ... This Court is justified in saying that there has been a failure of due process only in those cases where it cannot be said that the procedure adopted, fairly insures the protection of the interests of absent parties who are to be bound by it.[58]

According to the Court, then, the key in class-action litigation is that it must provide sufficient procedure so as to "insure that those present are of the same class as those absent and that the litigation is so conducted as to insure the full and fair consideration of the common issue." Where complex litigation satisfies these standards, it satisfies the Constitution.

The Court has thus closely guarded the rights of those that are not formal parties to the litigation. As a general rule, individuals will not be bound to a decision where they are not directly implicated in the suit. Class actions are an exception to this general rule. But, as seen in *Hansberry* v. *Lee*, adequate protections must exist to allow for this exception. In *Martin* v. *Wilks*,[59] the Court further expanded upon the protections that must be afforded to nonparties in a systemic claim. The Court acknowledged that there is "an exception to the general rule when, in certain limited circumstances, a person, although not a party, has his interests adequately represented by someone with the same interests who is a party ... [or] where a special remedial scheme exists expressly foreclosing successive litigation by non-litigants." The Court has emphasized that the burden of demonstrating the class-action exception is on the party seeking certification.

Similarly, in *Ortiz* v. *Fibreboard Corp.*,[60] the Court again addressed the tension between the desire to streamline mass litigation with concerns over due process rights of individuals. The Court emphasized that this tension "is only magnified if applied to damages claims gathered in a mandatory [class]."[61] In this regard, class-action cases require notice and an opportunity to be heard as well as an opportunity to "participate in the litigation." As *Ortiz* demonstrates, the Court – over the decades – has repeatedly put safeguards in place to assure that Rule 23 complies with due process principles.

Class-action litigation has thus long raised numerous constitutional issues over the years, and there can be little doubt that Rule 23 has been associated with various due process concerns since its inception. These concerns have been raised by the Supreme Court and in the academic literature.

Just like many of the other constitutional concerns raised by Rule 23, commonality presents its own set of problems. Where a systemic claim lacks commonality, defendants are potentially deprived of their due process rights. Though much of the due process concerns of Rule 23 are targeted at the plaintiffs' rights to their day in court, these constitutional issues cut both ways. Indeed, defendants are guaranteed the same type of process as others under the Constitution. Where defendants are subjected to massive complex claims with little in common, due process is also implicated. Such litigation has the potential to run afoul of due process guarantees by punishing defendants "without first providing an opportunity to present every available defense."

Commonality is thus one more fertile ground for due process concerns under Rule 23 – albeit from the defendant's rather than the plaintiff's perspective. Though the potential constitutional concerns raised by commonality have gone largely unexplored in the courts and academic literature, *Wal-Mart* signals a major change on this issue. This change has been in the works in recent years, and is highlighted by the Supreme Court's desire to protect defendants from unpredictable harm that is the result of unfair litigation.

Critiquing the Wal-Mart *Constitutional Argument*

A constitutional argument from *Wal-Mart* can be made that where a class-action case lacks sufficient commonality, the defendant is deprived of due process under the Constitution. From a practical standpoint, this means that *Wal-Mart*'s interpretation of the commonality standard *would apply not only to cases brought in the federal courts, but to systemic state causes of action as well.* This argument has two major components, which are derived from the principles enunciated in the Supreme Court's recent due process decisions discussed earlier.

The *Wal-Mart* constitutional argument specifies that to satisfy due process, a systemic claim must (1) provide proper notice to the defendant and (2) not subject the defendant to unreasonable or unexpected harm. The argument further maintains that *Wal-Mart* creates a constitutional floor. The Supreme Court's decision defined commonality, and any systemic claims that fail to satisfy that definition cannot meet the due process guarantees. This constitutional argument thus maintains that *Wal-Mart*'s definition of commonality extends beyond the Federal Rules, and applies to all state class-action claims as well.

This *Wal-Mart* "constitutional argument" is already percolating in the courts, and "[d]efendants have already begun to raise the constitutionalized commonality argument in a wide range" of litigation.[62] The argument has been raised in numerous cases, but has yet to form the basis for any high-profile decision. This constitutional argument has caught the attention of not only the defense bar, but major employer groups as well. Both the US Chamber of Commerce and the Equal Employment Advisory Council have filed amicus briefs in cases arguing that the commonality standard adopted by the Supreme Court should apply to all state law claims.[63] These groups have thus argued that the commonality standard established by the Supreme Court creates due process guarantees for *all* class-action claims, not just those brought in federal court.

In *Lubin* v. *Wackenhut*,[64] the Los Angeles County Superior Court addressed whether a wage/hour claim brought by nonexempt security officers should be certified.[65] In its amicus brief, the US Chamber of Commerce argued that even though "the *Wal-Mart* court centered its decision on the Rules Enabling Act ... such class action procedural 'protections [are] grounded in due process.'"[66] Similarly, in *Jacobsen* v. *Allstate Insurance Co.*,[67] the Montana Supreme Court addressed whether a class claim could be certified on the basis of an insurance carrier's claim adjustment guidelines, which allegedly discriminated against unrepresented parties. The Equal Employment Advisory Council filed an amicus brief in a petition for *certiorari* before the US Supreme Court.[68] That petition maintained that the requirements of Rule 23 and the *Wal-Mart* decision "are intended to comport with federal constitutional principles of due process designed ... to effectively limit the class claims to those fairly encompassed by the named plaintiff's claims."[69]

Though not yet developed in the courts, the *Wal-Mart* constitutional argument is compelling. As discussed earlier, Rule 23 has had a constitutional dimension since its inception, and there can be no doubt that all defendants are entitled to certain due process guarantees. The rule itself was put in place, at least in part, to protect the interests of defendants. Nonetheless, the *Wal-Mart* constitutional argument fails for several important reasons. While it is true that all parties are entitled to notice and an opportunity to be heard, the Supreme Court's decision in the case fails to address the constitutional limits of the commonality requirement. The Court did not intend for the case to create a constitutional benchmark for commonality. Nowhere in the Court's decision does it purport to create a standard in this regard. Indeed, the Court's decision on commonality never expressly uses the terms "notice" or "due process."[70]

Indeed, the Court is simply addressing the facts before it in one particular case. Also of note, the facts of that case are extraordinarily unusual. Indeed, as addressed by the Court, the *Wal-Mart* facts present "one of the most expansive class actions ever."[71] The Court set out not to define commonality on a constitutional level, but to determine whether commonality was satisfied under the facts of one extreme situation. The Court repeatedly emphasized the enormous size and geographic scope of the decision.[72] This emphasis clearly shows that the Court was concerned not with the constitutional dimension of the case, but with the specific (and unusual) facts before it.

Thus, the Court was concerned with the potential harm that a massive, amorphous lawsuit could cause to defendants. Indeed, such a lawsuit can bring the company to its knees and potentially force bankruptcy in certain situations. This is the type of case that the Court was addressing as evidenced by the reasoning of its decision. The Court emphasized the uniqueness of this particular factual scenario and did not expressly attempt to create a constitutional threshold for commonality. The decision undoubtedly fails to *expressly* create a due process standard. And to read the decision as *implicitly* creating one would be improper. Developing a constitutional standard for due process was simply not the issue before the Court.

In addition, the case is unique because there is a complete lack of commonality under the facts of the claim. The plaintiffs in the case – at least in the view of the majority decision – failed to demonstrate a "general policy of discrimination."[73] The "social framework" and statistical evidence offered by the plaintiffs were expressly disregarded by the Court. And, the "corporate policy" of "allowing discretion by local supervisors over employment matters" fails to provide any inference that the company was discriminating on a nationwide basis. In sum, the majority concluded that the plaintiffs in *Wal-Mart* were "worlds away" from establishing commonality.

The facts of *Wal-Mart*, then, present an extreme case where the Court believed that the commonality standard was not even closely met. In the Court's view, the plaintiffs in the case were largely dissimilar and failed to come anywhere near the Rule 23(a)(2) threshold. Given the complete lack of any common thread in the case, the decision offers a wholly undesirable vehicle for establishing the commonality standards on a constitutional level. A benchmark for constitutional due process in complex litigation does exist. That benchmark, however, is simply not created by the *Wal-Mart* decision, which only gives us an example of one case where the facts have "little in common" other than the plaintiffs' "sex and [the] lawsuit" in question.[74] Certainly, *Wal-Mart* provides some insight into "what is not" commonality, but it does very little to help shed any light on what type of notice and other due process requirements are actually necessary for class-action claims. The case does not provide us with the minimum standards of commonality under the Constitution, and we are left to speculate on this question.

Moreover, it is worth highlighting that the Court only resolved the dispute in *Wal-Mart* with respect to Rule 23(b)(2). The case cannot – and should not – be read as applying beyond this procedural rule. In its decision, the Court repeatedly discussed and defined Rule 23(b)(2), and evaluated whether the plaintiffs had satisfied this standard. The Court expressly set forth the entire text of the Rule in the case, and it specifically mentioned the rule over a dozen times over the course of its decision. In the case, the Court noted that the "Rule's … requirements – effectively 'limit the class claims to those fairly encompassed by the named plaintiff's claims.'"[75] The Court further stated that "[a] party seeking class certification must affirmatively demonstrate his compliance with the Rule";[76] and the Court provided that "[t]he crux of this case is commonality [under] the rule.'[77]

It is clear from the decision – which repeatedly addresses the contours of Rule 23(a) – that the Court is not intending to go beyond this Rule in its decision. The Court does not purport to interpret commonality under the Constitution, but rather defines the term specifically with regard to Rule 23(a). The Court's interpretation of commonality, then, while critical to cases brought in the federal courts, is not binding on claims brought in state court. Nor was it intended to be.

In sum, there can be little doubt that class actions have a constitutional component that provides defendants with certain due process guarantees. The *Wal-Mart* decision, however, does not define what these guarantees should be. Rather, the case is expressly decided under Rule 23(a) – a rule on which the Court relies repeatedly throughout the decision.[78] In addition, nowhere in the Court's decision can any discussion of the due process limits of commonality be found.[79] No serious argument can be made that the Court intended to establish a constitutional boundary for commonality without expressly providing that this was what it was intending to do. The Court has never been shy when developing the law, and it would be bizarre – to say the least – for the Court to create a new standard for due process without expressly saying that this was its intent. Finally, as noted, the facts of the *Wal-Mart* decision are extreme. The case involves over a million putative plaintiffs and the largest private employer in the country.[80] The Court repeatedly emphasizes throughout its decision the unique nature of the case before it.[81] Given the unusual circumstances of the case, the facts of the decision *cannot* be construed as creating a new standard for due process. It is true that the case does present one extreme factual scenario that fails to satisfy the commonality test, but it is difficult to read anything beyond this into the case.

At the end of the day, it is clear that a due process standard for commonality exists. It is equally as clear that the Court has yet to define this standard, and *Wal-Mart* only provided some general guidance on what commonality means under a single set of facts. Any argument that *Wal-Mart* did more – that it actually created a constitutional standard for commonality in class-action claims – must fail. *Wal-Mart* was intended only to apply to federal claims brought under Rule 23, and the decision cannot be extended to the state courts.

This obviously leaves unanswered the question of what commonality actually means under the Due Process Clause. If class actions do have a constitutional component to them – as this chapter argues – how is commonality defined under the broader due process test? This question is one that must be visited by the courts and academic literature.[82] In the short term, however, the *Wal-Mart* case should not be considered binding in state court decisions.

The *Wal-Mart* constitutional question thus has the potential to dramatically impact civil-rights litigants in state court. It will be important to follow how this issue progresses and whether the Supreme Court addresses the question. Most importantly, however, it is critical to be cognizant of this issue and its potential impact on workers.

4

Retaliation: The Last Safe Haven for Plaintiffs

Don't get mad, get even.

> – Robert F. Kennedy

Of course, you know this means war!

> – Groucho Marx

The tone of this book has been quite pessimistic for minority workers. As noted, the collective result of the Roberts Court's decisions has been to procedurally undermine the substantive rights of civil-rights litigants. While on the whole this trend has remained consistent, there has been one area where it is reasonable for plaintiffs to remain optimistic – claims of retaliation.

The Supreme Court and the lower courts in general have been far more receptive to claims of retaliation than to the underlying cause of action of the original complaint. As will be discussed, even in this area the high court has intervened to make things more difficult. However, as a general rule, plaintiffs will often get much further with a claim of retaliation than with a traditional civil-rights case under the current structure of our federal court system.[1]

This is true for a couple of important reasons. First, Congress was clear that it wanted to create a lower standard in these cases to prevent the rights of individuals from being chilled. Congress correctly believed when it added an antiretaliation provision to Title VII that it was critical to the statute as workers would not bring a claim if they feared retaliation from their employers.[2] Even with this statutory protection, countless viable claims go unpursued each year, as many employees are afraid to "stir the pot" or be labeled as a "troublemaker" in the workplace. Once a worker files a claim against the company, he is often viewed differently in that place of business, an unfortunate result given that victimized employees are simply availing themselves of their federally protected rights. For these reasons, Congress understood that it must include a vigorous antiretaliation clause in the statute, which (as discussed in greater detail shortly) is expressly enumerated in the law.

Second, the evidence in retaliation cases is frequently much stronger than it is for other claims of substantive discrimination. This is because employers are often caught off guard when they receive the discrimination charge and are extremely upset when accused by one of their workers of violating federal law. Oftentimes, these employers have not been properly trained by legal counsel on how to respond to a workplace complaint of discrimination. And, supervisors will often strike back at a complaining employee before even consulting with the company or its attorneys. The irony here is that the weaker the underlying case appears to be, the more likely it is that the employer will be upset by the charge and react negatively. In many cases, the employer might think that the claim is completely frivolous, and aim to get back at the worker for alleging purported violations of federal law. An immediate, "this means war," knee-jerk reaction to a discrimination charge can thus cloud an employer's judgment.

The case law is replete with instances where an employee has been fired shortly (or immediately) after receiving notice of a discrimination charge filed against the company.[3] Similarly, there are a number of cases where the employee has been able to secure direct evidence of retaliatory intent based on the comments that are made by the angry employer.

Thus, given that the standards in these cases are often strictly enforced, and that the evidence is frequently much stronger, it is not surprising that many believe that litigants tend to prevail at a higher rate in these cases at trial.[4] Further, it is unsurprising that thousands of retaliation claims are filed with the EEOC each year. Indeed, as shown in Figure 4.1, claims of retaliation far exceed any other type of charge filed with the agency.

Well over 40 percent of charges filed with the EEOC included a claim of retaliation. Race discrimination claims, which are the next most common charges, comprised 34.7 percent of the total charges in fiscal year 2015.[5] The pure volume and success of these claims make them an attractive area for plaintiffs to pursue. And, as will be discussed in the sections that follow, with a couple of notable exceptions, Congress and the Supreme Court have acted to make this area more easily accessible to litigants as a whole.

RETALIATION GENERALLY

Retaliation claims stem from the statutory language of Title VII, and have thus long been codified in the statute. All of the major federal employment-discrimination statutes have such prohibitory language including the ADEA, the ADA, and the Family and Medical Leave Act (FMLA). The language is quite similar among these

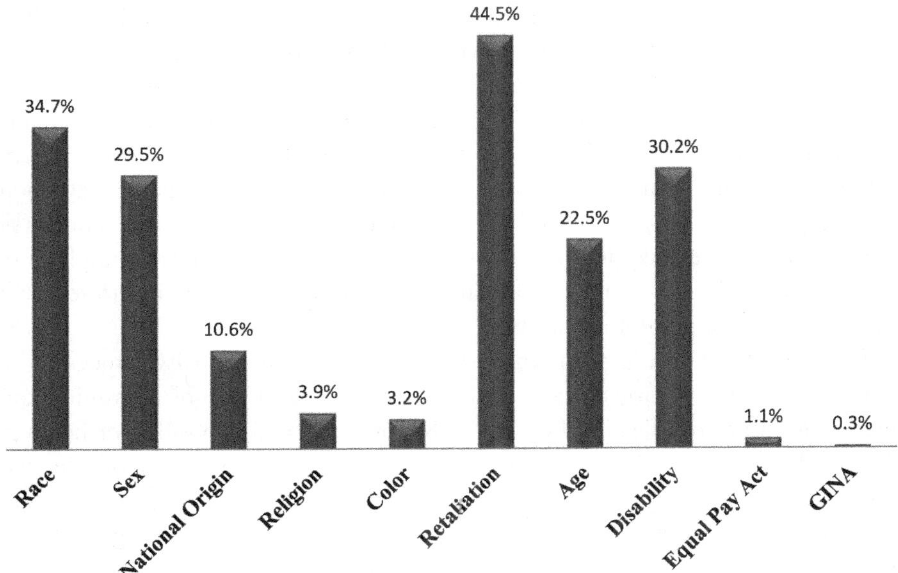

FIGURE 4.1 Comparison of types of discrimination charges, 2015. The types of discrimination claims brought against employers varies each year. This chart provides a snapshot of the composition of these claims in 2015.
Credit: EEOC, *Charge Statistics FY 1997 through FY 2015*, www.eeoc.gov/eeoc/statistics/enforcement/charges.cfm (last visited August 28, 2016).

statutes. More specifically, Title VII prohibits an employer from taking an adverse action against a worker "because he has opposed any practice made an unlawful employment practice by [Title VII], or because he has made a charge, testified, assisted, or participated in any manner in an investigation, proceeding, or hearing."[6]

The courts have varied in their description of the *prima facie* case of retaliation, but a typical formulation would include details from the alleged victim that "(1) he engaged in protected activity; (2) he was subjected to an adverse employment action; and (3) there was a causal link between the protected activity and the adverse action."[7]

The statute is quite broad and encompasses many aspects of the discrimination process. Initially, a plaintiff must establish that she has engaged in some type of activity that is protected under Title VII. Plaintiffs can establish this type of protected activity either through the participation or opposition clause of the statute. Thus, coverage is satisfied where a current (or former)[8] employee is able to establish that: (1) she has opposed some type of unlawful activity; or (2) she has participated in the process that is involved with an employment-discrimination claim.

The first category of workers typically includes those who have complained about discrimination internally at the company – usually to a supervisor or human resources representative. This type of complaint can take any form, but is often performed in person, by email, or in writing. Those workers engaging in this type of protected activity gain protection from retaliation, provided the complaint is reasonable in scope and manner. Thus, under the law, a person must reasonably believe that the statute has been violated for her to have this type of protection from retaliation. Similarly, a person must not complain in an unreasonable way, such as engaging in an illegal act. While these limitations on the scope and manner of a complaint can restrict the protections of some workers,[9] the typical complaint of race or sex discrimination made internally to the human resources department will be sufficient to gain statutory coverage.

Broader protection is given to those who "participate" in the EEO process. The participation clause covers those employees who file a charge of discrimination, cooperate in an investigation by the EEOC, or testify at a deposition or hearing. Thus, where a worker becomes involved in the more formal aspects of a federal complaint of discrimination, she will have complete protection under the statute. This protection is greater than that given to someone complaining internally to a corporate official, as there are no limitations on the scope or manner of the complaint itself. Thus, the participation clause gives blanket protection to workers complaining to the EEOC or participating in the federal government's investigation into discrimination. This is true regardless of the veracity of the individuals' participation in the investigation, or the nature of the charge filed.[10] Congress was clear that where the wheels of the federal process are invoked, individuals should be protected from retaliation, irrespective of the merit of the underlying claim.

The Supreme Court has recently broadly interpreted coverage under the statute. Thus, the question often arose in the lower courts whether – for example – an employee who complains of discrimination would have protection if his wife or close relative (who also worked at the same company) was terminated in retaliation for the complaint. In *Thompson* v. *North American Stainless, LP.* the Court held that an individual has protection if she "falls within the 'zone of interests' sought to be protected by the statutory provision whose violation forms the legal basis for his complaint."[11] Thus, "accidental victim[s]" or those that are "collateral damage" may not find coverage in the statute, but where injury "was the intended means of" the employer's retaliation, coverage will apply.[12] This "zone of interest" test is a broad application of the statute by the Supreme Court, but it is unclear how far it will extend and how it will be interpreted by the lower courts.

Once a plaintiff establishes that she has engaged in some type of protected activity pursuant to Title VII, she must also show that she has suffered an adverse action. What constitutes an adverse action is controversial and has never been addressed by the Supreme Court outside of the retaliation context. In traditional Title VII cases that do not involve retaliation, the issue has never been resolved, with some courts requiring the plaintiff to suffer an "ultimate employment action," and others applying a much lower "materially adverse" bar.[13] In the retaliation context, the lower courts were similarly divided, until the Supreme Court granted review in *Burlington Northern & Santa Fe Railway* v. *White*.[14] Many in the academic and legal community believed that the Court would use the case as an opportunity to further limit the civil-rights protections of affected workers. Surprisingly, however, the Supreme Court would adopt a more expansive view of what satisfies the adverse-action standard. That case will be discussed in greater detail in the sections that follow.

The final component of the *prima facie* case of retaliation involves an examination of whether there is a *causal link* between the adverse act and the protected activity. This causal link requires some showing that the employer took the adverse action against the employee *because of* the protected activity involved. There are a number of ways that this showing can be made. Most notably, the timing of the act itself can raise suspicions as to the employer's motivations. If an employee complains of discrimination and that worker is immediately fired, there would be a strong suggestion of causation in the case. This link becomes more tenuous as time passes, and an adverse action taken a year after a complaint was filed would likely not meet the *prima facie* threshold, without additional evidence of retaliatory motivations. The courts vary as to how much time between the complaint and adverse action is too much to raise suspicions, but the trend in the courts is to require more than simply timing alone where there is not an immediate retaliatory act. In many cases, there may also be retaliatory comments (constituting direct evidence of retaliation), that are made shortly after the claim is filed or received by the employer. Employers are often offended when accused of discriminatory activity and may react with anger or resentment toward the employee. Many cases provide evidence of this type of direct or circumstantial evidence of retaliatory conduct (e.g., "Can you believe that this employee has the nerve to accuse us of discrimination; we will show her.") and would satisfy the *prima facie* case of retaliation.

For example, in one case, *Shaver* v. *Independent Stave Co.*,[15] a plaintiff alleged that he had repeatedly been called "platehead" by his coworkers when they learned that he had undergone a surgery to implant a metal plate in his head to prevent serious seizures. He filed a complaint of disability harassment, and the Eighth Circuit Court of Appeals concluded that this conduct was not sufficiently severe or pervasive to support a claim. However, the Court did permit the retaliation claim to proceed, as the employer had allegedly responded to a job inquiry by telling the caller that the plaintiff "had a get rich quick scheme involving suing companies."[16] This case thus demonstrates the type of direct causal link that is often found in retaliation cases. It further shows the value of educating employers on the importance of not acting out against workers who have filed complaints for relief – even where those claims ultimately have no legal basis.

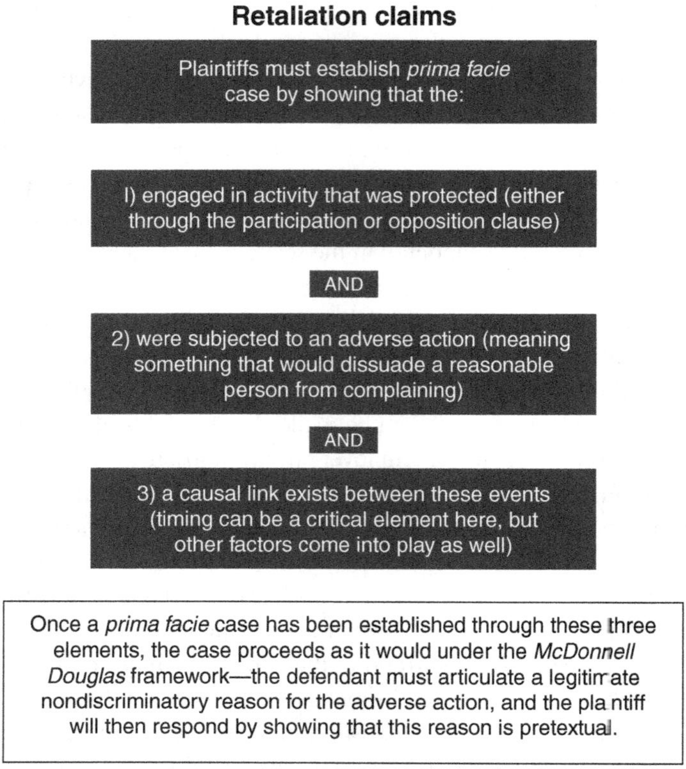

Retaliation claims

> Plaintiffs must establish *prima facie* case by showing that the:

> I) engaged in activity that was protected (either through the participation or opposition clause)

AND

> 2) were subjected to an adverse action (meaning something that would dissuade a reasonable person from complaining)

AND

> 3) a causal link exists between these events (timing can be a critical element here, but other factors come into play as well)

> Once a *prima facie* case has been established through these three elements, the case proceeds as it would under the *McDonnell Douglas* framework—the defendant must articulate a legitimate nondiscriminatory reason for the adverse action, and the plaintiff will then respond by showing that this reason is pretextual.

FIGURE 4.2 Retaliation claims chart. Retaliation litigation is a complex and confusing area of the law. This chart illustrates how these claims are analyzed by the courts.

While timing, direct evidence, and/or retaliatory comments are some of the more common ways of showing retaliation, there are countless other ways of establishing this final component of the *prima facie* case. Once this test has been satisfied, the claim is treated like any other case of circumstantial evidence of discrimination. An inference of discrimination arises in the case, and the defendant must articulate a legitimate, nondiscriminatory reason for the retaliatory act. The plaintiff then carries the ultimate burden of showing that the employer's provided rationale is pretextual. The Retaliation Claims chart set forth in Figure 4.2 reflects how the *prima facie* case is addressed by the courts in the retaliation cases.

TAKING AN EXPANSIVE VIEW OF RETALIATION CLAIMS

In *Burlington Northern*, the Court considered a case where the plaintiff, the only female working in a particular railway department, claimed retaliation as a result of her complaints of discrimination. The plaintiff in the case, Sheila White, was hired as a "track laborer," a position that involved moving and replacing track components and material. She also operated a forklift while on the job, which soon became her primary workplace duty. During her employment, White complained that her supervisor had made inappropriate comments to her and informed her that females should not work in her department. After an investigation into this complaint, the company suspended the supervisor for several days. Following the complaint, White was also removed from her forklift assignments and asked to perform the more standard laborer duties. White filed a complaint with the EEOC maintaining that this reassignment was the result of sex discrimination. After this complaint, she was also suspended without pay after an employment dispute arose with another worker. An internal company investigation revealed that White had done nothing wrong, and she was compensated for the thirty-seven days of pay that she had missed while the investigation was pending. The case subsequently went to trial, and a jury awarded White $43,500 for her retaliation claims.

In deciding this case, the Court considered whether the employer's two acts against White – assigning her to less desirable labor duties in place of her typical forklift responsibilities and suspending her for thirty-seven days without pay pending an investigation – were sufficiently adverse to rise to the level of actionability under Title VII. The Court looked at the two different standards that were applied by the appellate courts – ultimate employment actions and material adversity – and concluded that the latter was the better approach. The Court thus held that if an employer takes an action that is materially adverse to an employee based on that worker's complaint of employment discrimination, a violation of the statute has occurred.

The Court further defined what it means for an action to be materially adverse. Specifically, the Court noted that it was following the approach offered by the Seventh Circuit and D.C. Courts of Appeals that a retaliatory act must "dissuade[] a reasonable worker from making or supporting a charge of discrimination."[17] The Court was clear that not all retaliatory harm will be sufficient to satisfy the statute, and more precisely stated that "trivial harms" are not covered by Title VII.[18] Thus, the retaliatory act must be "significant," and "personality conflicts," "petty slights," "or minor annoyances" will not rise to this level under the statute.[19] When considering the facts of this case, the Court concluded that there was sufficient evidence to support the jury verdict on the plaintiff's claims. As to her concerns about her reassignment following her complaint, the Court stated that "one good way to discourage an employee ... from bringing discrimination charges would be to insist that she spend more time performing the more arduous duties and less time performing those that are easier or more agreeable."[20] The Court was also sympathetic to the claim of retaliation based on her suspension, noting that "White and her family had to live for 37 days without income."[21]

The Supreme Court's decision in this case came as a significant surprise to many in the legal community. The holding took a broad approach to retaliation claims and signaled a resistance on the part of the Court to permit employers to chill the Title VII rights of employees.[22] By choosing a more expansive definition of "adverse action" for retaliation claims, the Court helped preserve one of the most important areas of employment-discrimination law. As noted earlier, retaliation claims comprise a large portion of those charges against employers, and these claims are often highly successful where others fail. In maintaining a broad scope for retaliation claims, the Court did at least calm some critics on its increasing trend toward limiting the civil rights of employees.

After *Burlington Northern*, then, the standard for an adverse action was crystallized – plaintiffs need only show that their employer's action would have dissuaded a reasonable person from complaining. This lower threshold allows a more comprehensive view of retaliation generally and permits more cases to proceed in this area. By taking this more expansive approach to retaliation claims, the Supreme Court signaled its view that these claims are critical to enforcing civil-rights laws. If individuals are afraid to complain about discrimination, the laws in this area will be largely ineffective. The Court, though unreceptive to civil-rights claims generally, does clearly understand the importance of retaliation in preserving these individual rights.

WHY RETALIATION CLAIMS ARE DIFFERENT

Like Congress, then, the Court understands that the statute will have little effect if an employer can prevent an employee from bringing a claim in the first instance. According to the Court, this just makes "[c]ommon sense."[23] And the Court is correct here. On further reflection, it is not entirely unexpected that the Court would adopt this view. After all, acknowledging Congress's intent of incorporating the broad scope in retaliation claims into Title VII is simply recognizing the strong language used by the legislature in creating the law. Indeed, going against this clear reading might have even lead to congressional intervention – as it has in multiple instances where the Court has overstepped its grounds in discrimination cases in the past.[24]

To be fair, though, the *Burlington Northern* case does stand out as an outlier in the trend that can be found in the Court's decisions undercutting worker rights. This case presented the opportunity for the Court to again chip away at these protections. Yet the Court went in the other direction on this issue. Though the reason is not entirely clear, there is something unique about retaliation cases. These claims get more at the core of statutory authority and judicial enforcement than traditional employment claims. An employer who retaliates against an employee who complains of a violation of federal law is doing much more than discriminating – that employer is challenging the very foundation of the legal system. Retaliation is an act of defiance and clearly one that is viewed much more seriously by the Court in recent years than a traditional civil-rights violation.

In addition, in a more practical sense, retaliation is often easier to identify than discrimination itself. The facts often yield more direct type evidence of discrimination and often involve more suspicious timing. And, these claims are easy to recognize and understand. From the playground to the basketball court – those who retaliate are often more quickly identified and punished. Retaliation, then, creates a unique area of the law that has not been quite as trampled upon by the Court with procedural nuances and restrictions.

REFINING RETALIATION

Even with retaliation claims, though, there has still been a narrowing of worker rights through procedural mechanisms. This may be a signal of the increasing conservative nature of the Court on worker claims generally. *Burlington Northern* was decided more than a decade ago, and more recent case law has seen a pulling back on employee protections, even in the retaliation arena.

In particular, in *University of Texas Southwestern Medical Center* v. *Nassar*,[25] the contours of retaliation claims were revisited in a case involving a medical center operating within a university system that focused on medical education. Naiel Nassar was a medical doctor working with internal medicine for the employer. Another employee at the university, Beth Levine, was hired as the chief of Infectious Disease Medicine, and served as Nassar's superior. Nassar believed that Levine held certain animus against him as a result of his Middle Eastern background and religion. Nassar complained to the chair of Internal Medicine about this perceived harassment. Nassar eventually resigned his position, expressly stating that the harassment from Levine was the reason for his separation. The chair noted concern that Levine had been "publically humiliated" by Nassar's complaint, and took further steps to assure that Nassar would not be rehired at the hospital.[26]

Nassar alleged that his treatment resulted in an unlawful constructive discharge, as well as retaliation under Title VII. A jury awarded Nassar $400,000 in back pay and more than $3 million in compensatory damages – these amounts were subsequently reduced to comply with the statutory caps. On appeal, the US Court of Appeals for the Fifth Circuit vacated the constructive discharge claim for lack of evidence and affirmed the retaliation claim on a mixed-motives theory. The Supreme Court granted *certiorari* to consider whether the statute permits retaliation claims where there is only evidence to support that the retaliatory motives were a motivating (rather than but-cause) reason for the discrimination.

The Supreme Court concluded that "but-for" causation is a necessary element of a retaliation claim under Title VII. The Court relied heavily on statutory differences between the retaliatory discrimination provisions and the more traditional status-based discrimination in Title VII. As the Court emphasized, retaliation claims can be proven only where an adverse action was taken "because of" a protected characteristic, and not simply where retaliatory motives were a motivating factor in the decision. This "motivating factor" language is present in the statutory language for status-based discrimination but was omitted for retaliation claims. This distinction, the Court held, supports a finding that plaintiffs must establish a but-for causal link between the adverse action and the retaliation to sufficiently support the claim. The Court's finding was consistent with an earlier decision on claims brought under the ADEA, which also required but-for causation.[27] As the Court concluded, "[t]he text, structure and history of Title VII demonstrate that a plaintiff making a retaliation claim ... must establish that his or her protected activity was a but-for cause of the alleged adverse action by the employer."[28]

A vigorous dissent, authored by Justice Ginsburg, and joined by Justices Breyer, Sotomayor, and Kagan, strongly disagreed.[29] The dissent argued that the Court was inappropriately "reining in retaliation claims."[30] Justice Ginsburg noted that the majority's decision was "at odds with a solid line of decisions recognizing that retaliation is inextricably bound up with status-based discrimination."[31] The majority thus "reaches outside of Title VII to arrive at an interpretation of 'because' that lacks sensitivity to the realities of life at work."[32] Justice Ginsburg further accused the majority of being "driven by a zeal to reduce the number of retaliation claims against employers."[33] She thus urged Congress to intervene in this "misguided judgment" with "yet another Civil Rights Restoration Act."[34]

Nassar reflects the realities of employment-discrimination law in the workplace. While the Roberts Court has been sympathetic to retaliation suits, it has still taken a more narrow view of the procedural contours of these claims. Retaliation is unique and tends to be protected by the courts and legislature. However, the Supreme Court has its limits on how far it is willing to extend those protections. *Nassar* clearly illustrates the Court's limits, creating an additional procedural hurdle for employment-discrimination plaintiffs.

As Justice Ginsburg highlights, the primary problem with this decision is the practical difficulty of establishing but-for causation in the retaliation setting. It is simply human nature to harbor multiple motivations for retaliating against an employee. If a company can put forward other nondiscriminatory factors involved in the decision, the plaintiff will be unable to prevail. In simple terms, even if the employer retaliates against a worker for legitimately raising a claim of discrimination, that worker will be unable to have a successful cause of action if there are other nondiscriminatory motivations also in play. Employers can often point to such things as tardiness, insubordination, or poor work product in support of the disciplinary action of an employee, even if retaliatory animus was also involved. These employment deficiencies are often subjective in nature, making it even easier for employers to justify their decision to take an adverse action.

A NOTE ABOUT *BREEDEN*

In a decision issued prior to the Roberts Court, *Clark County School District* v. *Breeden*,[35] the Court also limited the scope of retaliation claims. In *Breeden*, a female employee met with her boss and another worker for purposes of evaluating certain job applicants. As part of the meeting, it was revealed that one of the job applicants had once stated to another worker that "making love to [her was] like making love to the Grand Canyon."[36] The supervisor looked at the plaintiff and remarked that he was unsure what the statement meant. The other worker stated, "Well, I'll tell you later," and both men in the room laughed.[37] After the plaintiff complained about this remark, she was punished. Considering whether these allegations satisfied the retaliation standard under Title VII, the Supreme Court concluded that "[n]o reasonable person could have believed that the single incident recounted above violated Title VII's standard."[38] The Court thus concluded that this incident was too "isolated" for anyone to believe that a violation of Title VII had occurred.[39]

Breeden is significant in that it raises the bar for what must be established in a retaliation case. It also creates difficulty for plaintiffs trying to navigate the complaint process. Indeed, as *Breeden* demonstrates, if a plaintiff complains too early, they will fail to have any protection in their complaint. In many ways, the decision thus fails to encourage early reporting of harassing conduct as an individual's complaint will lack protection until the events are more egregious in nature. Some lower courts have issued complementary decisions.[40]

One notable example occurred in *Jordan* v. *Alternative Resources Corp.*[41] In that case, the plaintiff was offended by a comment of a coworker who claimed that "they" should put the "two black monkeys" responsible for the D.C. sniper shooting "in a cage with a bunch of black apes and let the apes f-k them."[42] After complaining about this comment, the plaintiff received negative treatment. The Fourth Circuit rejected the plaintiff's retaliation claim, holding that "no objectively reasonable person could have believed that [the employer] was in the grips of a hostile work environment or that one was taking shape."[43] While it seems entirely appropriate for someone to complain of such a comment, such a complaint would not be protected in many jurisdictions. Rather, the plaintiff would need to wait until more incidents occurred to gain any protection under the law from retaliation.

The timing of a complaint – particularly in a harassment case – thus becomes critical after *Breeden* and its progeny. Complaining too soon leaves workers open to retaliatory conduct. However, waiting too long can raise the potential of silently encouraging continued discriminatory conduct. This Catch-22 faced by plaintiffs forces them to walk a narrow line when registering discriminatory complaints.

One potential resolution to this dilemma, however, is for the plaintiff to go directly to the EEOC, rather than complaining internally. Individuals who avail themselves of this governmental entity receive blanket protection under the participation clause of the statute. Nonetheless, as a practical matter, complaining to the federal government about one's employer can have its own set of difficulties. Many individuals would prefer to handle the matter internally rather than "making a federal case" out of what occurred. Regardless, as the law stands today, far greater protection is given to those who complain externally rather than internally.

LESSONS FROM *NASSAR* AND *BREEDEN*

From *Nassar* and *Breeden*, we learn that while the Court is generally more receptive to retaliation claims than other cases of discrimination, it is still quite wary of all employment cases generally. Thus, *Nassar* and *Breeden* represent a pulling back on the breadth of retaliation claims, and they provide yet another example of the Court's use of procedural mechanisms to limit the scope of employment cases.

There can be little doubt, though, that the courts still view retaliation claims far more favorably than other areas of civil-rights law.[44] Congress was clear when it passed Title VII that these claims must be given special attention and protection. Similarly, in *Burlington Northern*, the Supreme Court acknowledged the important role these cases play in the overall enforcement process. Retaliation thus remains one area where plaintiffs have still been somewhat successful in pursuing their claims and obtaining relief. With that said, the Supreme Court has still intervened in a couple of different instances to limit the breadth of the role played by retaliation.

Nassar teaches us that the Supreme Court will not permit anything other than but-for causation in retaliation cases. From a procedural standpoint, this means that plaintiffs must shore up any question early in the case as to the defendant's true motivations. This can be done through a variety of different mechanisms, including direct evidence of discrimination, discriminatory comments, statistical evidence, comparative evidence, or other circumstantial evidence of discrimination. The *Nassar* decision is particularly problematic as retaliation claims often involve multiple motivations. An individual who is generally a poor employee, for example, might not otherwise have been terminated if he had not filed a claim of discrimination. The employee's poor work history might, as a practical matter, provide an employer with the basis for the termination even if there is some evidence that retaliation also played into the decision. Therefore, plaintiffs must gather substantial evidence to put to rest anything other than a but-for link between retaliation and the protected conduct.

Breeden also demonstrates the need to gather substantial evidence in this area. If a plaintiff complains internally, she must also be able to demonstrate a reasonable belief that Title VII has been violated. In harassment cases, this means not acting too soon and gathering sufficient evidence to demonstrate a reasonable belief that the statute has been violated. *Breeden* also demonstrates the advantage of complaining to the EEOC – where blanket protection is provided – when alleging these claims. From a legal standpoint, then, there is a substantial advantage to complaining externally about Title VII violations. From a practical standpoint, however, there may be many drawbacks for an individual to raise a discrimination claim with the federal government.

SUGGESTED APPROACHES FOR THE PLAINTIFF

Retaliation claims are one of the few remaining fertile grounds for plaintiffs in employment-discrimination law. These claims comprise the most frequently brought Title VII actions – and for good reason. Evidence of suspicious timing and discriminatory, overt comments are often available in these types of claims. Plaintiffs and their attorneys should be vigilant in watching for these claims. They should also be proactive. Where an employee (or former employee) brings a case against the company, the plaintiff should further advise (in writing) the employer of the legal restrictions against retaliation. The attorney should thus advise the employer not to take any adverse actions against the employee – and notify the company that if an improper adverse action is taken, a separate charge of retaliation will be filed with the government. Plaintiffs' attorneys should be particularly cognizant of any activity that occurs immediately after a charge or claim of discrimination is filed. Documents sent to the employee (or of which the employee is aware) related to the claim should be gathered and maintained. Any comments made to the worker should be documented as well. The period of time immediately following the charge filing of the underlying claim can be critical to supporting a subsequent claim of retaliation.

Before filing a retaliation charge, employees should make certain that their claims satisfy the three-part test commonly adopted by the courts. In particular, they should make sure that their complaint can plausibly state that the worker has engaged in protected activity, has suffered an adverse action that would reasonably dissuade a typical employee from complaining, and that there is a causal link between these two events.

As noted, it is quite common for an employee to lose her underlying claim of discrimination but still prevail on a subsequent retaliation cause of action. Employers are all too often unprepared for claims and charges of discrimination and improperly lash out at workers even where there is no basis for the claim. The courts have been quite receptive in this area of the law, and plaintiffs should capitalize on these claims where appropriate.

Finally, as indicated, plaintiffs should not complain too early in harassment cases when doing so internally (rather than going directly to the EEOC). And, when complaining of retaliation generally, plaintiffs must make sure to have gathered sufficient evidence to establish a but-for causal link between the adverse action and the purported retaliation.

A DEFENSE PERSPECTIVE

Defendants should similarly be cognizant of the potential for claims of retaliation. As this is one area where plaintiffs may have the upper hand in certain instances, a corporate defense attorney should do her best to insulate the employer from liability. In particular, a company should be well prepared for the receipt of a charge or complaint of discrimination. All supervisory personnel should be trained to funnel such charges to a particular source (or sources, depending upon the size of the business).

Those authorized to receive a complaint should have undergone comprehensive training on how to handle claims of discrimination. They should know how to respond and notify legal counsel immediately if an action is brought. An appropriate response mechanism to the complaint must be in place. This will often include launching an investigation into the matter by individuals who are independent and unbiased on the issue. Harassment claims must be handled with particular care, and all claims must be kept strictly confidential – sharing information only with those workers who have a need to know.

Employers must be well advised on the potential problems they can face with retaliation. Management-level employees are often frustrated when they receive a discrimination charge and might be inclined to retaliate. All workers in a company must be informed of the critical importance of not retaliating against complaining employees. All too often employers face EEOC charges that include no viable claim of discrimination, yet the business finds itself on the hook because one of their management workers retaliated against the complaining individual.

At the end of the day, claims of retaliation present particular problems for employers, and all businesses should be cognizant and proactive in preventing these claims. Preparation and training in advance of discriminatory allegations is critical to preventing this potentially expensive and successful litigation against the business. This is particularly important in the present climate, where the courts appear far more receptive to retaliatory actions than to other types of discrimination claims.

A NOTE ON REFERENCES

Providing employee references can be a particularly troublesome area for employers. Employers would like to help their workers by providing an honest assessment of their work, but sharing this information comes with some risk. This is particularly true where the employee has already filed a discrimination complaint against the employer. If employees are dissatisfied with the reference that is given, they may claim that they have been retaliated against for having filed this complaint. Providing a reference thus exposes the employer to a potential federal claim (in addition to the more traditional common law claim of defamation).

A large portion of employers have adopted a policy that the company will provide prospective employers only with the basic information related to the employee.[45] Thus, they will refuse to provide any substantial critique of the worker's performance and will only detail the employee's dates of service, pay grade, and reason for separation. This type of policy helps insulate businesses from litigation for providing a retaliatory or defamatory reference to others. Although such a policy provides some comfort to employers, it also comes with a number of potential drawbacks. For instance, those seeking references may look to other potential sources of information at the company (former friends, colleagues, etc.), which will prove more unreliable and more likely to subject the company to litigation. Second, these types of policies unnecessarily restrict the flow of information. They generally prevent companies from properly gathering important knowledge about their workers. And, they potentially hurt good employees who are unable to demonstrate to prospective companies that they have excelled in their prior job.

A SUMMARY OF RETALIATION

Retaliation brings a unique opportunity for employees to pursue litigation that will be seriously considered by the federal courts. These claims are looked at quite closely in litigation and can be successfully brought in the courts. Retaliation, by its very nature, suggests that some employers may be flaunting the federal laws put in place by Congress. While the Supreme Court has restricted some parts of these claims through procedural mechanisms, it remains one area where plaintiffs should strongly consider litigation under the proper set of facts. In areas where the Court has constructed procedural barriers, litigants must proceed cautiously to avoid a misstep that could result in the dismissal of the case. The Court's decisions in *Breeden* and *Nassar* are particularly important for plaintiffs to understand and cautiously navigate.

5

Striking at Relief

A billion dollars to them is chump change.

–Member of jury that awarded $11.8 billion in
punitive damages in a case brought against Exxon Mobil Corporation[1]

Punitive damages were described by one early court as "an unsightly and an unhealthy excrescence." Another court called them "monstrous heresy."[2] Though punitive damages can be seen as "deforming the symmetry of the body of the law,"[3] there can be little doubt that one of the primary purposes of such relief is to help deter unlawful conduct.[4] Although views toward punitive relief have changed over the years, the debate over the availability of exemplary damages in the judicial system has remained controversial. No place is that controversy more aptly demonstrated than in employment-discrimination law, where punitive damages first became available in an amendment to Title VII of the Civil Rights Act of 1964 after a bitter congressional debate. Almost two decades ago, in *Kolstad* v. *American Dental Association*, the Supreme Court provided guidance on how punitive damages should be applied in discrimination cases brought under Title VII. *Kolstad* has only generated more confusion concerning the proper standard for exemplary relief, and recent district and appellate court decisions reflect this uncertainty.

This chapter will provide a historical review of punitive relief in employment-discrimination cases. It will explain how constitutional and statutory provisions have shaped the exemplary damages in workplace lawsuits. This chapter will explain the structure of those damages schemes that have been in place for years, and it will discuss the specific statutory relief made available by Title VII of the Civil Rights Act of

This chapter draws heavily from the following articles: Joseph A. Seiner, "The Failure of Punitive Damages in Employment Discrimination Cases: A Call for Change," *William and Mary Law Review* 50 (2008): 735; Joseph A. Seiner, "Punitive Damages, Due Process, and Employment Discrimination," *Iowa Law Review* 97 (2012): 473.

1964. It will further navigate the changes of the Civil Rights Act of 1991, which added jury trials, as well as compensatory and punitive damages, to the statute.

This chapter will then explore how more recent decisions of the Supreme Court have impacted the damages available to civil-rights litigants. In particular, it will look at the *Exxon* and *Philip Morris* decisions. While these recent cases arose outside of the workplace context, they have very real implications for employment cases. The text will explain how these cases will affect worker rights, and how they will potentially impact the damages available to employment plaintiffs. The *Philip Morris* decision serves as a potential threat to undermine the damages afforded to civil-rights litigants, while *Exxon* offers an opportunity for workers. This chapter will conclude with a proposed framework that will allow plaintiffs to minimize any negative effects of these Supreme Court cases. It will explain strategies workers can use to maximize relief. It will further provide a new model for analyzing the role of the Constitution when examining punitive damages under Title VII.

THE HISTORY OF PUNITIVE DAMAGES AND THE LAW

Evolution of Doctrine in American Law

Punitive (or "exemplary") damages are not a recent phenomenon and have been described as an "ancient curiosity."[5] Indeed, these damages date back over four millennia to 2000 BC and the Code of Hammurabi and evolved as part of the common law. Pursuant to the Code, for example, a man who stole an ox, sheep, or a pig from a temple or palace would be required to pay damages thirtyfold the worth of the animal.[6]

The theory of punitive damages persisted through the following centuries. For example, the Magna Carta contains three chapters on the system of amercements, that, in many respects, operated in a similar manner to punitive damages under the current US legal system. The amercement system allowed wrongdoers to buy back their "grace under the law" through payments to the Crown. A jury, rather than a judge, determined the amount of the payments and was instructed to consider "[t]he gravity of the offense and the wealth of the wrongdoer" in reaching an appropriate award.[7]

Over time, punitive damages came to satisfy the particular requirements of society, including "punishment and deterrence of wrongdoers, and [also] as a substitute for revenge."[8] Under English common law, punitive damages "appeared discreetly … overshadowed by the legal and moral issues" of the cases in which they were awarded.[9] Like in the American legal system, punitive damages in England have been the subject of controversy over the years, and these damages "practically were abolished" in the country in 1964.[10] Punitive damages in the American legal system can be traced to English common law.[11] In 1784, in *Genay v. Norris*,[12] an American state court adopted the theory of punitive relief enunciated by the English courts in a case in which the plaintiff became sick after drinking wine that the defendant had spiked with Spanish Fly. The court awarded "exemplary damages" to the plaintiff. Moreover, in 1791, a New Jersey court granted punitive relief for the explicit purpose of making an "example[]" of the defendant in an action that involved breach of promise to marry.[13]

By the mid-nineteenth century, punitive damages were well established in the United States.[14] In *Day* v. *Woodworth*,[15] the US Supreme Court resolved any question on the availability of punitive relief, stating that it was settled that "a jury may inflict what are called exemplary, punitive, or vindictive damages upon a defendant." The Court acknowledged that "the propriety of this doctrine has been questioned," but noted that "repeated judicial decisions" would support the view that punitive damages were appropriate, depending upon the particular circumstances and the "degree of moral turpitude or atrocity of the defendant's conduct."[16]

Punitive damages are presently a widely accepted form of relief under American law. It has been well established in the United States for "over a century that punitive damages are noncompensatory in character."[17] Almost all states allow some form of punitive relief upon a specified showing of proof. Punitive damages are, and have been for decades, a "fixture in American law."[18] Nonetheless, the debate over punitive damages persists. Many scholars evaluating punitive damages have agreed that this form of relief is "a necessary component in an efficient civil justice system."[19] Punitive awards, however, are also seen as "an anomaly" in the justice system that "should be abolished except where specifically authorized by statute."[20]

Purpose of Punitive Damages

Punitive damages are those damages that are "awarded in addition to actual damages when the defendant acted with recklessness, malice, or deceit."[21] The purpose of this type of relief is much more difficult to capture. For the most part, exemplary damages have been justified by three different rationales: retribution, deterrence, and education.

First, punitive relief is a form of retribution or revenge.[22] As one of the primary purposes of exemplary damages, this relief is viewed as a way of punishing the wrongdoer.[23] The retribution function serves not only the need of the individual victims, but also the society as a whole. Justice Oliver Wendell Holmes summarized the benefit of allowing the law, rather than individuals, to achieve some form of retribution when a wrong has been suffered, stating that "[i]f people would gratify the passion of revenge outside of the law, if the law did not help them, the law has no choice but to satisfy the craving itself, and thus avoid the greater evil of private retribution."[24] Perhaps an antiquated theory in support of punitive relief, revenge "seems incompatible with our modern conception of the judicial system."[25] Still, retribution is often cited as one of the primary bases for awarding punitive relief. Justice Sandra Day O'Connor has even described exemplary damages as "quasi-criminal" relief that is "specifically designed to exact punishment in excess of actual harm to make clear that the defendant's misconduct was especially reprehensible."[26]

Second, punitive damages are a way to deter the wrongdoer (or potential wrongdoers) from engaging in repeat conduct against the plaintiff.[27] This function of exemplary relief is premised on the economic theory that a wrongdoer who is required to pay a victim above and beyond the harm actually suffered will be less likely to engage in the wrongful conduct in the future. By deterring future misconduct, punitive relief serves to "enforce desireable [*sic*] social norms" and results in a "positive gain to society."[28]

Finally, punitive damages are a way of educating the wrongdoer and society as a whole. In this regard, exemplary relief affirms both the "protected right" of the plaintiff and the "correlative legal duty" of the defendant to respect the plaintiff's right.[29] And punitive damages demonstrate the disapproval "society attaches to [the] flagrant invasion [of a right] by the kind of conduct engaged in by the defendant."[30]

Though deterrence, retribution, and education are the primary rationales in support of punitive damages, this form of relief also serves to compensate victims where traditional compensatory awards are insufficient. In addition, punitive damages have also been said to serve a procedural law-enforcement mechanism, whereby they encourage "reluctant victims to press their claims and enforce the rules of law."[31]

PUNITIVE DAMAGES IN EMPLOYMENT DISCRIMINATION CASES

At the time of the passage of Title VII of the Civil Rights Act of 1964, victims of employment discrimination were limited to obtaining relief that was primarily equitable in nature. When Title VII was passed, the statute contained no provision for aggrieved individuals to obtain either compensatory or punitive damages. Though Title VII was extremely effective in helping to vindicate the rights of those individuals who had been discriminated against, the lack of compensatory or punitive relief in the statute was problematic. As one commentator noted less than a decade after the passage of Title VII, "[d]iscrimination is so obnoxious to our ideals and so injurious to the nation as a whole that this form of punishment and deterrence [in allowing punitive damages] is justified."[32] At the time, some believed that the lack of punitive damages in Title VII undermined the statute's ability to deter wrongful conduct. The addition of punitive damages, they argued, was necessary to help effectuate the enforcement of the statute, as this relief would encourage victims of discrimination to bring suit.[33] Under the original statutory scheme of Title VII, a successful plaintiff could expect to obtain relief that was "hardly enough to inspire such a plaintiff to stand up for her rights."[34] Others argued that Congress had originally intended for courts to be able to provide any type of relief that they deemed necessary, so adding punitive damages to Title VII would therefore "restore the statute to its originally intended role."[35]

Legislative History of the Civil Rights Act of 1991

In 1991, Congress passed the Civil Rights Act of 1991. Among other significant changes to Title VII, the Civil Rights Act of 1991 provided for compensatory and punitive damages. The legislative history of this amendment to Title VII demonstrates that Congress understood the need for adding punitive damages as a weapon for fighting employment discrimination. A House Report on the Civil Rights Act of 1991 explains that the summary and purpose of the amendment was to "strengthen existing protections and remedies available under federal civil-rights laws to provide more effective deterrence and adequate compensation for victims of discrimination."[36]

In considering the Civil Rights Act of 1991, Congress thus believed that the "existing protections and remedies" in the statute were not "adequate to deter unlawful discrimination or to compensate victims of intentional discrimination," and that the addition of exemplary relief was therefore necessary.[37]

Congress was thus clear that, based on the testimony before it, the addition of new remedial relief to Title VII was a critical component of deterring future wrongful conduct and encouraging "private enforcement" of the statute.[38] This "compelling need" for new relief would lead to the passage of the Civil Rights Act of 1991, which amended Title VII of the Civil Rights Act of 1964 to add punitive damages and compensatory relief.[39]

The Revised Statute

After two years of "often rancorous debate," Congress passed, and President George H. W. Bush signed into law the Civil Rights Act of 1991.[40] The addition of punitive damages to Title VII would "fundamentally" alter the "legal model underlying federal employment discrimination laws," shifting the focus of the statute from conciliation and employer change to a model similar to tort law that was targeted more at obtaining monetary relief.[41] It was argued that the amendments were "among the most sweeping civil rights legislation to be passed by Congress," and that the act provided exemplary damages that were "sorely lacking from previous legislation."[42]

Under the revised statute, a plaintiff is now entitled to pursue punitive damages if that individual can show that the defendant "engaged in a discriminatory practice" with "malice or with reckless indifference to the federally protected rights of an aggrieved individual."[43] As part of a compromise, the statute also contains limitations (or statutory caps) on the size of the potential award.[44] Maximum award amounts vary depending upon the size of the employer, with a maximum potential liability of $300,000 for companies with 500 or more employees. In addition to the statutory cap, plaintiffs can also obtain back pay, front pay, and certain interest.

THE SUPREME COURT ADDRESSES PUNITIVE
DAMAGES UNDER TITLE VII

Kolstad v. American Dental Association

Nearly two decades ago, the Supreme Court provided the seminal case on punitive damages in Title VII employment-discrimination matters in *Kolstad* v. *American Dental Ass'n.*[45] The Supreme Court granted *certiorari* in the case to resolve a split in the circuits over whether a showing of egregious conduct is necessary for a punitive damage claim to go to the jury. In analyzing the damages provision of Title VII, the Court noted that the Civil Rights Act of 1991 limits punitive awards to cases where the plaintiff has demonstrated that the discrimination was "intentional." The Court rejected the lower court's conclusion, however, that a plaintiff must show that the intentional discrimination involved in the case was also egregious in nature. Looking to the plain terms of the statute, the Court noted that the text does not require a demonstration of an employer's outrageous behavior. Rather, the statute focuses on only "an employer's state of mind."[46]

The Court acknowledged, however, that not all cases of intentional discrimination warrant an instruction on exemplary damages. Instead, the statute requires a showing that the defendant acted with "malice or with reckless indifference to the [plaintiff's] federally protected rights." This requirement relates to "the employer's knowledge that it may be acting in violation of federal law, not its awareness that it is engaging in discrimination." The Court went on to explain that a plaintiff can show malice or reckless indifference by demonstrating that the employer "discriminate[d] in the face of a perceived risk that its actions [would] violate federal law." The Court acknowledged that by requiring this showing it was narrowing the cases of intentional discrimination in which exemplary relief would be appropriate, and noted that "[t]here will be circumstances where intentional discrimination does not give rise to punitive damages liability."

In addition to demonstrating malice or reckless indifference, the Court also held that the victim must impute liability for exemplary relief to the defendant. Referring to the *Restatement (Second) of Agency*, the Court advised that punitive liability is imputed in those cases in which "an employee serving in a 'managerial capacity' committed the wrong while 'acting in the scope of employment.'" Even in those cases in which punitive damages are imputed to the employer, however, the defendant can avoid liability by demonstrating that it has engaged in "good faith efforts at Title VII compliance." Such good faith efforts can be demonstrated, for example, where the employer has effectively maintained and implemented a policy or program attempting to prevent discrimination. By allowing this employer defense, the Supreme Court attempted to "promote prevention as well as remediation" and thereby effectuate the "purposes underlying Title VII." In conclusion, in light of the new standards that it announced on the issue of punitive damages, the Court vacated the appellate court's order and remanded the case.[47]

Interpreting Kolstad

The *Kolstad* decision is important, as it is the Supreme Court's clearest statement on the standard necessary to establish a punitive damages claim pursuant to Title VII. Nonetheless, there has been significant confusion in the lower courts over how exactly to apply this standard.[48] This uncertainty is likely caused by the fact that the Supreme Court did not define certain critical terms in its analysis, such as "managerial capacity" and "good faith efforts."

The academic scholarship is mixed on the effect of *Kolstad*. Some have argued that the decision was an enormous victory for employers, and that by permitting companies to avoid punitive damages for the unlawful conduct of their managerial employees "without establishing a clear good-faith-effort standard, the Court rendered Title VII's most powerful deterrent mechanism – punitive damages – ineffectual."[49] By failing to consider the "broader purpose" of Title VII and the Civil Rights Act of 1991, the Supreme Court did not recognize that potential liability for punitive damages "could spur employers to work tirelessly to prevent unlawful discrimination in their workplaces." Even employer defense firms announced that companies "can breathe a bit easier" after the decision.[50]

Others have taken a contrary view of the decision. One commentator suggested that *Kolstad* "created more continuity than change and more opportunity than limitation for plaintiffs to be awarded punitive damages."[51] Another further maintained that while the effects of *Kolstad* would largely depend upon how it is applied, the decision "may mean that most employers sued under Title VII will face paying thousands of dollars in punitive damages."[52] The confusion in the lower courts over how to apply the *Kolstad* case, combined with the conflicting views in the academic literature regarding the impact of the Supreme Court's decision, leave much uncertainty over the effectiveness of punitive damages in deterring discriminatory behavior. A study of the decisions that followed *Kolstad* is therefore necessary to help shed light on whether the Civil Rights Act of 1991 provided an effective remedial structure.

SUPREME COURT CASE LAW

In recent years, the Supreme Court has provided substantive guidance on the applicability of punitive damages to civil cases. Little of this guidance has been in the employment-discrimination context, however. The seminal case in this area, *Kolstad*

v. *American Dental Association*, is now almost twenty years old, and represents the Court's clearest expression of how to assess punitive damages in the workplace.

More recently, the Supreme Court has expounded upon its punitive damages jurisprudence, though outside of the workplace context. In *Philip Morris USA v. Williams*, the Court addressed the question of whether a company can be subjected to punitive damages for harm to third parties that are not part of the litigation.[53] The *Philip Morris* decision threatens to undermine the ability of civil-rights plaintiffs to obtain damages in discrimination cases.

In *Philip Morris*, an individual's estate sued a cigarette manufacturer under state law for negligence and deceit related to his death, which was the result of smoking. Finding for the plaintiff, the jury awarded $821,000 in compensatory damages and $79.5 million in exemplary relief.

The company objected to the verdict on the grounds that the ratio of compensatory relief to punitive damages was in excess of what the Constitution allows. In addition, Philip Morris argued that the trial court had erred in failing to instruct the jury that punitive damages could not be awarded to punish the company for harms on behalf of others not party to the litigation. Specifically, the company noted that plaintiff's counsel had referenced the widespread damage that Philip Morris cigarettes had caused to the general population, and the company maintained that this was an improper consideration for awarding punitive relief.

Addressing the question of whether a jury may award punitive damages on the basis of third-party effects, the Court held that "the Constitution's Due Process Clause forbids a State to use a punitive damages award to punish a defendant for injury that it inflicts upon nonparties or those whom they directly represent." The Court noted that due process requires that an individual cannot be punished without having the opportunity to present a full defense. A defendant will be unable to avail itself of an adequate defense where the accusations of injury come from "strangers to the litigation." Thus, in this case, the company would be unable to establish that individuals injured from cigarette smoking "knew that smoking was dangerous or did not rely upon the defendant's statements to the contrary," if those persons were not party to the litigation. Perhaps more importantly, the Court warned that allowing punishment for nonparty harm would result in "a near standardless dimension to the punitive damages equation."[54]

Thus, the Court was clear that exemplary relief cannot be used to "punish[] a defendant for harming others." The Court did acknowledge, however, that a jury may consider *reprehensibility* when awarding punitive damages and that nonparty harm may factor into that determination.[55] The Court therefore distinguished reprehensibility from punishment when considering third-party harm for purposes of awarding exemplary relief. Interestingly, the *Kolstad* Court downplayed the importance of considering reprehensibility when awarding punitive relief for *workplace* claims, stating that "the reprehensible character of the conduct is not generally considered apart from the requisite state of mind."[56]

Having concluded that a jury may consider harm to strangers for purposes of considering reprehensibility – but not punishment – when awarding punitive damages, the Court remanded the case for the lower court to apply this new standard.[57] The Court further found it unnecessary to address the question as to whether the award itself was "grossly excessive."[58]

In *Exxon Shipping Co.* v. *Baker*,[59] the Supreme Court again addressed the appropriateness of an award of punitive relief. In *Exxon*, the Court examined a case where an oil tanker was grounded off of Alaska, resulting in a spill of an enormous amount of crude oil into Prince William Sound. Joseph Hazelwood, who captained the tanker, was a recovering alcoholic. There was evidence to suggest, however, that Hazelwood had relapsed and that Exxon management was aware of his difficulties. Indeed, there was testimony that on the night of the spill the captain consumed approximately five double vodkas prior to departing on the ship. Hazelwood left the bridge two minutes before a critical turn needed to be made, and those left to man the ship failed to properly navigate the vessel. The ship crashed into a reef, resulting in an oil spill of 11 million gallons.

Exxon stipulated to negligence before the District Court for the District of Alaska, and a trial was held on the issue of recklessness. After this trial, the jury concluded that the captain and Exxon were reckless and could thus be subject to exemplary damages. In the next phase of the trial, the jury awarded compensatory relief of $287 million. In the final phase of the trial, the jury awarded $5 billion in punitive damages against the company. This award was reduced to $2.5 billion on appeal. The Supreme Court granted *certiorari* to determine whether this award was appropriate under maritime law and the Clean Water Act (CWA).

The Court considered Exxon's argument that the CWA preempts an award of exemplary relief under maritime common law. Rejecting the company's position, the Court saw "no clear indication of congressional intent to occupy the entire field of pollution remedies." The Court thus turned to the amount of the punitive damages award and Exxon's position that the relief "exceeds the bounds justified by the punitive damages goal of deterring reckless (or worse) behavior and the consequently heightened threat of harm." Tracing the history of exemplary relief, the Court noted that the current consensus is that this form of relief is "aimed not at compensation but principally at retribution and deterring harmful conduct."[60]

The Court further pointed out that larger punitive damages awards are considered particularly appropriate where it is difficult to detect the wrongdoing, and where injury and compensatory awards are likely to be low. Examining the literature, the Court noted that there is "an overall restraint" in the courts when awarding punitive relief, with a median ratio of punitive to compensatory damages "less than 1:1."

The Court further stated that while due process concerns can be implicated with large punitive damage awards, this case was brought under federal maritime law, and thus "precedes and should obviate any application of the constitutional standard." Indeed, the Court's "due process cases … have all involved awards subject in the first instance to state law." Thus, the Court's "enquiry differs from due process review because the case arises under federal maritime jurisdiction, and we are reviewing a jury award for conformity with maritime law, rather than the outer limit allowed by due process."[61]

Considering several studies on punitive damages, and rejecting the approach used by several states, the Court concluded that a 1:1 ratio of punitive to compensatory damages "is a fair upper limit in such maritime cases." The Court noted that this upper threshold will still protect the goals of deterrence and punishment necessary for effective exemplary relief, while preventing "unpredictable and unnecessary" awards in maritime cases. The Court further found this ratio appropriate in light of the criminal penalties set forth in the CWA. And, though the case was not considered under due process principles, these guidelines further support the ratio established by the Court. The Court noted that its previous jurisprudence in this regard concluded that "a single-digit maximum is appropriate in all but the most exceptional of cases."

Applying these principles to the facts of the case, the Court concluded that the punitive damages in the case should not exceed the compensatory award of $507.5 million. The Court thus vacated the $2.5 billion punitive award, and remanded the case to the appellate court.[62]

KOLSTAD REFINED

The recent Supreme Court decisions in *Philip Morris* and *Exxon* provide substantial guidance for awarding exemplary relief in all areas of the law. These cases similarly help refine the *Kolstad* decision and provide significant direction for plaintiffs seeking relief as a result of workplace discrimination. Much more guidance is needed, however, as the lower courts remain confused over when exemplary relief is appropriate for workplace claims.

Kolstad *Revisited*

Though *Kolstad* fails to offer any substantial guidance on the *purpose* underlying exemplary relief, the decision provides an important backdrop for punitive damages in Title VII cases. Though problematic in many respects, the decision remains the best statement of when exemplary relief can be awarded to employment-discrimination plaintiffs. Thus, *Kolstad* is the best – and really only – Supreme

Court decision explaining the parameters of punitive relief in the workplace context. Despite the confusion that *Kolstad* creates, it offers a few clear-cut principles for employment-discrimination litigants. It is helpful to briefly highlight these principles before moving on to the more difficult aspects of the decision.

Initially, and importantly, the decision resolves the difficult question of how liability can be imputed to an employer. In many ways, it is counterintuitive to punish a corporation or other "employer" for unlawful conduct when it is an individual – not the company – that has taken the inappropriate action. This inquiry becomes even more difficult when the individual taking the unlawful action is doing so against the express policies of the employer. *Kolstad* makes clear that, like other areas of the law, we must rely on agency principles when considering whether to impute liability to the employer. Thus, according to the Court, liability can be imputed where a supervisor "authorizes or ratifies the agent's tortuous act," or where the individual perpetrating the discrimination is a manager "acting in the scope of employment." After *Kolstad*, then, a key question in a typical employment-discrimination case is whether the manager acting in an unlawful manner is also acting within the scope of employment.

In addition, *Kolstad* resolves the question of whether there is a certain amount of egregiousness that a plaintiff must show in order to be entitled to exemplary relief. The Supreme Court made clear that plaintiffs were not required to demonstrate a particular amount of egregiousness on the part of the defendant to be entitled to punitive relief. Instead, the Court determined that the proper inquiry was whether or not the defendant "discriminate[d] in the face of a perceived risk that its actions will violate federal law to be liable in punitive damages." The Court explained that an employer can establish this by showing that the supervisor in question was acting with knowledge that she was violating federal law. More precisely, "the reprehensible character of the conduct is not generally considered apart from the requisite state of mind."[63]

Finally, the decision is important because it creates a number of incentives for employers to be proactive in identifying and preventing discrimination in the workplace. In this way, *Kolstad* creates an affirmative defense for employers who act in good faith and attempt to comply with the statute. An employer who sufficiently demonstrates its good-faith efforts at compliance will immunize itself from any potential liability for punitive damages. To do so, employers generally will have to establish that they have conducted training or implemented policies or programs targeted at avoiding employment discrimination.

The lessons from *Kolstad* are thus relatively simple. In order to be entitled to punitive relief, a plaintiff must first establish that the individual perpetrating the unlawful conduct is a manager acting within the scope of employment – thus imputing liability to the employer. Next, the plaintiff must demonstrate that the defendant knew that its actions were in violation of federal law (or acted recklessly in this regard). Finally, the defendant may avoid liability for punitive damages by affirmatively demonstrating that it acted in good faith.

Though these basic principles certainly provide a significant amount of guidance in addressing whether an employment-discrimination plaintiff is entitled to punitive relief, the decision still leaves questions. As already noted, the relief provisions of Title VII require a plaintiff to establish that the employer acted "with malice or reckless indifference." Perhaps most problematically, then, *Kolstad* fails to address the difficult question of how we specifically define what malice or reckless indifference really means. Though the principles outlined in *Kolstad* start us down the path of defining these critical terms, the parameters of this showing still remain largely undefined. This leaves the lower courts without any real guidance on how to apply the clear terms of the statute. Recent Supreme Court decisions, however, do provide some additional instruction for workplace litigants seeking punitive relief.

Exxon *and* Philip Morris *in the Workplace Context*

The Supreme Court's recent decisions in *Exxon* and *Philip Morris* arose well outside of the workplace arena. Nonetheless, these decisions have critical implications for punitive damages in the employment-discrimination context and offer important lessons not found in the *Kolstad* decision.

Most notably, the Supreme Court's decision in *Exxon* provides important guidance on the relevance of constitutional concerns when awarding punitive damages pursuant to Title VII and offers an opportunity for civil-rights litigants pursuing exemplary relief in employment-discrimination cases. In this regard, the Supreme Court has previously made clear – outside of the Title VII context – that punitive damages must generally comport with the due process considerations of the Constitution. In *BMW of North America* v. *Gore*, the Court held that a "grossly excessive" punitive damages award can be considered so arbitrary as to run afoul of the Due Process Clause of the Fourteenth Amendment.[64] In reaching this conclusion, the Supreme Court provided three guideposts for the courts to consider when evaluating the constitutional fairness of an award of punitive relief – the degree of reprehensibility, the disparity between the harm suffered by the plaintiff and the award of exemplary damages, and the difference between the punitive award and awards permitted in similar cases.

In addressing these guideposts, the Court placed significant emphasis on the ratio of the punitive damages awarded to the actual harm (or compensatory damages) suffered by the plaintiff in the case, rejecting a "breathtaking" award of exemplary relief that was 500 times the harm actually incurred by the plaintiff.[65] In *State Farm Mutual Automobile Insurance Co.* v. *Campbell*, the Supreme Court provided additional guidance on the "guidepost" analysis, and further refined the ratio inquiry set forth in *Gore*.[66] In this regard, the Court rejected a ratio of punitive damages to actual harm that was 145 to 1, and advised that it "should be obvious" that "[s]ingle-digit multipliers are more likely to comport with due process, while still achieving the State's goals of deterrence and retribution, than awards with [much higher] ratios."[67]

The extent to which *Gore* and *State Farm* – both of which addressed the excessiveness of punitive damages under state law – would apply to federal statutory claims was unclear. What is noteworthy about the *Exxon* decision is that the case helps resolve this issue and carves out a critical exception for these constitutional questions when a federal statute is involved. In *Exxon*, the Court considered the appropriateness of punitive damages awarded under maritime law and the CWA. Acknowledging its prior precedent addressing the due process issues raised by exemplary awards, the Court dismissed those concerns in the case because the matter did not involve a state issue. Rather, the case was brought under *federal* maritime law, and thus "precedes and should obviate any application of the constitutional standard."[68]

There can be little doubt after *Exxon*, then, that the due process issues raised in *Gore* and *State Farm* are inapplicable to employment-discrimination claims brought under Title VII or other federal statutory law. The *Exxon* Court specifically acknowledged that when a federal scheme is in place to address punitive relief, the due process concerns of the Fourteenth Amendment are not implicated.[69] Thus, after *Exxon*, employment plaintiffs should no longer need to address the "guideposts" set forth in *Gore*. The Court's holding under the CWA is entirely consistent with Title VII, and it is likely that the Court would extend its reasoning to punitive damages awarded in the workplace. Indeed, two decades of decisions have helped develop a large body of case law establishing the parameters of these awards. Just like the CWA and federal maritime law, then, Title VII case law has created a federal scheme that satisfies any constitutional concerns over the excessiveness of punitive awards.

Beyond the case law, however, it is clear that Title VII satisfies any due process concerns as it specifically sets forth the limits of punitive relief, limiting exemplary awards based on the size of the business.[70] As already noted, depending upon the size of the employer, a plaintiff can attain a combined total of between $50,000 and $300,000 in punitive and compensatory damages.[71] Employers are on notice, then, that if they intentionally discriminate against employees on the basis of race, color, sex, national origin, or religion, they can be subjected to the punitive penalties set forth in the statute. Because the amendments to Title VII have been in place for nearly two decades, there can be little doubt that employers have received more than sufficient notice of the employment laws and potential damages that flow from violating these laws, thus obviating any due process issues. Where a "congressionally-mandated, statutory scheme" sets forth the clear financial implications for intentionally violating federal law, any award within the confines of that scheme "provides strong evidence that a defendant's due process rights have not been violated."[72]

In addition, given even the upper limits of the potential punitive awards – which have remained static since the amendments went into effect – there is no need for employers to be concerned with the multimillion-dollar verdicts that have arisen in other contexts, excluding those workplace cases arising as part of class-action litigation. The federal case law of Title VII, then, combined with the punitive damages limits of the statute, work together to assure that "a penalty [is] reasonably predictable in its severity," and is not "eccentrically high."[73] Certainly, Title VII punitive awards must still be reviewed by the federal courts, but it is now clear that due process concerns should no longer be the focus of the courts' analyses.

Similarly, the inquiry into the ratio between actual harm to punitive damages – which formed part of the Supreme Court's due process analysis in *Gore* – now seems largely irrelevant to workplace claims for due process purposes. However, the degree of actual harm may still prove important as part of the consideration of the overall appropriateness of a punitive award, although this determination will likely take place outside of the due process context.

In addition to the critical importance of *Exxon* to employment-discrimination plaintiffs, the Supreme Court's decision in *Philip Morris* has significant implications for workplace litigants. In particular, *Philip Morris* provides important guidance to Title VII plaintiffs on the importance of harm an employer might cause to third parties when it intentionally discriminates against an individual on the basis of a protected characteristic. Though a somewhat complex case, the holding of *Philip Morris* is straightforward: a jury may consider harm incurred by strangers to the litigation for purposes of considering reprehensibility – but not punishment – when awarding punitive damages. This holding threatens to negatively impact civil-rights litigants bringing claims in the workplace.

To the extent the case is applicable to a *federal* statute (an issue discussed in more detail shortly), the decision clarifies that employment-discrimination plaintiffs may not argue for enhanced exemplary relief to *punish* an employer for similar harms it caused other individuals in the workplace. Thus, for example, where an employer discriminates against three workers on the basis of race and only one employee files a claim, punitive damages cannot be used to punish the employer on behalf of those that did not bring an action. Just like the defendant in *Philip Morris*, an employer in this situation will be unable to properly defend itself where the accusations of injury come from "strangers to the litigation."[74]

Nonetheless, the employer's conduct toward nonparties to the litigation may still be addressed when the jury considers the reprehensible nature of the conduct when awarding punitive relief. In *Philip Morris*, the Court did acknowledge that a jury may consider *reprehensibility* when awarding punitive damages, and that nonparty harm may factor into that determination. Thus, to the extent that an employer's conduct harms several individuals in the workplace, a jury may award greater punitive relief to a single individual bringing a claim if it finds the conduct particularly reprehensible. This distinction – that a plaintiff may be awarded punitive relief for harm caused to nonparties on the basis of reprehensibility, but not punishment – may prove critical at the conclusion of Title VII litigation.

Indeed, the issue of third-party harm will have broad implications in the employment-discrimination context. An employer who discriminates against one individual will often discriminate against others as well. And, victims of employment discrimination are particularly hesitant to bring claims for fear of retaliation, disruption of the workplace environment, or concern over the perception of their coworkers. Thus, it would not be unusual for an employer who maintains a workplace permeated with discrimination to be sued by only one or two individuals. After *Philip Morris*, a strong argument can be made that these individuals will be unable to use the discriminatory experiences of their coworkers to further punish the employer. These individuals would be left to couch the experiences of their coworkers in terms of the reprehensible nature of the employer's conduct.

Of course, it can be argued that *Philip Morris* is inapplicable to employment-discrimination cases and the decision is easily distinguishable from traditional workplace claims. The case arose as a question of state law, and the Court addressed whether the Due Process Clause of the Constitution prohibits a state from punishing a defendant for nonparty harm. The Court's holding is thus premised on the notion that due process requires that an individual cannot be punished without having the opportunity to present a full defense – which it is unable to do where it is being accused of harm by nonlitigants. Just like *Exxon*, then, *Philip Morris* addresses the due process concerns of a punitive damages award issued under state law. A defendant facing an employment-discrimination claim under Title VII, however, may not have these same due process arguments. Indeed, as discussed earlier, Title VII defendants have full knowledge of the amount of punitive relief they can be subjected to under the federal statute and case law. These amounts are relatively low and do not reflect the type of "runaway" jury awards that the Court may have been attempting to address in its recent cases.[75] It may well be, then, that the primary holding of *Philip Morris* is inapplicable to Title VII claims, and future litigation may help resolve this issue. Nonetheless, even if the holding itself does not apply in the workplace context, the federal courts are still free to use the tenor of the decision when reviewing punitive damages awards. Certainly, in determining whether a jury's award of exemplary relief is excessive, the federal courts could consider whether punishing an employer for harm to third parties is fair and equitable under the particular circumstances of the case. At a minimum, then, *Philip Morris* provides substantial guidance to the litigants and courts on the potential impact of nonparty harm in the employment-discrimination context. Future litigation may well provide the exact contours for how that guidance will be applied to workplace plaintiffs.

Confusion in the Courts

Not surprisingly, the lack of clear guidance on the applicable standard for awarding punitive damages in the employment-discrimination context has resulted in conflicting and confused decisions in the lower courts. The more recent Supreme Court cases only add to that confusion, as the extent to which their holdings apply in the employment-discrimination context is still unclear. The Title VII statutory standard for punitive relief provides that an employer must take an unlawful action "with malice or reckless indifference," but this standard can be – and has been – interpreted by the courts in a variety of ways. Though *Kolstad* provided some direction for employment-discrimination litigants, the decision failed to offer clear guidance on how the malice or reckless indifference standard should be applied. The confusion over this standard, as well as how to analyze workplace punitive damages claims more generally, has resulted in varied opinions in the federal courts.

An excellent example of the confusion in the lower courts on the question of exemplary relief was provided by the US Court of Appeals for the Eighth Circuit in *EEOC* v. *Siouxland Oral Maxillofacial Surgery Associates*.[76] In that case, the court considered whether the district court had improperly failed to instruct the jury on punitive damages in a pregnancy discrimination case that was brought pursuant to Title VII. A receptionist in the case worked for a medical clinic and informed the partnership shortly after being hired that she was pregnant and would eventually need about six to eight weeks of leave as a result. After the managing partner found out about the pregnancy, he stated in a meeting that "[i]t doesn't make any sense to begin training her ... we are going to have to let her go." She was terminated shortly thereafter and was told that "your baby is going to be due during our busy season," and that the partnership wouldn't have employed her "if they had known she was pregnant." When looking for *another* candidate to fill the vacant position, one applicant was subsequently told by a supervisor that it was "a problem" that she was four months pregnant, and that she should "just continue her pregnancy, have the baby, have her maternity leave," and then the partnership would consider her. This same supervisor wrote on the top of the applicant's resume that she was "4 months pregnant!"[77]

The EEOC subsequently filed suit alleging that the partnership had terminated the receptionist and failed to hire the subsequent applicant on the basis of pregnancy – a clear violation of Title VII. The district court allowed the case to go to the jury, but granted the defendant judgment as a matter of law on the issue of whether punitive damages were available in the matter. The district court determined that "it has not been shown that there was a perceived risk that the actions [of the defendant] would violate federal law to be liable on punitive damages." Following a trial, the jury concluded that the partnership had discriminated on the basis of pregnancy and awarded $15,341 in back pay to the receptionist and $5,757 in back pay to the subsequent applicant for the position.[78] The EEOC appealed on the punitive damages question.[79]

In considering the issue, the Eighth Circuit summarized the guidance provided by the *Kolstad* decision on the question of exemplary relief for Title VII claims. The court concluded that the managing partner who fired the receptionist had been warned that he should not do so on the basis of her pregnancy. Similarly, the supervisor who rejected the subsequent applicant for the position testified that she was aware that pregnancy discrimination was unlawful. Given that both decisions were made by individuals with supervisory authority and that both individuals were aware that their conduct was illegal, the court concluded that a punitive damages instruction should have been given to the jury. The court thus determined that the conduct of those involved could properly be imputed to the partnership itself and that the district court erred in failing to give the punitive damages instruction. The court therefore remanded for a new trial solely on the question of exemplary relief.[80]

This decision provides an excellent illustration of the existing confusion over when punitive damages are appropriate under Title VII. The district court in this case refused to give the question to the jury because it believed that there was insufficient evidence to demonstrate that the employer's conduct was performed under "a perceived risk" of "violat[ing] federal law."[81] The Eighth Circuit properly recognized, however, that there was sufficient evidence that those involved in the unlawful conduct had supervisory or managerial authority and they were aware that their conduct might violate pregnancy discrimination law. Though the appellate court likely got it right in the end, it is disturbing that the federal courts can so plainly disagree on the appropriate standard for sending a punitive damages question to the jury and that the courts can view the same evidence so differently. The unfortunate result in this case is that the question of exemplary relief must be remanded for a new trial, resulting in substantial inefficiencies for both the court and litigants.

Unfortunately, this case is not isolated in its confusion over this issue, and the lower courts routinely grapple with the proper standard to apply to workplace punitive damages claims. It is not uncommon for the appellate courts to reverse the district courts on the question of exemplary relief, particularly in employment-discrimination cases. For example, in *EEOC* v. *Heartway*, the US Court of Appeals for the Tenth Circuit reversed a district court's decision not to give a punitive damages instruction in a disability case and remanded for a new trial on that issue.[82] In that case, a nursing home employee with hepatitis was terminated by the facility administrator after he found out about her condition, despite the fact that the administrator was aware "that it was against the law to fire someone because they had a disability." Finding that the administrator's unlawful conduct and knowledge of the law could be imputed to the company, the appellate court reversed for a new trial on punitive damages.[83] Similarly, in *EEOC v. Stocks, Inc.*,[84] the US Court of Appeals for the Fifth Circuit found that the district court had erred in failing to give a punitive damages instruction to the jury in an employment-discrimination case. Again, there was evidence in the case that showed the unlawful acts "were taken by management-level employees acting within the scope of their employment" and the "decision-makers were aware of their responsibilities under Title VII."[85]

As a final illustrative example, in *Canny v. Dr. Pepper/Seven-Up Bottling Group, Inc.*, the Eighth Circuit reached a completely different result from those decisions discussed previously, *vacating* a district court's award of exemplary relief in an employment-discrimination case.[86] In *Canny*, a jury awarded $100,000 in punitive damages to a former route supervisor for a beverage company who was terminated after he was diagnosed with a degenerative eye condition and could no longer maintain a driver's license. The appellate court was persuaded that the employer did not reassign the plaintiff to an available warehouse position because of genuine safety concerns that the company maintained and therefore did not act maliciously. Because the employer reasonably believed that it was "caught" between OSHA safety regulations and the ADA, the company "made a culpable, but not *malicious or reckless*, decision based upon safety concerns." The court thus vacated the punitive damages award.[87]

As this sampling of cases demonstrates, there is a significant amount of confusion over when punitive damages are appropriate in an employment-discrimination matter. This confusion seems largely caused by the ambiguous "malice or reckless indifference" standard set forth in the statute, as well as the lack of clear guidance on how to analyze these cases more generally. It is almost impossible to know how widespread this problem is, as many litigants may choose not to even appeal an adverse determination on exemplary relief, particularly where they have prevailed in other aspects of the case. Nonetheless, these cases are sufficient to demonstrate the extreme difficulty that the lower courts are facing when applying the Title VII punitive damages standard. Though *Kolstad* was helpful in providing a basic framework from which the courts could consider whether to award punitive relief, the decision failed to go far enough in defining when exemplary damages are appropriate. The consequence of the Supreme Court's failure in *Kolstad* is the current confusion in the lower courts, as clearly seen in the cases discussed earlier.

A NEW MODEL

The Supreme Court has provided little guidance on interpreting the statutory standard for exemplary relief in Title VII cases. Now that *Kolstad* is almost two decades old, it is time to reassess the guidance we have been given and identify those remaining areas of the law that still require clarity. A new model for awarding punitive relief in employment-discrimination cases is needed to simplify this area of the law, and to provide a blueprint for the litigants and courts when assessing whether exemplary relief is appropriate. The confusion that currently exists in the law has resulted in conflicting opinions in the federal courts and significant inefficiencies for the judicial system. This chapter seeks to put an end to this confusion by providing an analytical framework for evaluating whether exemplary relief is appropriate for a given workplace claim. In developing this analytical model, we must first briefly reassess what we have learned from *Kolstad* and the subsequent Supreme Court decisions on punitive relief. Though these cases lack clarity for employment-discrimination litigants, the decisions do provide a baseline from which we can begin analyzing Title VII claims.

Initially, from *Kolstad* we learned that when awarding punitive relief we must look to agency principles to impute the unlawful conduct of a supervisor or manager to the employer itself. And, as outlined earlier, *Exxon* makes clear that the due process issues raised in *Gore* and *State Farm* are inapplicable to employment-discrimination claims brought under Title VII or other federal statutory law. Finally, after *Philip Morris*, we know that it may be difficult for victims of employment discrimination to use the discriminatory experiences of their coworkers to further punish the employer, though these experiences can still be used to show the reprehensible nature of the employer's conduct.

With these principles from *Kolstad*, *Exxon*, and *Philip Morris* in mind, then, this chapter proposes a five-part analytical framework for analyzing whether punitive damages are appropriate for a Title VII claim. Navigating these Supreme Court decisions, and keeping in mind the goals of exemplary relief, the proposed framework will serve as a blueprint for litigants and courts to evaluate punitive damages in employment-discrimination cases. And, perhaps most importantly, this model helps resolve the question of what evidence is necessary to establish that an employer has acted with malice or reckless indifference – a standard that has confused and plagued the lower courts for years. It is worth noting that this framework focuses exclusively on punitive damages in Title VII cases and does not explore the question of exemplary relief under other civil-rights statutes, such as 42 U.S.C. § 1981. Where the proposed model mentions employment discrimination or workplace plaintiffs, then, it is specifically referencing those individuals bringing claims pursuant to Title VII.

Thus, the following five elements should be evaluated at the close of trial to determine whether a punitive damages jury instruction should be given to the jury in a case of intentional discrimination brought under Title VII.

Management-Level Employee

When evaluating whether there is sufficient evidence to award punitive damages in an employment-discrimination case, the first inquiry that must be made is determining whether a supervisor or manager is responsible for the unlawful conduct. If a supervisor or manager is involved, the inquiry is satisfied and we can move on to the other aspects of the analytical framework. If a supervisor or manager is not involved in the conduct, the inquiry is over, and punitive damages are not warranted in the case. Though the question seems relatively straightforward, determining which employees have sufficient supervisory authority to impute liability to the employer is not always easy.

As we learned from *Kolstad,* we must rely on the principles of agency when attempting to impute malicious or reckless conduct to the employer. And, *Kolstad* makes clear that liability can be imputed where the employer "authorizes or ratifies the agent's tortuous act" or where the individual perpetrating the discrimination is a manager "acting in the scope of employment." To determine whether an employee is a supervisor, the courts should examine the authority that the individual is given and "the amount of discretion that the employee has in what is done and how it is accomplished."[88] Mid-level managers would satisfy the Court's standard (as adopted from the *Restatement*), as the individual "must be 'important,' but perhaps need not be the employer's 'top management, officers, or directors,' to be acting 'in a managerial capacity.'"[89] Knowing that mid-level managers or supervisors are sufficient to impute liability to the employer for punitive damages is helpful, but it still leaves a significant amount of ambiguity as to which employees satisfy this standard. Even *Kolstad* acknowledges that "no good definition of what constitutes ... managerial capacity has been found."[90]

The Court has further clarified who is a supervisor in *Vance* v. *Ball State*.[91] In that case, the Court held that only those who have the authority to take a tangible employment action are supervisors. To satisfy this standard, a worker would generally be required to be able to hire, fire, or transfer an employee to a position with substantially different job requirements.[92]

One special circumstance to consider is the potential for punitive damages where *coworkers* are responsible for the illegal conduct – a situation likely to arise in the harassment context. The Supreme Court has made clear that an employer may be held liable for discrimination under Title VII where that employer knew or should have known that coworker harassment was present in the workplace but failed to take appropriate remedial action.[93] In this context, however, liability for *punitive damages* is less clear as the individual perpetrating the unlawful conduct is a coworker (rather than a managerial employee, which *Kolstad* seems to require). Nonetheless, *Kolstad* acknowledges that liability for punitive damages may be imputed where the employer "authorizes or ratifies the agent's tortuous act."[94] It thus seems a fair inference that if a manager ratifies the harassing (or otherwise unlawful) conduct of the victim's coworker, the first prong of the analytical framework will be satisfied, as a supervisor is ultimately endorsing the discrimination. While there can be little doubt that something beyond mere negligence will be required to hold the employer liable for punitive relief in the coworker discrimination context, the contours of this issue are still developing in the lower courts.

In summary, to satisfy the first prong of the proposed framework, a supervisor with authority to effectuate a tangible employment action must be involved in the unlawful conduct. If a supervisor is involved but is merely endorsing the discriminatory acts of a coworker, or if the supervisor involved has only limited authority to act, the specific facts of the case and law of the jurisdiction must be looked at more closely.

Manager Had Knowledge of Title VII

An employer must discriminate "in the face of a perceived risk that its actions will violate federal law" to be liable for punitive damages under Title VII. To satisfy the second prong of the analytical framework, then, the plaintiff is required to produce sufficient evidence to establish that the employer had knowledge that its actions were in violation of Title VII. This inquiry can be a bit tricky, as uncovering an employer's knowledge of federal law is not always an easy task.

Unfortunately, there is no exhaustive list of ways to establish an employer's knowledge of the statute. One common way of establishing a supervisor's knowledge of Title VII, however, is through testimony at trial or during a deposition. Indeed, in an effort to avoid the underlying liability for allegations pertaining to discrimination, company officials may be particularly willing to acknowledge that they are well aware of federal employment-discrimination law and indicate that their conduct was entirely consistent with these laws. Simply asking whether the supervisor in question has knowledge of Title VII is likely the easiest way for a plaintiff to establish an employer's familiarity with employment-discrimination law.

Similarly, a plaintiff can establish the requisite mental state by showing that the employer has conducted training on employment-discrimination law that the supervisor(s) in question attended. Or, the victim can show that the company maintained an explicit policy prohibiting discrimination covered by Title VII of which the supervisor was aware. Finally, another common way of showing the requisite mental state is through the employer's deception. If company workers "lied, either to the plaintiff or to the jury, in order to cover up their discriminatory actions," this evidence would go directly to the employer's knowledge that its conduct was unlawful.[95] In some respects, the sheer fact that Title VII has been in place for nearly half a century will make it difficult for managers to deny their familiarity with its operative provisions. Given the history and widespread nature of federal employment-discrimination law, then, some courts might even be willing to assume that managers (particularly at large corporations) are aware of Title VII's provisions, though it is certainly best for a plaintiff not to rely solely on this presumption.

The knowledge requirement is likely the most difficult element of the analytical framework for the plaintiff to establish. Indeed, there are a number of readily available explanations for an employer's discriminatory conduct, which often have nothing to do with a desire to intentionally violate federal law. Some of the most common explanations for why an employer might run afoul of Title VII – without acting with malice or reckless disregard – were set forth by the Supreme Court in *Kolstad*, and include cases where

> the employer may simply be unaware of the relevant federal prohibition. There will be cases, moreover, in which the employer discriminates with the distinct belief that its discrimination is lawful. The underlying theory of discrimination may be novel or otherwise poorly recognized, or an employer may reasonably believe that its discrimination satisfies a bona fide occupational qualification defense or other statutory exception to liability.[96]

Thus, an employer will not be acting with the requisite mental state to warrant the imposition of punitive damages where that employer is not aware of Title VII, where the employer believes its discriminatory conduct is lawful, where the basis for liability is new or undeveloped, or where the employer reasonably believes its conduct falls within a statutory exception. Certainly, we must look to the facts and circumstances of the particular case to determine if one of these explanations adequately applies, keeping in mind that it is the plaintiff's ultimate burden in the matter to establish liability for punitive relief.

Nonetheless, simply asking during a deposition or at trial whether those involved in the unlawful conduct were aware of, or had training in, Title VII may often yield the evidence necessary to establish this second prong of the proposed analytical framework. And, as discussed, there are a variety of other ways to go about establishing an employer's knowledge of Title VII's provisions. Finally, it is worth noting that there are likely additional ways – beyond simply demonstrating an employer's familiarity with the statute – to establish that a company discriminated "in the face of a perceived risk that its actions will violate federal law." Establishing knowledge of Title VII, however, is the most common way of demonstrating the requisite mental state of the employer.

Manager Acting within the Scope of Employment

The third prong of the proposed analytical framework – demonstrating that the manager involved acted within the scope of employment – will typically be the easiest to establish. The *Restatement (Second) of Agency* permits an award of punitive damages against a principal as a result of the acts of a managerial employee if that employee is "acting in the scope of employment."[97] Under *Kolstad* and the *Restatement*, this means that the manager's actions are of "the kind [the employee] was employed to perform," the conduct "occurs substantially within the authorized time and space limits," and the actions are "actuated, at least in part, by a purpose to serve the employer."

As discussed in greater detail here, *Kolstad* suggests that almost all adverse employment acts taken by a supervisor against an employee will fall within the scope of employment, even where those acts are intentional. This is true because when an employer violates Title VII, it has taken an action against an employee that affects the "terms, conditions, or privileges of employment" of that individual. A manager's violation of Title VII, then, will typically occur at work, during normal business hours, and with the authority given to that supervisor – thus placing the conduct squarely within the scope of employment. Obvious exceptions certainly come to mind – such as where a supervisor harasses an employee after hours and away from the place of business. But even this kind of harassing conduct will typically still involve some type of workplace component. And, where there is simply no relationship to the conduct in question and the workplace environment, it is likely that the actions will not fall within the ambit of Title VII at all, let alone give rise to an entitlement to punitive damages.

Thus, to satisfy the third component of the proposed model, an employee must demonstrate that the offending manager was acting within the scope of employment. In the typical Title VII case – where a supervisor has taken an adverse action against the worker that affects the terms, conditions, or privileges of employment – that supervisor will be acting within the scope of employment as interpreted through the rules of agency and the *Kolstad* decision. Nonetheless, litigants should still make certain that the facts do not present an unusual set of circumstances where this component of the proposed model would be called into question.

Good-Faith Efforts

The fourth prong of the proposed analytical model for punitive damages provides an affirmative defense for employers. Under this defense, if the employer can demonstrate that it made good-faith efforts at complying with Title VII, it can completely evade liability for punitive relief under the statute. This defense has its roots in the *Kolstad* decision and the principles of agency.

As noted earlier, the Restatement requires that a manager must be acting within the scope of employment to subject an employer to liability for punitive damages. While this rule is straightforward, the *Kolstad* Court expressed concern over applying the "scope of employment" concept to workplace punitive damages. In this regard, the Court found it problematic that, under the rules of agency, "an employee may be said to act within the scope of employment even if the employee engages in acts specifically forbidden by the employer and uses forbidden means of accomplishing results."[98] Thus, the Court was worried that if the rules of agency were strictly applied they could potentially subject an employer to liability for punitive damages for the unlawful conduct of a managerial employee even where the company "makes every effort to comply with Title VII."[99]

As a result of these concerns, the *Kolstad* Court modified the scope of employment concept to include a "good-faith efforts" exception for the employer. Under this defense, for purposes of punitive damages, "an employer may not be vicariously liable for the discriminatory employment decisions of managerial agents where these decisions are contrary to the employer's good-faith efforts to comply with Title VII." By creating this defense, the Court hoped to avoid the possible "perverse incentives" of the scope of employment concept, as well as to "promote prevention as well as remediation" by encouraging employers to comply with the terms of the statute. In the Court's view, such a defense would likely promote the use of antidiscrimination polices and training on employment-discrimination laws by employers.

After *Kolstad*, then, we look to a modified "scope of employment" test when considering whether punitive damages are applicable in the case. Thus, in addition to considering whether the manager involved in the unlawful conduct was acting within the scope of employment, we should also examine whether the employer made good-faith efforts at complying with the statute. This raises the obvious question of what facts are necessary to establish whether the employer is acting in good faith. The *Kolstad* decision suggests that implementing an antidiscrimination policy and conducting training on employment-discrimination laws for workers could be two ways of demonstrating an employer's good faith. Indeed, having an effective policy in place and training workers on the provisions of Title VII are often cited by the lower courts as important considerations when evaluating an employer's purported good faith.

By surveying the decisions of the lower courts, it becomes much more clear what type of conduct an employer must exhibit to avoid punitive damages liability through its good-faith efforts. The first – and most important – hurdle in this regard is that the employer *must* have some type of antidiscrimination policy in place. Without an antidiscrimination policy, it will be almost impossible for an employer to avail itself of this defense. Having a clear, definite, and extensive policy will also prove helpful to the employer. In addition, a company must do more than simply adopt an antidiscrimination policy – it must demonstrate that the policy is effectively maintained and enforced. In this regard, the employer should strive to abide by its policies and try not to apply them inconsistently. A company should also educate and train its employees both on its policies and how to prevent employment discrimination more generally. Finally, an employer must respond to employee complaints that it receives through the mechanisms established in its policies. Whether an employer engages in good-faith efforts at complying with Title VII is certainly a fact-intensive inquiry. However, by adopting an extensive antidiscrimination policy, which is both effectively and consistently maintained and enforced, an employer will go a long way toward satisfying this good-faith inquiry, as well as the fourth prong of the proposed analytical framework.

One final consideration for the good-faith efforts defense is where the burden of proof lies with this element. There is no definitive rule for which party bears the burden of proof with this test, though *Kolstad* seems to treat the good-faith efforts inquiry as an affirmative defense for the employer. In addition, the lower courts have generally placed the burden of proof for the good-faith compliance question on the company.[100] Thus, while there is not a definitive answer to where the burden of proof lies for this inquiry, both the reasoning of the Supreme Court and the trend in the lower courts strongly suggest that this is an affirmative defense for the employer to establish. As such, the analytical framework for punitive damages proposed here will similarly place the burden of proof on the employer for this good-faith test.

Judgment as a Matter of Law

The final element of the proposed analytical framework for analyzing whether a punitive damages jury instruction is appropriate in a Title VII employment-discrimination case is *optional* and proposes giving the jury this instruction even in those circumstances where the court is otherwise inclined to *deny* the plaintiff's request for exemplary relief. In these situations, the court should strongly consider allowing the jury to decide the issue, but entertain a renewed motion for a Judgment as a Matter of Law (JMOL) from the defendant following the trial.[101] Thus, if the court permits the jury to resolve the underlying question of whether the employer intentionally discriminated against the employee, at a minimum, the court should further give the jury the question of what amount of punitive relief is appropriate in the case (if any). Whether the court ultimately allows the jury's punitive damages verdict to stand, however, is ultimately within its own discretion.

Jury trials are expensive and time-consuming endeavors. If a district court declines to give a punitive damages instruction to a jury and is subsequently overturned, another jury must be empaneled to resolve this question. Indeed, in at least one jurisdiction, the entire case may have to be retried if the appellate court overturns the lower court on the question of exemplary relief.[102] And, as demonstrated earlier, it is not an uncommon result for a district court to be overturned on its decision to restrict punitive damages in an employment-discrimination case. To save significant judicial resources in these matters, then, a district court – when inclined against awarding punitive relief – should still ask the jury whether punitive damages are appropriate and in what amount they should be awarded. The court may then strike the award following the defendant's renewed motion for JMOL. If the district court is subsequently overturned on the punitive damages question, the jury's verdict could then be reinstated, completely obviating the need to retry the matter.

There may be some concern that providing the jury with this somewhat advisory determination of exemplary relief may distort the verdict. In this regard, perhaps a jury would have awarded a victim greater compensatory damages or backpay if it believed that punitive damages were unavailable in the case. While the proposed approach may present this practical difficulty, it should be noted that juries should not be adjusting their other award determinations based on the availability of punitive relief. And, given the significant efficiencies of allowing the jury to reach the punitive damages issue, these benefits significantly outweigh any concerns that juries may inappropriately adjust their overall damage determination based on the instruction.

Thus, the final component of the proposed analytical framework is optional and is targeted primarily at enhancing efficiencies in the judicial system. Where a court is inclined not to allow punitive damages in a case that will otherwise be decided by a jury, the model strongly proposes that the court still allow the jury to consider the question of exemplary relief on an advisory basis.

Other Considerations

In addition to the five-part proposed analytical framework for analyzing punitive damages claims set forth earlier, there are some additional considerations that the litigants and courts should evaluate when addressing these issues. These concerns arise primarily from the *Philip Morris* and *Exxon* decisions on punitive damages already discussed. Though not arising in the employment-discrimination context, these cases are instructive and the courts should still consider the possible implications of the decisions. As already noted, the primary holding from *Philip Morris* is that a jury may consider harm incurred by strangers to the litigation for purposes of considering reprehensibility – but not punishment – when awarding punitive damages.

The main lesson from *Philip Morris* for employment-discrimination litigants is that Title VII plaintiffs may be unable to use the discriminatory experiences of their coworkers to further punish the employer. Instead, these individuals would be left to couch the experiences of their coworkers in terms of the reprehensible nature of the employer's conduct. To the extent *Philip Morris* is applicable to a federal statute such as Title VII, then, the federal courts should strongly consider restricting the use of evidence of third-party harm for the purpose of attempting to punish the employer through punitive relief. Thus, after *Philip Morris*, a court should carefully evaluate how this type of evidence is presented to a jury, if at all.

Similarly, in *Exxon*, the Supreme Court held that when a federal scheme is in place to address punitive relief, the due process concerns of the Fourteenth Amendment are not implicated. After *Exxon*, then, it is clear that the due process issues raised in *Gore* and *State Farm* are inapplicable to employment-discrimination claims brought under Title VII. When evaluating a jury's award of punitive relief after *Exxon*, the court and litigants should therefore not be concerned with the "guideposts" set forth in *Gore* or (more specifically) with the ratio of punitive relief to actual harm in a Title VII case. Any award of exemplary relief that falls within the permitted statutory range – up to $300,000 for the largest employers – should satisfy the constitutional standards.[103] The Court's decision in *Exxon* thus makes it much more likely that a jury's award of punitive damages in a Title VII case will stand and makes the court's job much easier in reviewing the award.

Certainly, a punitive damages award may still be reviewed for excessiveness, and there may well be circumstances where a reduction of the award is still appropriate. The most obvious scenario where an award should be reduced, for example, would be where the amount is in excess of the statutory limits. Nonetheless, after *Exxon*, given the limited circumstances under which the Due Process Clause could be implicated in a jury's award of punitive relief under Title VII, a court's role in reviewing the *amount* of the award should be fairly limited in an employment-discrimination case.

In sum, despite the fact that the recent *Philip Morris* and *Exxon* Supreme Court decisions did not involve Title VII, the cases certainly have strong implications for employment-discrimination claimants that seek punitive relief. The courts and parties should thus strongly consider whether these cases impact the facts or claims of any workplace litigation.

Summary of Proposed Framework

The five-part analytical framework for evaluating punitive damages in employment-discrimination cases attempts to provide clarity to an otherwise confused area of the law. The model navigates the *Kolstad*, *Philip Morris*, and *Exxon* Supreme

Court decisions to provide a simplified test for the courts and litigants to use when analyzing these cases. And, most importantly, this model answers the difficult question left by *Kolstad* – what malice or reckless indifference means for the typical workplace litigant. In conclusion, when analyzing whether a punitive damages instruction should be given to a jury in an employment-discrimination case brought pursuant to Title VII, the courts and litigants should evaluate:

1. Whether a supervisor is responsible for the unlawful conduct;
2. Whether the supervisor had knowledge of Title VII;
3. Whether the supervisor was acting within the scope of employment;
4. Whether the employer was acting in good faith; and
5. Whether the court should allow the punitive damages question to go to the jury even where it is inclined to reject the instruction.

In analyzing these factors, the burden of proof is also critical to consider. The employee must produce sufficient evidence to satisfy the first three elements of the framework by demonstrating that a management-level employee – acting within the scope of employment – was both responsible for the unlawful conduct and aware of the requirements of the statute. The employer may still avoid punitive damages for the unlawful conduct if it can satisfy the fourth element of the test by showing that it made good-faith efforts at complying with Title VII. Finally, if the court is inclined against awarding punitive relief, it should still ask the jury whether punitive damages are appropriate and in what amount they should be awarded. The court may then strike the award following the defendant's renewed motion for JMOL. If the district court is subsequently overturned on the punitive damages question, this jury verdict could be reinstated, avoiding the need to retry any part of the case.

When considering the presentation of evidence on punitive damages to the jury, the court should also keep in mind the possible limitations of *Philip Morris*. Thus, a court should be hesitant to allow the jury to punish an employer for harm caused to strangers to the litigation, though such evidence can be used for purposes of showing reprehensibility. Similarly, once the jury awards punitive damages in a Title VII case, the court may analyze the award for excessiveness. After *Exxon*, however, the court's role in reviewing the amount of the award for due process concerns will be extremely limited.

By analyzing whether punitive damages are appropriate pursuant to this proposed analytical model, the court and litigants will inherently satisfy the standards set forth in *Kolstad* and the recent Supreme Court decisions on this issue. Though the proposed model is simply one way of examining these cases, it can be used for most Title VII claims. And, while the courts have struggled with how to comply with *Kolstad*, the proposed model clearly and concisely articulates whether an employment-discrimination plaintiff is entitled to exemplary relief.

LIMITATIONS OF THE PROPOSED MODEL

Though the analytical model for examining punitive damages in the workplace will provide simplicity to a currently confused process, it is not without its limitations. Most notably, the proposed model is intended to apply only to individual cases of disparate treatment discrimination. Though the same basic principles set forth in this chapter can also be applied to class-action or systemic litigation, such cases must be analyzed much more carefully when determining whether exemplary relief is appropriate. As punitive damages are appropriate only in cases where *intentional* discrimination has been established, the model would certainly be inapplicable to disparate impact cases (which involve unintentional discrimination).

The model set forth here should also be used only at the close of evidence in a Title VII case, when determining whether a punitive damages instruction should be given to the jury. The model should not be used at earlier stages of the litigation, other than as a guide for the basic principles of punitive damages in the workplace. As noted throughout this chapter, the model is also intended only for cases brought pursuant to Title VII (which prohibits discrimination on the basis of race, color, sex, national origin, and religion)[104] as well as disability cases brought under the ADA. It is not intended for claims brought under other civil-rights statutes, such as 42 U.S.C. § 1981. In particular, it is worth noting that claims brought under § 1981 will deserve special analysis, as this statute does not impose statutory caps on punitive relief like Title VII.[105] Thus, although beyond the scope of this chapter, the question of the extent to which the *Exxon* decision will apply to § 1981 claims should be addressed.

In addition, the model proposed here must be adapted to the principles set forth in the Supreme Court's decisions in *Faragher v. City of Boca Raton*[106] and *Burlington Industries, Inc., v. Ellerth*[107] when considering whether punitive damages are appropriate in harassment cases. Similarly, the Court's jurisprudence on retaliation claims, as discussed in *Burlington Northern & Santa Fe Railway Co. v. White*,[108] must be considered when determining whether punitive relief is appropriate for a case alleging unlawful reprisal. Harassment claims and retaliation cases present special Title VII factual scenarios, then, and the proposed model should be used only with these Supreme Court cases in mind.

As these limitations make clear, the model proposed here is simply one way of analyzing whether punitive damages are appropriate in cases involving workplace discrimination. Certainly, there are many other ways of determining whether exemplary relief is appropriate, and the facts of each particular case must be carefully analyzed. Nonetheless, the model set forth in this chapter provides a simple, straightforward way of analyzing punitive damages in the vast majority of Title VII employment-discrimination cases.

FRAMEWORK IMPLICATIONS AND CONCLUDING THOUGHTS ON RELIEF

The model proposed here for analyzing workplace punitive damages claims has many implications for this area of the law. Perhaps the most significant benefit of the proposed model is its simplicity. The framework takes a confused area of the law and provides a straightforward way of resolving the otherwise complex issue of exemplary relief. The courts and litigants should thus easily be able to apply this model to Title VII cases to determine whether punitive relief is appropriate. And, the model simplifies and explains how the recent Supreme Court cases on punitive damages should apply in the employment-discrimination context. Similarly, the model clearly addresses what evidence is necessary to establish malice or reckless indifference after the Court's decision in *Kolstad*. Thus, a plaintiff successfully navigating the elements of the proposed analytical framework will inherently have established (under the statute and relevant Supreme Court precedent) the requisite mental state of the employer. As demonstrated earlier, this question resulted in conflicting decisions in the federal courts. The model thus makes sense of *Kolstad*, *Philip Morris*, and *Exxon* and explains – in simple terms – how these decisions should be applied to employment-discrimination cases arising under Title VII.

By providing a uniform model, the proposed framework should also bring much more certainty to the damages analysis of workplace discrimination claims. Cases analyzing workplace punitive damages have resulted in varying opinions and confused analyses. By bringing uniformity to this area of the law, the courts and litigants will much more easily be able to evaluate the potential damages in a particular case. And with more certainty in the process comes the increased likelihood that more workplace claims will settle before reaching litigation.[109] Through simplicity and uniformity, then, the proposed analytical framework set forth in the chapter should help the parties to better evaluate workplace punitive damages claims, and thus better allow the statute to effectively achieve the goals associated with exemplary relief.

Some might argue that the proposed model is too rigid and takes necessary discretion away from the courts when analyzing workplace discrimination claims. While there should be concern over adopting an inflexible model, the framework set forth in this text is not intended to be overly rigid and the courts have significant leeway in applying the various factors to the specific facts of the case. In addition, as already noted, this model is simply one way of evaluating whether punitive damages are appropriate in a particular case. The courts and parties are free to use other methods of evaluating the cases as well, particularly where there is an unusual fact pattern that would call for a more specialized analysis.

It could also be argued that the proposed model is unnecessary as the courts have been resolving workplace claims for over a decade after the *Kolstad* decision.

While *Kolstad* certainly helped provide much-needed guidance on when punitive relief is appropriate in employment-discrimination cases, in many ways the decision generated more questions than answers, resulting in confused lower court decisions. The model proposed here assists the courts in evaluating employment-discrimination claims and finally brings some uniformity to this process. Thus, while the courts have used the *Kolstad* decision to analyze workplace claims, the analytical framework proposed here simplifies the analysis. Moreover, the proposed model makes sense of the much more recent Supreme Court decisions in *Philip Morris* and *Exxon.* By explaining how these cases should apply to Title VII claims, the analytical framework could help avoid years of unnecessary litigation on this topic.

In the end, any concerns over the proposed punitive damages model are outweighed by the simplicity and uniformity that the framework brings to Title VII claims. By providing greater efficiency to the judicial process, the analytical framework set forth in this chapter should greatly enhance the evaluation of punitive relief in employment-discrimination cases.

Through its recent decisions in *Philip Morris* and *Exxon,* the Court has acted to further limit the punitive damages available to litigants. At a minimum, these cases serve to confuse civil-rights law. The model proposed here adds clarity to this field and provides a roadmap for plaintiffs seeking relief in this area.

6

The On-Demand Economy Example

The guys who invented the steam engine, if you met them you might say they were a bunch of arrogant assholes. But the steam engine still changed the world. It doesn't matter.

–Bill Gates[1]

The problems presented thus far in this text would apply across the employment spectrum. It is impossible to discuss all of the different ways the Supreme Court's recent decisions could cause additional hurdles for minority workers in the context of this book. It can be helpful, however, to look at how the problems have arisen in one particular context and how the frameworks proposed here could be adapted to fit one specific industry. The tech sector has recently undergone substantial strain and growing pains with respect to particular employment questions. This chapter will examine how the Supreme Court's actions have directly impacted that sector and how litigants can still navigate around the Court's decisions to successfully proceed with their claims.

Disputes over numerous labor and management issues continue to percolate in the lower courts. One trend that will likely reach the Supreme Court in upcoming terms is the role of the more modern worker in the technology sector. This topic resonates with the issues addressed in this text for two important reasons. First, the critical question that arises in many of these cases is the issue of whether or not technology workers are employees or independent contractors. This is a threshold question in these cases, and one that will often be addressed at the pleadings stage of the proceedings. Thus, the Supreme Court's guidance in *Twombly/Iqbal* – discussed in Chapter 2 – would require that a plausible case be pled with respect to coverage under the statute. Second, these cases lend themselves to the class-action mechanism, and numerous

This chapter draws heavily from the following articles: Benjamin Means and Joseph A. Seiner, "Navigating the Uber Economy," *University of California Davis Law Review* 49 (2016): 1511; Joseph A. Seiner, "Tailoring Class Actions to the On-Demand Economy," originally published in *Ohio State Law Journal* 78 (2017): 21.

systemic claims have already been brought in this sector. As discussed in this book, the Supreme Court's view on commonality in the *Wal-Mart* decision will become critical as these gig-sector cases are more clearly defined in the lower courts.

Thus, the modern economy provides an excellent example for viewing how the Supreme Court's procedural decisions will impact a growing sector. *Twombly, Iqbal,* and *Wal-Mart* have had very practical substantive impacts, despite arising largely through procedural questions. The current labor and employment laws were formulated at a time when businesses tended to operate in more traditional brick-and-mortar facilities. The forty-hour work week was far more standard and there was not as much mobility in the workforce. Working from home was also far less common. The gig sector economy, driven by such companies as Uber and Lyft, has transformed the modern workplace. The traditional model contemplated decades ago when most major workplace statutes were enacted is no more in this sector. The courts and litigants have struggled to make sense of these old laws in the new economy. Ultimately, either Congress or the Supreme Court will have to step in to provide much-needed guidance in this new sector.

In the meantime, workers and the courts are left with little guidance when navigating these cases. This chapter provides some helpful insight in this critical new area, with an eye toward the pleading and class-action cases discussed earlier.

THE ON-DEMAND ISSUE

One of the most controversial issues in labor and employment law concerns how workers should be categorized in "on-demand" businesses that rely more on smartphone applications and internet connections than on hierarchical supervision within traditional brick-and-mortar workplaces.[2] For example, (former) drivers for ride-sharing companies Uber and Lyft have brought lawsuits alleging that they were improperly classified as independent contractors and denied employment benefits.[3] The companies have countered that they do not employ drivers but instead license access to a platform that matches those who need rides with nearby available drivers.[4]

At stake are the prospects, not only for Uber and Lyft, but also for a nascent, multi-billion dollar, "on-demand" economy that relies upon independent contractors to offer goods and services as varied as home cleaning, software development, household errands, personal training, and apartment or home rentals. Employees typically cost more than independent contractors because businesses are responsible for, among other things, payroll taxes, workers' compensation insurance, health care, minimum wage, overtime, and the reimbursement of business-related expenses. If saddled with those costs, the on-demand business model might not survive, at least not in its current form. At the same time, the importance of adequate protections for workers does not diminish simply because workers' tasks are coordinated through a high-technology platform.

Unfortunately, existing laws fail to provide adequate guidance regarding the distinction between independent contractors and employees, especially when applied to the hybrid working arrangements common in a modern economy. Under the Fair Labor Standards Act (FLSA) and analogous state laws, courts consider several factors to assess the "economic reality" of a worker's alleged employment status; yet, there is no objective basis for prioritizing those factors. As one court observed recently, deciding whether an on-demand driver is an independent contractor or an employee under current law is like being "handed a square peg and asked to choose between two round holes."[5]

WHO IS AN EMPLOYEE?

Most labor and employment laws apply only to those who are classified as employees. Often, the laws define the concept of employment broadly. However, courts must still interpret statutory language in light of the preexisting common law divide between independent contractors and employees. The factors relevant to the common-law analysis generally concerned the principal's vicarious liability for the conduct of agents, rather than the principal's obligations to those agents.

A Multifactor Approach to Worker Classification

According to the FLSA's somewhat circular definition, an employee is "any individual employed by an employer."[6] The employment relationship covered by the statute is broad – to "[e]mploy includes to suffer or permit to work."[7] That language was drawn from existing state laws and was designed to "reach businesses that used middlemen to illegally hire and supervise children."[8] Thus, the FLSA's broad language suggests that Congress intended to prevent employers from manipulating the form of the working relationship in order to circumvent their responsibilities.

The courts have elaborated several factors to assist in determining the economic reality of disputed working relationships. Specifically, the courts look to: (1) the level of control the employer maintains over the worker; (2) the opportunity for profit or loss maintained by the worker in the business; (3) the amount of capital investment the worker puts into the process; (4) the degree of skill necessary to perform the job; (5) whether performance of the job is integral to the operation of the business; and (6) the permanency of the relationship between the worker and the employer.[9] Under this multifactor, evaluative approach, "employees are those who as a matter of economic reality are dependent upon the business to which they render service."[10] Yet, when the factors conflict, courts need guidelines for deciding which factors best illuminate the economic reality of the situation. As discussed in the next section, no such guidelines exist – to advert to economic reality, as if it could supply the missing guidance, is to mistake a label for the analysis necessary to support it.

Classifying Workers in the On-Demand Economy

In typical cases involving on-demand businesses, the traditional factors for assessing economic reality can be marshaled to establish that a worker is an independent contractor or, equally plausibly, that the worker is an employee. On the one hand, a worker may access work assignments via a smartphone app (an instrumentality of the business) and will, as a condition of access, agree to abide by guidelines for how the work should be performed. The work may well be integral to the operation of the business. On the other hand, the working relationship may also be impermanent, involve no in-person interactions, and permit the worker to work whenever she wishes. Often the worker will bring her own equipment to the job: a computer for software development, a car for ride-sharing, or an apartment for vacation rental.

As evidenced by two recent class-action cases involving Uber and Lyft, respectively, the traditional factors alone cannot resolve classification disputes in the on-demand economy because the factors merely illuminate what is already evident – that neither category neatly fits hybrid circumstances. The factors that courts have previously identified are potentially useful, but they lack an organizing framework. What is missing, then, is a higher-level conceptual analysis that would enable courts to adapt existing categories in a manner consistent with the economic reality of an on-demand economy.

In *O'Connor* v. *Uber Technologies, Inc.*,[11] the court rejected Uber's motion for summary judgment and concluded that whether Uber's drivers are employees or independent contractors under California's Labor Code is a mixed question of law and fact that would have to be decided at trial. Although Uber characterized itself as a "technology company" rather than a "transportation company," a point hotly contested by the plaintiffs, many of the basic facts were not in dispute. Essentially, Uber matches those who need rides with available drivers through a smartphone application. The company sets the fare for each ride and processes payments from passengers, reserving a percentage for itself. To become an Uber driver, applicants must pass a screening process and background check, as well as a "city knowledge test."[12] There is also an interview process, after which successful applicants must sign a contract with Uber (or a subsidiary) indicating that they are purely independent contractors – there is no employment relationship.

The parties disagreed principally regarding the amount of control Uber has over its drivers. Uber argued that it lacks control because it simply provides a software platform for independent contractors who use their own vehicles, set their own schedules, and operate with very little supervision. The plaintiffs disputed those characterizations and maintained that Uber markets itself as a transportation company, selects its drivers, monitors their performance (largely through customer ratings), and disciplines individuals who fail to meet company standards.[13]

Under California law, which closely resembles the FLSA, the classification of workers as employees or independent contractors requires consideration of several factors.[14] The *O'Connor* court noted the importance of control, but also a number of other factors quite similar to the FLSA test the types of services performed, whether the work is done at the direction and supervision of the company, the amount of skill required to perform the job, who supplies the instrumentalities of the job, the length of time that the services are rendered, the method of payment, whether the work is a "regular" part of what the company does, and whether the parties intended to create an employment relationship.[15]

While the court was skeptical as to whether those factors ought to control the classification of workers in a modern "sharing economy," it was nevertheless bound to apply existing law and concluded that there was a mixed question of law and fact that could not be resolved before trial. The court rejected Uber's argument that it was merely a "technology company" and held that it was "most certainly a transportation company, albeit a technologically sophisticated one."[16] Thus, the work performed by the drivers was for Uber, and the question of classification could not be avoided.

In *Cotter v. Lyft, Inc.*,[17] issued on the same day as the *O'Connor* decision involving Uber, the court rejected Lyft's motion for summary judgment regarding the classification of its drivers under California law. Like Uber, Lyft uses a smartphone application that matches drivers with individuals in need of transport. The company initially provided a guide for drivers to follow when addressing passengers, which was subsequently replaced by a "frequently asked questions" section placed on its website.[18] The company further reserves the right to investigate workers and ultimately terminate them "at any time, for any or no reason, without explanation."[19] Drivers typically select their work schedule by either submitting requests in advance with the company or logging onto a website to reserve available hours.

Given these facts, drivers might plausibly be placed in either category. The court observed that "[a]t first glance, Lyft drivers don't seem much like employees," then added, "[b]ut Lyft drivers don't seem much like independent contractors either."[20] The court noted the amount of control exerted by the company over the drivers, including its detailed guidelines concerning how drivers are to perform their job. Also, the company reserved "a broad right to terminate drivers for cause" or for no reason at all. Thus, in some respects, the Lyft drivers appear to be employees.

Yet, in other respects, the drivers look like independent contractors. As in *O'Connor*, the drivers provide their own vehicles and choose their own work schedules. Ultimately, although most of the relevant facts were not in serious dispute, the court could not decide as a matter of law which classification was appropriate. Accordingly, just like the court in *O'Connor*, the *Cotter* court decided that the case should proceed to a jury on the question of whether Lyft drivers were employees or independent contractors.[21] However, as the court understood, committing the question for jury determination was simply an admission that the law provides no clear answer.

Nor are problems of worker classification limited to the most cutting-edge, high-technology businesses. In a case involving the classification of migrant workers who picked cucumbers, Judge Easterbrook authored a separate opinion arguing that it is absurd to decide the economic reality of a worker's situation through a multifactor balancing test: "My colleagues' balancing approach is the prevailing method, which they apply carefully. But it is unsatisfactory both because it offers little guidance for future cases and because any balancing test begs questions about which aspects of 'economic reality' matter, and why."[22]

If the multifactor approach to worker classification is unpredictable, even when applied to migrant farm workers, it is still more difficult to apply in cases involving on-demand businesses. But the basic problem in any context in which the classification issue arises is that the concept of economic reality has no clear meaning.[23] Assuming that all the factors previously identified by courts are potentially relevant, they do not all point in the same direction. The lack of guidance creates uncertainty and wastes judicial resources, encouraging an expensive litigation process. By leaving open the specter of punitive damages for misclassifications, pursued through class-action litigation as in the *O'Connor* and *Cotter* cases, the current climate of legal uncertainty threatens to diminish what has become a vibrant and promising sector of the economy.

THE PLEADING PROBLEM IN THE GIG SECTOR

As *Uber* and *Cotter* clearly show, there is widespread uncertainty in the courts and among the litigants in attempting to define who is an employee and who is an independent contractor in a case brought in the technology sector. When pleading these claims after *Iqbal* and *Twombly*, it will be difficult – if not impossible – for the plaintiffs to understand what facts would make a "plausible" claim in this area. Two uncertain questions – what "employee" means in the gig sector, and what it takes to establish a plausible pleading in this area – now combine to create unprecedented confusion in this field of the law. This problem will continue to persist until more clarity is given by the Supreme Court in both of these areas.

Ultimately, the Court must help define what plausibility means in workplace claims. And, the Court will have to provide some guidance on how to define "employee" in the technology sector. Until then, the courts – like those in *Uber* and *Cotter* – will openly struggle with how to address these claims.

In the meantime, from a practical perspective, plaintiffs are best off "overpleading" their case, including as many factors as possible to establish the elements of their claims. Given the level of uncertainty that currently exists, gig-sector plaintiffs should err on the side of caution in preparing the complaint. Though the danger always exists that including too many facts can create additional problems for the litigants, best practices currently suggest that plaintiffs should plead as comprehensive and as exhaustive of a complaint as possible.

CLASS ACTIONS AND THE ON-DEMAND ECONOMY

As *Uber* and *Cotter* clearly demonstrate, many of the employee/independent contractor questions impact entire companies in the technology sector. For this reason, this issue is ripe for class-action litigation. Just like determining who is an employee or independent contractor, the courts have struggled with how (and when) to aggregate these cases. This section looks at some of the best indicia to apply when attempting to classify groups of workers.

As discussed in the section that follows, the question of sufficient commonality presented by *Wal-Mart* will pervade the technology sector. As more class cases emerge in this context, we will see the lower courts struggle with this standard.

Grubhub, DoorDash, Amazon, and More

Though this chapter focuses on the litigation against Uber and Lyft, these cases really represent only the tip of the iceberg. There is also substantial other litigation pending against businesses throughout the on-demand economy. Many of these cases involve the question of worker misclassification and are worth brief exploration. These cases underscore the prevalence of this issue, and the increasing importance of finding a way to address class actions in the technology sector.

Grubhub and DoorDash

Grubhub and DoorDash provide on-demand delivery food services, allowing customers to order from local businesses through online and mobile applications.[24] On September 23, 2015, delivery drivers for Grubhub brought a class action in California state court alleging that they were misclassified as independent contractors, when they should have been classified as employees for purposes of wage payment law.[25] The drivers for Grubhub receive a flat fee for each delivery as well as any tip added by the customer.[26] The drivers allege that they are employees because they sign up for shifts in advance.[27] Grubhub controls the drivers' work by instructing them where to report, how to dress, where to go to pick up deliveries, and how to handle the food and timeliness of the deliveries themselves.[28] However, Grubhub required the drivers to bear the expenses of their vehicle, gas, parking, and phone data.[29] A similar complaint was also filed against DoorDash for the misclassification of workers as independent contractors in California state court.[30] These cases are both pending.

Instacart

Similarly, Instacart is an on-demand "grocery delivery service."[31] The company hires workers to purchase and deliver grocery orders for Instacart's customers.[32] The company has been extremely successful and boasted an impressive $2 billion valuation in 2015.[33] However, it has been entangled in litigation over the classification of its workers.[34] In February 2015, several workers initiated a class action lawsuit in the Northern District of California claiming that Instacart misclassified the workers as independent contractors.[35] The plaintiffs claimed that they were entitled to a minimum wage, overtime pay, and employment-related expenses such as automobile maintenance, fuel, and insurance.[36] The plaintiffs further alleged that Instacart asserted extensive control over its workers as evidenced by the company's control over "when and where [workers] were to collect and deliver groceries," the manner by which workers interfaced with customers, and the requirement that workers dress in clothing displaying the Instacart logo.[37] Furthermore, Instacart could fire workers at will,[38] determined workers' wages[39] and the prices charged to customers,[40] required workers to work in shifts,[41] and constantly monitored workers' actions.[42] The courts have consistently granted Instacart's motions to compel arbitration.[43]

Amazon

Amazon Prime Now provides a benefit to users of Amazon Prime that allows the members to place orders for same-day delivery in select zip codes through the use of a mobile application.[44] The drivers of Amazon Prime Now filed a class-action suit in California state court on October 27, 2015, alleging misclassification as independent contractors and failure to pay minimum wage.[45] The drivers state that they work regular shifts for hourly pay in order to deliver only the packages that Amazon Prime specifically assigns to them while wearing an Amazon uniform.[46] Amazon provides the drivers with a smart phone to use for the deliveries, but drivers must provide their own vehicle and fuel.[47] The drivers work fixed shifts in which they check in with the dispatcher to receive their package assignments.[48] They can neither reject assignments nor request to work in a particular geographic area.[49] Amazon determines the sequence of their deliveries as well as the routes and can track the drivers while they are out on delivery.[50] The drivers do not have the ability to negotiate any aspect of their compensation.[51] The Amazon Prime Now class-action suit awaits possible certification by the superior court of California.

Yelp

Yelp was founded as a means of connecting customers with local businesses.[52] Through the Yelp platform, consumers can find local businesses and leave reviews for the companies that they have visited.[53] Business managers can set up accounts to post photos of their business and message customers.[54] Yelp reviewers filed a class-action suit in federal district court against the company alleging that the reviewers should be considered employees.[55] However, the court granted Yelp's motion to dismiss for failure to state a claim on August 13, 2015.[56] The court emphasized that the language used by the plaintiffs to assert that they were "hired" by Yelp should reasonably be inferred to refer to a process by which any person can sign up on Yelp and submit reviews.[57]

Handy

Handy (previously Handybook) is an online platform that connects individuals looking for household help, like cleaning or handyman services, with independent professionals.[58] Cleaning professionals book their work through the list of available jobs provided by the application.[59] Handy retains control over the cleaning professionals through its ability to terminate at will and through its control over the location of the cleaning job and amount charged to the customer.[60] These independent professionals filed a class-action suit alleging that Handy was misclassifying its employees as independent contractors and failed to pay the workers overtime compensation.[61] The complaint was filed on October 30, 2014.[62] The court granted the cleaning service's motion to compel arbitration.

Postmates

Postmates is a courier service that connects "customers with local couriers who can deliver anything from any store or restaurant in minutes."[63] Couriers have filed several class action lawsuits against Postmates for worker misclassification.[64] A class action complaint filed in the Northern District of California alleges that Postmates misclassifies its couriers as independent contractors and failed to pay a minimum wage, overtime, and various expenses that an employer should incur.[65] The complaint further alleges that couriers "are required to follow detailed requirements imposed on them by Postmates, and they are graded, and are subject to termination, based on Postmates' discretion and/or their failure to adhere to these requirements (such as rules regarding their conduct with customers, their timeliness in picking up items and delivering them to customers, the accurateness of their orders, etc.)."[66] Couriers are responsible for many of their work-related expenses, such as transportation and phone costs.[67] The class action "has been stayed pending mediation."[68]

CrowdFlower

CrowdFlower is a data enrichment, data mining, and crowdsourcing company.[69] Customers upload their data onto the CrowdFlower website and set up instructions to create their job.[70] Once the job has been created, people will task on the job until it has been completed.[71] Individuals who performed some of these tasks for CrowdFlower brought a class-action suit against the company alleging that they were misclassified as independent contractors and paid less than the legal minimum wage.[72] The parties entered a settlement in the case in which defendants agreed to pay $585,507 to be distributed among the plaintiffs and plaintiffs' counsel.[73] The settlement was approved on July 2, 2015.[74]

Homejoy

Homejoy was an on-demand start-up that connected independent professional cleaners with customers.[75] The company classified its 1,000-plus cleaners as independent contractors.[76] At the outset, the company enjoyed considerable growth and raised a significant amount of venture capital financing.[77] Despite its early successes, workers filed a series of lawsuits, including three class actions, against Homejoy alleging that the company's cleaners were improperly classified as independent contractors.[78] Each complaint asserts that Homejoy exerted a substantial amount of control over its cleaners, and therefore, misclassified its workers as independent contractors.[79] A class action complaint filed on March 19, 2015, in the Northern District of California alleges Homejoy failed to compensate cleaners for overtime and work-related expenses that Homejoy should have reimbursed.[80] A separate class action complaint filed in California state court alleges that the company's cleaners could not "negotiate their pay," and had no discretion over which homes to clean or the amount of time spent cleaning a home.[81] In addition, Homejoy could fire a cleaner at any time or place a cleaner on "performance improvement plans."[82] The complaint further alleges that Homejoy could change a cleaner's schedule with very little notice,[83] determined the cleaning fees,[84] mandated a "minimum number of jobs" per week,[85] and required cleaners to wear a shirt emblazoned with the company's logo.[86] Furthermore, the cleaners were required to adhere to a cleaning checklist provided by Homejoy and could not determine "cleaning tasks" within the home.[87] In July 2015, Homejoy announced that it would cease operations primarily due to pending lawsuits over worker misclassification.[88]

Washio

Washio was an on-demand dry cleaning and laundry service that hired drivers to pick up and deliver laundry to customers.[89] Washio drivers filed a class action lawsuit on June 29, 2015, in California state court alleging that they were improperly classified as independent contractors.[90] The complaint claims that Washio required its drivers to adhere to rules dictating client interactions and how drivers should "store clothes in their vehicles."[91] In addition, Washio drivers were evaluated on how quickly they completed pick-ups and drop-offs, and the company could fire workers at will.[92] The complaint further alleges that Washio required drivers to consent to an exclusivity agreement, which prohibited drivers from working for Washio's competitors.[93] Washio ceased operations in August 2016, though the company cited reasons other than litigation for shutting down.[94]

As these cases demonstrate, there is a vast amount of litigation against technology-sector companies on the worker-classification issue. This litigation has had differing results. Some cases have been allowed to proceed, others have been dismissed, others have settled, and still others have found their way to arbitration.

More importantly, these cases emphasize the varied fact patterns that can give rise to technology-sector working relationships. While the ultimate question is one of control, there is no uniform set of facts in these cases that will help provide guidance on how that control should be measured. Indeed, these cases emphasize how this question is highly individualized in nature. With regard to control in this economy, we see that Grubhub controls where to report, how to dress, where to pick up deliveries, and how to address timeliness issues.[95] Amazon Prime Now controls the application that drivers use, the appearance of drivers, and the rate of pay.[96] Yelp maintains almost no control over its reviewers or those providing services for the company.[97] And, there is an additional panoply of businesses that have yet to see litigation in this area, but that are ripe for a potential dispute on this question.

Regardless of the potential company involved, the worker classification question will continue to arise in numerous contexts within the modern economy until more guidance is given in this area. This chapter seeks to provide a framework with which to address these issues on a class-wide basis.

REDIRECTING THE CLASS-ACTION INQUIRY: WEIGHING INDICIA OF EMPLOYMENT

The difficulty highlighted with litigating class-action cases in many of the technology-sector jobs already discussed is also, somewhat ironically, one of the greatest benefits associated with this type of employment–worker flexibility. Workers in the gig economy enjoy an unprecedented amount of flexibility in many instances, and often choose when, where, and how to carry out their job duties. While this workplace flexibility often works to the benefit of individuals, it makes aggregation of claims far more difficult. Unlike a traditional brick-and-mortar type place of employment, or a factory assembly line setting, workers in the gig industry often do not perform identical services or work similar hours.

THE INDICIA OF EMPLOYMENT TEST

The problem with using the class-action mechanism in many of these cases is the lack of *commonality* that often exists among workers in the technology sector. The key inquiry here, which will continue to be a question for years to come, is whether or not a worker is an employee or an independent contractor. But this question is very difficult to answer on an aggregate level – the workers are often too varied in these cases. This is not to say that in certain circumstances (or in particular employment settings) workers cannot be aggregated. However, each case must be examined on an individualized basis. Indeed, there may be groups of workers that have similar employment characteristics that would allow them to be aggregated for purposes of systemic litigation. Or, there may be subclasses that would work in the particular litigation. The major point here, however, is that there is often no "one-size-fits-all" answer to this question for technology sector cases. Rather, the best that we can do is to provide some general guidelines on how – and when – to aggregate these claims.

In analyzing the case law and reviewing the litigation, I have developed a framework that helps identify those technology-sector cases that would be appropriate for aggregation on the employee/independent contractor question. Through an extensive review of the case law, several factors emerged that help clarify which cases should be permitted to proceed on a systemic level. The key component of this framework is an emphasis on the level of *commonality* of the workers as required by the Supreme Court's *Wal-Mart* decision discussed earlier. Those workers who have more in common with each other share a number of similar characteristics, which are identified in the model proposed here.

This framework sets forth five different characteristics that the courts and litigants should consider when evaluating class-action litigation on the employee/independent contractor question. These characteristics should only serve as a guideline and are not dispositive. Each case – particularly in this emerging economy – is unique and should be evaluated on its own merits. The model, however, is sufficiently comprehensive to help the courts navigate this complex area of the law. It also provides some basic guidelines to consider when evaluating the appropriate scope of a class on this commonality question. Each of the five factors should be carefully considered by the court when addressing this type of systemic litigation.

These factors can help shape a systemic class when considering the independent contractor/employee issue, and should be examined when any aggregate litigation is proposed on this question. It is important to note that these factors should not be confused with the test for determining the existence of an employment relationship (though the considerations are quite similar). Rather, these factors are intended primarily to help evaluate the more precise question of whether worker claims should be *aggregated* on the independent contractor/employment issue. Each factor should be evaluated separately when examining this issue, and the weight given to any specific factor will depend on the particular case. These factors are nonexhaustive. Indeed, it is entirely possible that factors not contemplated here may still play a major role in shaping a proposed class. Nonetheless, the following framework attempts to provide some basic guidelines for considering how to aggregate a class in the technology sector.

These five factors – which are unweighted – are set forth here:

The Time that the Work Occurs

When an individual performs work is a critical component of that individual's status as an employee.[98] Thus, when aggregating claims, the courts should closely examine the timing of the work itself. If an individual works exclusively on evenings, that individual's experience may be far different from someone who is employed only during the day. Thus, individuals who perform work at similar times will be more likely to satisfy the commonality component of Rule 23. Timing is simply one factor – but an important indicia of employment that should be considered when grouping plaintiffs in systemic litigation on the independent contractor question.

The Place Where Work Is Performed

The place where the work is performed is a critical factor that helps differentiate individuals. Workers will likely vary in where their job duties are executed, such as at home, in an office, or even in their car. Those that carry out their tasks in a similar physical location will be far more likely to satisfy the commonality necessary to be part of a class action. Individuals who work at different locations may be too different from one another to warrant class certification.

The Frequency of Work Performed

Frequency is likely the most important factor in the five-part framework, as it helps clarify which workers are truly similar to each other. Frequency is a term that is malleable to the specific workplace, but in most contexts – as in the technology sector – it can be more simply defined as *how often* the work is performed. In the context of Uber, for example, the frequency of work would mean the number of hours that a driver performs her duties – how often the driver is actually on the road transporting customers.

The *frequency factor* – at least in the technology sector – is where employees will likely diverge substantially from one another. Some drivers might work forty to sixty hours a week, whereas other drivers may treat their employment as a part-time job, working only a few hours a week to make extra money on the side. Frequency of work can be, and often is, driven by a number of different criteria. Individuals who are unemployed could see being a full-time Uber driver as an excellent employment opportunity. Individuals who are currently employed in other parts of the economy may quit their jobs to make more money at Uber full time. Or, workers might have other full-time employment, be full-time students, or simply only want to work for the company for a limited number of hours per week. Irrespective of the particular worker's situation, however, *how often* the work is performed will be a critical (and often overlooked) criteria for aggregation on the employee/independent contractor question.

Manner of Work Performed

The manner of work performed can more simply be defined as how a worker performs his job. This factor is important, but often not likely to differ between workers in technology-driven jobs. In the *Uber* case, for example, courts could look at whether the individual drives her own car or whether she utilizes a vehicle owned by the company. Or, the court could examine whether some workers perform their jobs under particularly high-stress conditions, whereas others do not face the same obstacles or difficulties. How a particular individual's work is evaluated and/or supervised is another critical factor that forms part of this inquiry.

Like the other factors, those that perform work in a similar manner will be more likely to satisfy the commonality component as defined by the Supreme Court. This factor should thus be carefully scrutinized when evaluating the scope of a particular class action in the workplace.

Pricing Models

Price is a particularly unique component of the framework set forth in this chapter. The other factors – time, place, frequency, and manner – all go to the core of *how* work is performed. Pricing questions can reveal the level of control an employee exerts in the working relationship with the company. Those individuals who are able to set their own pricing models for their services will be far more likely to be independent contractors than those who do not have this amount of control. Similarly, class actions on the question of the employee/independent contractor issue should be grouped among employees who have similar levels of control over setting their own pricing structure for their particular services. Those workers who have different levels of power in setting prices should not be considered as part of the same class on this question, as they are far different in their status as employees.

The five-part model set forth here is intended to serve only as a guide and to provide common markers for courts to look to when assessing the scope of a class claim. The framework addresses the appropriate breadth of a class on the question of whether workers are independent contractors or employees. The model should not be used on the more precise question of whether workers actually *are* employees or independent contractors (though again the considerations are similar).

Attempting to define an appropriate class on this issue can be a difficult task, and the model offered by this chapter is simply one approach to this type of aggregate litigation. This model should serve as a guide to systemic litigation in this area of the law – one of the many tools practitioners and the judiciary can use to help establish the parameters of this common type of class-action litigation. This is not to say that there cannot be other approaches to class-action cases, however, as there are surely other indicia the courts can look to when considering the independent contractor/employee issue. The model is thus not intended to be exhaustive and serves as a single formulation to help better define this complex area of the law.

In addition, the technology cases in this area are often highly individualized. The model offered here attempts to be broad enough in scope to help account for specific variances in the cases. However, the model is malleable and may need to be adjusted in specific situations that do not fit neatly within its parameters. As the modern economy is constantly evolving, the framework offered here must only be considered as a guide – and some businesses may fall outside of the factors contemplated.

In short, no model can account for all of the potential variances in a constantly changing industry. This chapter offers a basic framework to address the bulk of the cases, but should be considered flexible and may need to be adapted to more unique or novel situations. Nonetheless, this model provides an important framework for evaluating the scope of much of the class-action litigation in the modern economy.

IMPLICATIONS OF THE PROPOSED MODEL

Adopting the framework proposed here would have several important implications for the courts and the litigants. There are a number of specific advantages of the model that are worth highlighting. Perhaps most importantly, the proposed framework offers a level of certainty to an otherwise confused area of the law. It navigates a complex field and breaks down the cases in this area into a workable five-part test for the courts and litigants that they can easily follow. The straightforward model thus synthesizes the law and federal rules in this area, and allows the courts to aggregate cases pursuant to a much more simple formula. This is not to say that the goal of choosing appropriate groupings of workers could not be accomplished in the absence of the formula offered here. The proposed framework makes the process much more straightforward, however, and far less susceptible to error.

Although simplicity is an important goal and advantage of the test, the framework proposed here offers far more. It has the further advantage of assuring commonality in diverse cases frequently brought in the technology sector. So-called gig-sector cases are notoriously difficult to navigate, and finding a common thread with which to aggregate these matters can be hard to identify. The Supreme Court's definition of commonality in the *Wal-Mart* case has made aggregating employment cases difficult under the Federal Rules of Civil Procedure. The Court's heightened commonality standard can be difficult to apply to claims brought in the on-demand economy. The framework offered here helps ensure that commonality is achieved in these difficult cases, and that the Supreme Court's new standard is adequately satisfied. Quite simply, the framework proposed here makes certain that workers share enough similar characteristics to proceed in a class-action case.

The proposed model also helps balance the interests of all parties in the litigation. By providing a fair test, it allows the scope of the litigation to be framed in an appropriate way. Similarly, the framework provides fairness to defendants, who can more precisely defend against this more focused class-action litigation. The model proposed here is far more useful than the approach currently used in the courts, which essentially involves scattered attempts by the judiciary to make sense of a hodge-podge of case law in this area.

This is not to say that there are not some drawbacks to the offered approach. Though the framework offered here would bring much-needed simplicity to this area of the law, it would also lead to additional litigation in some instances. More cases – both individual or otherwise – likely means more litigation time for the courts and the parties, and less efficiency. Nonetheless, the importance here is that the courts "get it right." By assuring that only similar claimants with common characteristics are aggregated together, the framework offered here helps achieve a proper result. And, by proposing a more straightforward, streamlined approach, the model offers many efficiencies that are not currently realized by the current system.

Some might also argue that by including an additional framework to certain class-action cases, the model proposed here adds one more layer of complexity to an already complex process. While it is a fair concern that the framework offered here could make the class-action process *more* difficult, that is not the intent of the model. Indeed, the factors suggested here are simply meant to serve as nonexhaustive, unweighted guidelines to assist the courts to help construct a proper class in gig-sector cases. The framework is *not* intended to introduce an additional rigid, inflexible test into an already cumbersome process. It is thus meant to serve as a tool to assist the courts in working through cases in an emerging, ill-defined area of the law.

At the end of the day, no approach is perfect. The model offered here simplifies a complex area of the law, proposes a straightforward framework for the courts to follow, and ensures that Supreme Court case law and the federal rules are being followed. The approach should strongly be considered for this type of technology-driven litigation.

As a final consideration, it is worth highlighting that the approach described in this chapter may apply more broadly than simply to cases brought in the on-demand economy. The independent contractor/employee question pervades many areas of the law beyond the technology sector. While this test could certainly be adapted to other areas of the economy, it was formulated specifically for cases brought in the technology sector. As this is the area that is currently the most divisive and complex, and as the cases are rapidly evolving in this sector, this chapter attempts to bring clarity to this specific field. The considerations addressed here, however, could certainly be easily tailored to other areas of the law as well.

It is also worth noting that this book offers an early attempt in the academic literature to streamline gig-sector class-action cases. As such, it primarily attempts to open a dialogue on this topic. As already noted, the factors here should not be considered exclusive, and others are encouraged to weigh in on possible elements that could be used to help define systemic litigation in this area. And, others may even disagree over how much weight should be assigned to particular factors (or may even take issue with some of the elements that have been proposed here). The courts, litigants, and others in the academic community should further attempt to find ways to simplify this confusing process, and bring clarity to these often cumbersome class-action cases.

CONCLUSION

The Supreme Court's procedural decisions have created confusion across the board. As we see with the on-demand economy, there is confusion specifically as to the pleading standards for who is an employee and how to aggregate claims after *Wal-Mart*. This chapter establishes a patchwork approach to these issues, essentially advocating for "overpleading" on the issue of who is an employee and establishing a framework for evaluating whether the aggregation of claims is proper.

This type of piecemeal approach to the broad-based procedural problems created by the Court is the only effective way for litigants to proceed at this time. This type of uncertainty will continue to lead to inconsistent decisions, and larger-than-necessary settlements, as the litigants struggle to make sense of this area. The on-demand economy example demonstrates that it is still possible to successfully litigate in an emerging and confusing area of the law. Nonetheless, congressional intervention could help clarify this area and level the playing field for civil-rights litigants.

The following chapter brings together the various frameworks proposed throughout this text, discussing how these models must be crafted to fit the particular case and industry – just as we see here with the technology sector example. As seen here, and as detailed in the next chapter, only congressional intervention can truly fix the procedural problems created by the Roberts Court.

7

The Solution

If you get tangled up, just tango on.

– Scent of a Woman, 1992[1]

As a caveat, the title of this chapter is intended to be a *dramatic* overstatement. In reality, there is no perfect fix for what the Supreme Court has done by undermining substantive worker rights through procedural mechanisms. The law in this area has become quite tangled up, and to proceed effectively now means that litigants must proceed cautiously and simply tango on. As I will argue later in this chapter, congressional intervention is the only true "solution" to the ongoing problem. But with tens of thousands of charges of discrimination filed with the EEOC each year, the civil-rights community cannot afford to wait in hopes that Congress will intervene as it has done in the past.

So how can civil-rights lawyers still proceed with their claims in this area? How do workplace plaintiffs "tango on" while waiting for a true legislative fix? This text, while identifying the problem, has sketched out a number of different ways around the Supreme Court's restrictive procedural decisions. A large part of the problem in this area is that the Court has now set several traps for unwary plaintiffs. Many attorneys find themselves overwhelmed when trying to navigate these potential pitfalls, and this book attempts to simplify and break down the problem to help litigants proceed when filing these claims. The current "solution" to the procedural hurdles erected by the Roberts Court is really just a *patchwork* approach to fixing the problem while we await legislative intervention. The best many litigants can do is to try and avoid springing the traps set by the Court.

This chapter brings the numerous individual "solutions" identified throughout the text together in an easy and workable format. Thus, it outlines how to navigate the recent difficulties created by the Roberts Court in the following areas: pleading employment-discrimination claims, addressing systemic workplace issues, litigating retaliation claims, and pursuing relief in this area. It further emphasizes the need for a legislative solution and identifies what this type of congressional action would look like. At the end of the day, congressional intervention is needed. For now, however, we must do our best to carefully navigate the murky waters created by the Court. Although some of the information discussed in this chapter may seem repetitive, it is useful to condense the numerous frameworks proposed throughout this book in a single workable format.

A CAUTIONARY NOTE

As seen throughout this text, the procedural problems created for civil-rights litigants by the Roberts Court apply to all areas of workplace cases. Plaintiffs in a wide variety of contexts and industries will face difficulties when trying to litigate their claims. As a cautionary note, then, it is important to highlight that the proposed frameworks must always be tailored to the particular case. The models set forth here are general in nature, and must be crafted to fit the given situation. As seen in the technology sector example discussed in Chapter 6, a given "solution" must be adapted to the context in which the "problem" arises. Just like the on-demand economy example, then, litigants must tailor the following proposals to fit the particular case at hand.

FILING THE CLAIM

As discussed in detail throughout this text, the Roberts Court has erected numerous barriers to workplace plaintiffs when pleading their claims in federal court. In essence, the Court has changed the pleading standard from one that could be supported through "any set of facts" to a standard requiring plausibility on the face of the complaint itself. The import of this change cannot be overstated, and litigants, legislators, and academics have all weighed in on the problem created by these new standards for the civil-rights community. In employment-discrimination cases, the major obstacle created by this new case law is the difficulty plaintiffs will have *pleading discriminatory intent* without access to discovery in the case. This problem will persist until addressed by Congress. In the meantime, plaintiffs are still left with the practical problem of attempting to successfully plead their plausible workplace claims without access to discovery. Fortunately, as discussed earlier, a safe harbor was created by the *Swierkiewicz* decision. If plaintiffs plead a *prima facie* case of discrimination under the four-part test articulated by this case, they should be permitted to proceed with their claim.

With this test in mind, plaintiffs should do their best to support their complaints with the following information, which should be sufficient to avoid dismissal:

1. The victim of the alleged discrimination;
2. The approximate time that the discrimination occurred;
3. The protected characteristic at issue;

4. The qualifications of the victim for the position;
5. The nature of the discrimination suffered;
6. Other evidence of discrimination (that others outside the protected class were treated better, statistical data, or discriminatory comments); and
7. That the discrimination by the employer was because of the plaintiff's protected characteristic.

This straightforward test can be easily applied and navigated. Perhaps more importantly, it can be used to analyze whether a claim should be filed in the first place, as well as to assess the amount of risk that a particular allegation might be dismissed in the case. Where plaintiffs can satisfy all of these elements, attorneys should feel confident that they will be permitted to proceed with their claims. If an element is missing, litigants should understand that the claim may be a bit riskier and, if at all possible, attempt to ferret out additional information prior to filing the complaint. Certainly, it will not always be realistic to obtain all of the information necessary to bring such a substantiated claim this early in the litigation. Nonetheless, this test gives the courts and litigants a way of evaluating where any weaknesses may exist with a particular allegation.

Indeed, perhaps the most troubling aspect of the *Twombly/Iqbal* decisions is the amorphous nature of evaluating civil-rights claims in their wake. Plausibility is an ambiguous term and one that seems to have been created by the Roberts Court out of whole cloth. The Court abrogated decades of pleading precedent and left no clear guidance on how to sufficiently allege employment-discrimination claims. The framework proposed here provides some clarity to this confused area and some reassurance to plaintiffs that, by establishing a certain set of facts, their allegations will survive.

This test is not meant to create any type of *threshold* requirement. Indeed, there will likely be numerous valid workplace claims that are plausible on their face where attorneys are unable to satisfy all seven elements of the test. Discovery is often needed – and should be granted liberally – in employment-discrimination cases. As noted throughout this text, discriminatory intent is extraordinarily difficult to establish, and plaintiffs should be given substantial leeway when trying to uncover this type of animus. Thus, the seven-part framework offered here can be described as more of a safe harbor than a minimum requirement. Where the elements are established, the claim should be permitted to proceed in all but the most extraordinary of circumstances. A claim that satisfies the elements of this framework is inherently plausible on its face.

THE AFFIRMATIVE DEFENSE

As discussed in this text, defendants in employment-discrimination cases may face a similar uphill battle when pleading an affirmative defense. There remains substantial debate as to whether the *Twombly/Iqbal* standard would apply to these types of defenses. Thus, it is unclear whether a defendant must plead a "plausible" affirmative defense. As set forth earlier, there are strong arguments on both sides of this debate and the courts have yet to clearly decide the matter. Though this book is targeted at the uneven playing field for civil-rights litigants in this area, it is worth considering that the ambiguity created by the Roberts Court negatively impacts defendants in other circumstances as well.

Just like plaintiffs, then, there is a certain amount of uncertainty for defendants in this area of the jurisprudence. The Supreme Court has yet to decide the issue and until it does, this uncertainty will remain. During this interim period, defendants should act just as cautiously as plaintiffs when asserting their affirmative defenses. Defendants should do their best to include enough facts to state a plausible defense in their answers. This will typically not prove difficult given that there is not the same type of intent hurdle faced by plaintiffs when addressing an affirmative defense. And, as a general matter, defendants tend to have more information in their possession than plaintiffs with regard to these claims at the earlier stages of the litigation.

Given the myriad ways that these defenses may arise, it is impossible to articulate a specific overarching framework for alleging the affirmative defense. There are some common considerations, however, that an employer should contemplate when responding to the complaint, such as basic times, dates, locations, and actors involved. As detailed earlier in this text, for example, asserting an affirmative defense in the sexual-harassment context can be relatively straightforward when carefully evaluated by the defendant. The specificity that is required depends precisely on the exact defense that is being asserted. Just like plaintiffs, defendants should be wary of falling into a trap of making statements that are *too conclusory* and merely parrot the statutory or legal standard implicated. Employers should be cautious – at least during this time of uncertainty – to *overplead* the defense and include any facts related to the defense that are available.

It is unclear, then, exactly how precise defendants must be when asserting an affirmative defense. What is clear, however, is that best practices dictate that defendants include relevant facts wherever possible. The more facts that are included in the answer, the less likely it is that such a defense will be rejected by the courts on the basis of plausibility. This cautious approach is needed by defendants until the Supreme Court weighs in on the issue or until additional case law makes clear what facts are necessary.

THE CLASS-ACTION CLAIM

As discussed in this text, one area where the Roberts Court has undermined worker rights is in the class-action context. Systemic claims are critical for employment-discrimination plaintiffs and for attempts to eradicate unlawful employer behavior. By weakening these types of claims, the Court has hit at the core of the ability of plaintiffs to vindicate their rights. Indeed, many workplace victims would never seek relief on an individual basis. Only through aggregate litigation, then, are many aggrieved employees able to be made whole for an employer's discriminatory behavior.

The crux of the Supreme Court's action in this area can be seen in the *Wal-Mart* decision. This case makes it far more difficult for employment-discrimination plaintiffs to aggregate their claims by raising the bar when interpreting Rule 23. More specifically, after *Wal-Mart*, plaintiffs must do far more to show sufficient *commonality* in a case involving workplace claims. As discussed in this text, there are many policy reasons that cause this decision to be problematic for civil-rights litigants. Although these policy rationales are well considered, they do little to offer a solution in this area. This book has attempted to provide some guidance on how groups can proceed when they have been discriminated against on a systemic level. These suggestions must be tailored to the individual case as there are a number of different ways that the civil-rights community can proceed when attempting to address an aggregate claim after *Wal-Mart*. Some suggestions are more general in nature, while others are more specific to the case at hand. Each should be reviewed in turn.

The Governmental Approach

The EEOC is not subject to the *Wal-Mart* decision. As the agency need not comply with the requirements of Rule 23 – including its now more restrictive commonality requirement – the EEOC should do far more to bring widespread systemic litigation claims. The EEOC is in a unique position to bring these claims as it has the first opportunity to review and investigate charges of discrimination that are of a systemic nature. As noted in this text, there are a number of practical benefits with this type of governmental systemic litigation. Nonetheless, there are drawbacks. As the EEOC receives limited funding, it would thus likely forego other more victim-specific litigation to bring these types of aggregate claims. This approach, then, raises important policy questions as to where the government should direct its resources. In the current climate of restrictive class-action cases, however, I would suggest that more resources be directed toward systemic claims.

Procedural Responses

There are a number of procedural workarounds to the *Wal-Mart* decision that can be effectively pursued by litigants. The first procedural response, the offensive use of collateral estoppel, has enormous potential value for class-action cases. This approach suggests that plaintiffs more aggressively use collateral estoppel as part of their litigation strategy. This procedural mechanism could thus be considered where victims face similar issues or fact patterns arising from a single employer. Collateral estoppel serves to prevent important issues from being re-tried in subsequent litigation. As it is not uncommon for an employer to discriminate against multiple individuals and discrimination often occurs at a single employment site, many cases of discrimination involve the same set of facts and policies. As outlined in this text, there are many circumstances where the use of collateral estoppel would be quite attractive. This procedural tool is concededly not as strong as the class-action mechanism itself; however, this approach would still help resolve many of the problems created by the *Wal-Mart* decision and avoid the re-litigation of issues that have already been resolved in an employment-discrimination matter.

Similarly, consolidation under Rule 42(a) offers another opportunity to fill the void left by the *Wal-Mart* decision. Consolidation offers the possibility of streamlining employment-discrimination claims, just like collateral estoppel. Unlike collateral estoppel, consolidation allows important issues to be resolved *at the same time*. Thus, consolidation involves the resolution of issues as part of a single proceeding. This procedural tool is typically used where there are common issues of law or fact involved in numerous cases. By trying multiple claims or issues in a single trial, the courts are able to simplify the litigation. Such trials can be resolved more quickly and inexpensively than multiple proceedings. And, there is less possibility of inconsistent judgments. Again, this approach is not as attractive as the class-action mechanism itself, but still offers a number of procedural benefits. The benefits and drawbacks of this approach should be weighed by the courts and individual litigants.

This text further argues that cabining *Wal-Mart* could be an effective approach for plaintiffs pursuing class-action litigation. This approach suggests that plaintiffs attempt to distinguish their systemic claims from the *Wal-Mart* case. Almost all claims can be distinguished from the *Wal-Mart* decision as that case was quite unique in its facts. Indeed, the Supreme Court repeatedly emphasized the massive size of the *Wal-Mart* case, which proposed a systemic claim involving more than one million individual victims. Plaintiffs can, and often should, attempt to distinguish their claims from this enormous case. Litigants can argue that the heightened commonality standard should apply only in these massive cases. Cabining *Wal-Mart* in this way would have obvious procedural benefits for the plaintiffs. Indeed, an effective use of this approach could largely distinguish *Wal-Mart* away, and the decision would have little or no impact on the legal landscape. This approach would certainly be dependent upon the receptiveness of the argument in the lower courts. The argument to limit *Wal-Mart* is sound, as the Supreme Court was notably preoccupied with the enormous size of the case. The receptiveness of this argument in the lower courts, however, is still quite unclear. The benefits and drawbacks of this approach are more fully outlined in Chapter 3, which fully discusses these arguments.

An additional procedural approach suggested in this book would be to take *Wal-Mart* at its word, and to embrace the application of the Court's holding to all employment-discrimination matters. By taking *Wal-Mart* at its word, plaintiffs that might otherwise pursue class-action claims should instead file suit individually against the employer. By filing thousands of individual cases against an employer, the company may ultimately become overwhelmed and completely bogged down by this type of litigation. Instead of defending against one suit, then, corporations could find themselves litigating individual cases across the country. This proposal involves massive organization by plaintiffs' attorneys and a careful analysis of which suits to bring – and in what jurisdiction. This type of organization has been achieved in other civil-rights pursuits in the past. There are risks with this approach, however, as detailed in the text. And there are obvious financial costs as well. Taking *Wal-Mart* at its word may thus be an effective procedural strategy for plaintiffs, but there are implications involved in using the Court's decision in this way.

A final procedural approach to *Wal-Mart* involves Rule 23(c)(4) – issue class certification. This rule allows a group of plaintiffs to certify certain issues common among them, even when the putative class itself has not been certified. Issue class certification is quite useful in class-action, employment-discrimination cases, particularly after the *Wal-Mart* decision. This is because workplace systemic claims often present the two criteria required for issue class certification: (1) aggregate litigation involving a common set of facts; and (2) varying degrees of harm among the individual plaintiffs. Given the similarities and differences of typical workplace claims, which are discussed in greater detail in this book, employment-discrimination disputes are often ripe for issue class certification under Rule 23. Because they inherently vary, discrimination claims will not always be suitable for traditional class treatment under the Federal Rules, as the *Wal-Mart* case clearly demonstrates. But as these claims frequently involve a common set of facts, including the same policies, practices, and personnel – there will often be similar issues that can be separated out and certified as an issue class. By resolving these common issues once as an issue class, litigants can proceed much more efficiently with these claims. And, as demonstrated by the Seventh Circuit decision authored by Judge Posner, this type of issue class certification has already been approved after *Wal-Mart* in an employment-discrimination case.[2] This approach is thus far more practical than theoretical and should strongly be considered by litigants when pursuing their workplace claims.

Revised Relief

An additional approach that can be used to navigate the *Wal-Mart* decision discussed herein is concededly far less practical, but should be strongly considered as well – revised relief. More specifically, this text noted the similarities between punitive damages and class-action, employment-discrimination litigation, both of which serve many of the same functions. In light of this, I argue here for the more aggressive use of punitive damages in workplace cases. The government and civil-rights groups should actively seek out those cases to prosecute that meet the standard for punitive relief. Also, the courts should be particularly sympathetic to claims of punitive relief against employers. This text identifies a new proposed framework for evaluating when punitive damages may be awarded in a discrimination case. The litigants and courts should closely evaluate the facts of the claim to help identify those cases that satisfy these factors. An employment-discrimination claim should thus satisfy the following five elements to be an appropriate case for punitive relief:

1. Whether a supervisor is responsible for the unlawful conduct;
2. Whether the supervisor had knowledge of Title VII;
3. Whether the supervisor was acting within the scope of employment;
4. Whether the employer was acting in good faith; and
5. Whether the court should allow the punitive damages question to go to the jury even where it is inclined to reject the instruction.

In considering these factors, the courts and litigants can more appropriately understand when a punitive damages jury instruction should be given. As detailed in far greater length in this text, these elements can be quite instructive on the issue of exemplary relief.

After *Wal-Mart*, the time is also now right for Congress to more aggressively consider revising the punitive damage caps. These damages have remained static since 1991. For punitive damages to be an effective substitute for class-action cases, the existing caps must either be raised substantially or completely eliminated. This approach is not novel as others have argued for this type of revised relief. However, this debate should be revisited in light of the controversial *Wal-Mart* decision and the overlapping goals of systemic litigation and punitive relief. In short, the government and civil-rights groups should be more aggressive when attempting to obtain punitive relief. Congress should similarly consider revising the structure of punitive damages in employment cases.

ARBITRATION

Like class-action claims brought in federal court, the Supreme Court has also struck at aggregate litigation in the arbitration setting. Arbitration involves claims brought outside of the court system. A private referee, or arbitrator, will evaluate these claims. This text addresses the restrictions the Supreme Court has placed on such aggregate litigation in the arbitration setting. The Supreme Court's decision in *Concepcion* discussed earlier raises the bar for these claims, just like the bar was raised in federal court aggregate litigation under Rule 23. Although there is no real solution to the hurdle created by the Court here, litigants must be cognizant of these new restrictions and evaluate the best way to proceed when addressing private arbitration agreements. There are pros and cons to arbitration generally that must be considered, and the additional restrictions on aggregate arbitration provide one further obstacle for individuals litigating in this arena.

RETALIATION

As discussed, retaliation remains one area where the Supreme Court and lower courts have tended to be more sympathetic to workplace litigants. There is a clear understanding that if retaliation claims are restricted, workplace statutes will become far less effective. If victims of discrimination are afraid to bring a claim at all, other workplace protections will have little purpose. This perception of the importance of retaliation claims is consistent with the role Congress viewed for these claims when enacting workplace legislation.

Despite this important – and well-recognized – role for retaliation claims, there have nonetheless been some efforts by the Supreme Court to curtail retaliation litigation through procedural mechanisms. In particular, in *Nassar*,[3] the Court required the plaintiffs to establish but-for causation when bringing a retaliation claim. And, in *Breeden*,[4] the Court raised the bar for the conduct necessary to establish retaliatory conduct under Title VII.

Though there is no "solution" to the procedural hurdles created by *Nassar* and *Breeden*, the cases are instructive of the types of retaliation claims necessary for litigants to be successful under Title VII. Retaliation victims thus must proceed cautiously to make certain that their claims satisfy the standards established by the Supreme Court in these cases. In particular, *Nassar* teaches us that the Court will not permit anything other than but-for causation in these cases.

From a procedural standpoint, this means that plaintiffs must shore up any questions about the defendant's true motivations early in the case. This can be done in a variety of different ways, including securing strong circumstantial or direct evidence of discrimination. *Breeden* also demonstrates the need for plaintiffs to gather sufficient evidence to create a reasonable belief that plaintiff's Title VII protections have been violated. There is also a procedural benefit of complaining directly to the federal government of discrimination, which would give workers blanket protection under the statute.

In light of *Nassar* and *Breeden*, then, plaintiffs must cautiously assess their claims and evidence prior to proceeding with a case of retaliation. Procedurally, plaintiffs should carefully consider where and when to even raise a complaint of discrimination in the first place. Only legislative intervention could completely undo the effects of these cases on workplace retaliation victims. Absent Congress's intervention, plaintiffs must be well aware of the case law and carefully navigate these standards. Failure to do so can have devastating effects on a plaintiff's claim, including dismissal of the case.

STRIKING AT RELIEF

This text sets forth in great detail a five-part framework that should be considered for punitive damages in employment-discrimination cases. This test is intended to help the courts and litigants identify when exemplary relief may be appropriate in a case, and therefore when a punitive damages instruction should be given to a jury. Beyond these factors, however, litigants must now strongly take into consideration the *Philip Morris* and *Exxon* Supreme Court decisions. Thus, a court should be hesitant to allow the jury to punish an employer for harm caused to strangers to the litigation, though such evidence can be used for purposes of showing reprehensibility. Similarly, once the jury awards punitive damages in a Title VII case, the court may analyze the award for excessiveness. After *Exxon*, however, the court's role in reviewing the amount of the award for due process concerns will be extremely limited.

By analyzing whether punitive damages are appropriate pursuant to this proposed analytical model, the court and litigants will inherently consider the standards set forth in *Kolstad* and the recent Supreme Court decisions on this issue. Though the proposed model is simply one way of examining these cases, it can be used for most Title VII claims. And, while the courts have struggled with how to comply with *Kolstad*, the proposed model clearly and concisely articulates whether an employment-discrimination plaintiff is entitled to exemplary relief.

CONGRESSIONAL INTERVENTION

This chapter takes a broader, more comprehensive approach to resolving many of the issues created by the Supreme Court. As explained here, the Court's decisions have struck at the core of several of the important protections for employees in the workplace. As this text has threaded these cases together, it has identified the extensiveness of the problem created by the Court. Workers are now in a disadvantaged position when trying to bring litigation, to aggregate their claims, to attain protection for retaliation, or to pursue sufficient relief. This chapter attempts to provide a number of broad-based solutions for these workers.

This chapter thus provides a basis for civil-rights plaintiffs to navigate the recent decisions of the Court. However, no model can completely undo what the Roberts

Court has accomplished in the past decade with respect to stripping away the rights of minority workers. The systematic eradication of employee rights cannot be completely reversed. Nonetheless, through strategic considerations, there are still numerous opportunities available that will allow civil-rights litigants to successfully pursue their claims. This chapter thus summarizes those opportunities and proposes various models that will allow minority workers a greater chance of prevailing with their cases. This framework thus provides workers a roadmap for bringing their claims and maximizing potential relief.

This chapter also signals to Congress, governmental entities, and civil-rights advocates the need for change in this area. There are certainly ways – as identified in this text – for minority workers to prevail with their claims. Change is nonetheless sorely needed. The Supreme Court has quietly eroded the protections of workplace claimants. Legislative and executive intervention is likely the only way to adequately restore the rights that Congress afforded employees through Title VII and its subsequent amendments. Thus, while this chapter proposes various models that will permit workers to navigate their claims, it also identifies the critical need for more robust legislation in this area.

Congressional intervention could take myriad forms to help resolve the problems created by the Supreme Court. Perhaps the most straightforward approach would be for the legislature to step in and expressly overturn the cases that have created difficulty for civil-rights litigants. I would advocate for clear congressional intervention in each of the procedural areas identified as problematic in this text.

In particular, Congress could expressly reject the standard created by the Court in *Twombly* and *Iqbal* and provide a law that clearly states a more favorable pleading standard. Congress could therefore legislate a different standard than the "plausibility" requirement articulated by the Supreme Court. The legislature could provide a standard that was either similar or identical to the *Conley* "any set of facts" language specifically abrogated by the Court in its more recent pleading decisions. Attempts to restore the *Conley* standard have already been advanced in both the House of Representatives and the Senate.[5] However, these efforts have gone nowhere and attempts to overturn these cases have failed. Nonetheless, as this book and other literature begin to make clear, the highly negative impact of these decisions should result in more robust efforts to overturn these cases. While this text identifies various patchwork approaches for litigants to mitigate the effects of these cases, the only true solution is for Congress to intervene and overturn these highly damaging decisions. As this text has identified the impact of the Court's pleading decisions on access to justice issues, it will hopefully provide a greater sense of urgency for the need for new legislation in this area.

Congressional intervention is also needed with respect to systemic class-action claims – both from a private litigant's standpoint in federal court as well as those claims proceeding in arbitration. The interpretation of these systemic-type cases in both *Wal-Mart* and *Concepcion* should be rejected by the legislature. The commonality standard of *Wal-Mart* places too high a burden on litigants and it should be rejected by Congress. Similarly, the legislature should expressly provide the opportunity for litigants to more easily aggregate workplace claims in the private arbitration setting. Congress could accomplish these goals by creating a law that would establish a lower threshold for litigants when attempting to aggregate their employment-discrimination claims. Such laws are necessary to return the jurisprudence to a pre–*Wal-Mart* setting. In short, Congress should reject the current high bar of commonality created by the Roberts Court if it wants to restore the protections of civil-rights litigants in systemic litigation.

In addition, Congress should revisit the but-for causation standard and reasonable belief standard created by the Supreme Court in *Nassar* and *Breeden* for retaliation claims. These standards have a chilling effect on victims of discrimination in the workplace and should thus be reversed. While the Court has generally been permissive of retaliation claims, Congress should reevaluate these standards where they have been narrowed by the Court.

Moreover, Congress should revisit the level of relief provided to employment-discrimination plaintiffs. There are many different ways through which this goal could be accomplished. The most pressing need – as discussed in this text – arises in the punitive damages context. The $300,000 cap on punitive and compensatory relief combined put in place for employment-discrimination plaintiffs has remained static for far too long. The effects of inflation have largely eroded the impact of these damages, as the caps have not changed in more than twenty-five years. These low caps now serve as a deterrent for aggrieved individuals to pursue employment-discrimination cases, and there is also less of a deterrent to prevent employers from discriminating in the first instance. It is important for Congress to revisit the statutory caps and to strongly consider raising these limits, indexing the limits to inflation, and/or eliminating the caps altogether. Again, such efforts could go a long way toward restoring the workplace protections of civil-rights litigants.

The legislation I propose here, which would overturn the *Twombly* and *Iqbal* decisions, eliminate the commonality standard created in *Wal-Mart*, allow victims of discrimination to more freely bring retaliation claims, and relax the overly static nature of relief in employment-discrimination cases, is only a starting point. Any of the problematic cases discussed in this text could largely be legislated away by Congress. A new Civil Rights Act – like the one put in place in 1991 – could amend Title VII, create additional law, and otherwise change the playing field in favor of civil-rights litigants. The deck has been stacked against these individuals for far too long and it is now time for Congress to act again. In dissenting opinions, members of the Court have already signaled that Congress should intervene to overturn the majority's decisions in certain cases. As we saw in the *Ledbetter* case discussed in Chapter 1, Congress has the ability to act when the Supreme Court has overstepped its bounds. In that case, Congress expressly overturned the *Ledbetter* decision and created new law with respect to the timing of employment-discrimination claims. The statute was the first one signed into law by President Obama and clearly showed that Congress has the will and ability to act when employment-discrimination protections are eroded too far by the Supreme Court. This book outlines a number of ways these erosions have continued to progress and congressional intervention is now necessary in these areas as well. As Justice Ginsburg argued in her dissenting opinion in *University of Texas Southwestern Medical Center* v. *Nassar*, now is the time for Congress to act with "yet another Civil Rights Restoration Act."[6]

THE ADA EXAMPLE

Proposing such congressional intervention is ambitious but not fanciful. As noted, Congress recently acted after the *Ledbetter* case to undo the Supreme Court's procedural timing limitation on victims of pay discrimination. Perhaps an even more poignant example occurred under the ADA, as it involved a series of Supreme Court cases that eroded the protections of those in the disability community. This text does not purport to undergo an exhaustive examination of the ADA and its subsequent decisions, which deserve separate treatment. Nonetheless, it is worth briefly noting a judicial trend under the ADA, which closely tracks the theme of this text – the use of procedural-type decisions to undermine the substantive rights of workers.

The ADA was passed in the early 1990s with overwhelming support by both the House and the Senate, and the statute was signed into law by President George H. W. Bush. In many ways, the ADA tracks Title VII, as it makes it an adverse employment action to discriminate on the basis of a worker's disability. There are a couple of notable differences, however, such as protections that are provided in the statute for employers where a worker would present an undue threat, as well as a separate requirement that employers reasonably accommodate employees in certain circumstances.

Perhaps the most substantial difference between Title VII and the ADA is the most basic – coverage under the law. For disability claims, one must show an actual, perceived, or historical disability. Essentially, this means establishing a physical or mental impairment that is substantially limiting, an employer's perception of such an impairment, or a record of this type of impairment. Though alleging that one is disabled seems relatively straightforward, it is actually quite complex under the law.

The EEOC has issued regulations on the meaning of the terms in the statute and the federal courts have helped to further define these terms. The courts, of course, have given varying interpretation to the complex language of the statute.

FIGURE 7.1 President George H. W. Bush signs the Americans with Disabilities Act, July 26, 1990. The ADA has fundamentally changed discrimination law and provided important rights for many employees in the workplace.

The Supreme Court, in a number of high-profile (and controversial) decisions, has also weighed in on the meaning of the law.

For example, in *Sutton* v. *United Airlines, Inc.*,[7] the Supreme Court held that mitigating measures *should* be considered when addressing whether an employee is disabled. Though the case arose in the context of whether an individual wearing eyeglasses is disabled, it can further be applied to such mitigating measures as artificial limbs and medication. In essence, then, the Court held that someone with a prosthetic leg who can ambulate as well as the average person is *not* disabled under the ADA. Nor would someone taking insulin who can accomplish her major life activities as well as the average person in the population. Under *Sutton*, then, the Court made it far more difficult to be considered "disabled" and to attain coverage under the statute. Though this holding was made well before the Roberts Court, it plays directly into the theme of this text. The Court used a highly technical reading of the statute to help undermine the substantive provisions of a widely popular civil-rights law.

The ADA also provides a nice example of the potential ramifications of this type of action by the Court. Indeed, Congress would subsequently step in to largely overturn *Sutton* (with the exception of contact lenses and eyeglasses) as well as other disability-related decisions that were limiting the intended breadth of the statute. These amendments to the statute – better known as the ADA Amendments Act – went into effect in 2009.

Just like Congress's negative response to the procedural limitations put in place by the Court for the ADA, there is now much needed legislative intervention on the more recent procedural rulings of the Court that have limited substantive civil rights in other areas of the workplace. The ADA is a clear example and illustration that such congressional intervention is entirely possible. Congress must now act in other areas as well.

CONCLUSION

The Supreme Court has systematically eviscerated the rights of minority workers through subtle changes in procedural law. These procedural changes have eroded the substantive protections of civil-rights litigants. This book has proposed a workable model for navigating these recent changes, and proposes a way for plaintiffs to successfully proceed with their claims during this difficult era. As seen with the on-demand economy discussed in the prior chapter, each "solution" must be carefully crafted to fit the particular case and industry in question. The framework set forth here is thus more general in nature and should be tailored to the claim at hand.

While it is still possible for minority workers to attain relief through the models set forth in this text, more broad-based legislative or executive action is needed to reverse the course set by the Court over the past decade. This book has thus identified the problems created by the Roberts Court. The most important contribution of this text to the scholarship is thus to spark a dialogue on this issue. The subtleties of the Court's decisions that are identified here have stripped workers of their statutory rights. It is now time for a discussion of these cases to begin. And it is time for the legislature to respond.

Notes

1 THE SUPREME COURT, EMPLOYMENT DISCRIMINATION, AND AN OVERVIEW OF CIVIL RIGHTS

1 564 US 338 (2011).
2 550 US 618 (2007).
3 557 US 557 (2009).
4 Bell Atl. Corp. v. Twombly, 550 US 544 (2007); Ashcroft v. Iqbal, 556 US 662 (2009).
5 133 S. Ct. 2434 (2013).
6 133 S. Ct. 2517 (2013).
7 42 U.S.C. § 2000e-2(a).
8 411 US 792 (1973).
9 Ashcroft v. Iqbal, 556 US 662 (2009); Bell Atl. Corp. v. Twombly, 550 US 544 (2007).
10 550 US 618 (2007).
11 Ibid., 621.
12 Ibid., 621–22.
13 Ibid.
14 Ibid., 632.
15 Ibid., 644.
16 Ibid., 659–61.
17 2012 Democratic National Convention, Charlotte, North Carolina (September 5, 2012).
18 Pub. L. No. 111–2, 123 Stat. 5 (to be codified in scattered sections of 29 and 42 U.S.C.).

2 ACCESS TO THE COURTS AND ENFORCEMENT

1 Martin Luther King Jr., "Address at Western Michigan University," in *MLK at Western* (Kalamazoo, MI: Western Michigan University Archives and Regional History Collections and University Libraries, Dr. Martin Luther King Jr. 1963 WMU Speech Found 1963), http://wmich.edu/sites/default/files/attachments/MLK.pdf; Justin Taylor, "Martin Luther King Response to "You Can't Legislate Morality; You have to Change Hearts First," *TGC: The Gospel Coalition*, September 20, 2008, https://blogs.thegospelcoalition.org/justintaylor/2008/09/20/martin-luther-king-response-to-you-cant/.

2 In 1998, South Africa enacted the Employment Equity Act, which provides a hugely comprehensive definition of sexual harassment that is broader than the definition in the United States. The promotion of Equality and Prevention of Unfair Discrimination Act was passed in 2000, and it further supplements the EEA. Deborah Zalesne, "Sexual Harassment Law in the United States and South Africa: Facilitating the Transition from Legal Standards to Social Norms," *Harvard Women's Law Journal* 25 (2002): 147; Rika Joubert and William E. Thro, "Sexual Harassment in Elementary and Secondary Education: A Comparative Analysis of South Africa and the United States," *Education Law Report* 233 (2008): 16; Julie Goldscheid, "Gender Violence and Work in the United States and South Africa: The Parallel Processes of Legal and Cultural Change," *American University Journal Gender Social Policy and Law* 19 (2011): 933.

3 Zalesne, "Sexual Harassment Law," 194–95; see also Michelle J. Anderson, "Rape in South Africa," *Georgetown Journal Gender and Law* 1 (2000): 813; Goldscheid, "Gender Violence," 933; Joubert and Thro, "Sexual Harassment," 16.

4 King, Jr., "Address at Western Michigan University, 1963."

5 H. R. 7152. Passage, Govtrack, www.govtrack.us/congress/votes/88–1964/h128 (last visited August 26, 2016).

6 EEOC, *Charge Statistics, FY 1997 through FY 2015*, http://eeoc.gov/eeoc/statistics/enforcement/charges.cfm (last visited August 26, 2016).

7 See, e.g., Hilal Elver, "Racializing Islam Before and After 9/11: From Melting Pot to Islamophobia," *Transnational Law and Contemporary Problems* 21 (2012): 140; Ross Johnson, "A Monolithic Threat: The Anti-Sharia Movement and America's Counter-Subversive Tradition," *Washington and Lee Journal of Civil Rights and Social Justice* 19 (2012): 185; Yaser Ali, "Shariah and Citizenship–How Islamophobia Is Creating a Second-Class Citizenry in America," *California Law Review* 100 (2012): 1044.

8 See Theodore J. St. Antoine, "ADR in Labor and Employment Law During the Past Quarter Century," *American Bar Association Journal of Labor and Employment Law* 25 (2010): 418; Maurice E. R. Munroe, "The EEOC: Pattern and Practice Imperfect," *Yale Law and Policy Review* 13 (1995): 270 (discussing staffing and funding issues of EEOC).

9 See, e.g., Mark D. Robins, "The Resurgence and Limits of the Demurrer," *Suffolk University Law Review* 27 (1993): 640.

10 Ibid., 641.

11 Ibid., 643.

12 See Linda S. Mullenix, "The Counter-Reformation in Procedural Justice," *Minnesota Law Review* 77 (1992): 380.

13 Federal Rules of Civil Procedure 8(a)(2).

14 355 US 41 (1957).

15 Ibid., 45.

16 Ibid., 48.

17 Adam N. Steinman, "The Irrepressible Myth of Celotex: Reconsidering Summary Judgment Burdens Twenty Years After the Trilogy," *Washington and Lee Law Review* 63 (2006): 87.

18 See Arthur R. Miller, "From *Conley* to Twombly to *Iqbal*: A Double Play on the Federal Rules of Civil Procedure," *Duke Law Journal* 60 (2010): 7; Amber A. Pelot, Note, "*Bell Atlantic Corp.* v. *Twombly*: Mere Adjustment or Stringent New Requirement in Pleading?," *Mercer Law Review* 59 (2008): 1371.

19 534 US 506 (2002).

20 Bennett v. Schmidt, 153 F.3d 516, 518 (1998).
21 Ibid.
22 550 US 544 (2007).
23 556 US 662 (2009).
24 15 U.S.C. § 1.
25 Twombly v. Bell Atl. Corp., 313 F. Supp. 2d 174 (S.D.N.Y. 2003).
26 Twombly v. Bell Atl. Corp., 425 F.3d 99 (2d Cir. 2005), *rev'd*, 550 US 544 (2007).
27 *Twombly*, 550 US at 573.
28 556 US 662 (2009).
29 *Iqbal*, 556 US at 678.
30 Ibid., 681.
31 Ibid., 687.
32 Ibid., 687–99.
33 See Federal Rules Civil Procedure 26, 34 (requiring initial disclosure and guidelines for requests to produce evidence).
34 See EEOC, FY2015 Performance and Accountability Report 11 (2015).
35 551 F. Supp. 2d 439 (E.D.N.C. 2008).
36 Joseph A. Seiner, "The Trouble with *Twombly*: A Proposed Pleading Standard for Employment Discrimination Cases," *University of Illinois Law Review* 2009, 1031.
37 Joseph A. Seiner, "Pleading Disability," *Boston College Law Review* 50 (2010): 118.
38 Additionally, it is entirely possible that many plaintiffs abandoned their claims after seeing the test created by the Court in *Twombly*. This would skew the meaning of the numbers being achieved by the data set of later cases.
39 See David Freeman Engstrom, "The Twiqbal Puzzle and Empirical Study of Civil Procedure," *Stanford Law Review* 65 (2013): 1205 n.7 (listing twenty studies published and unpublished studies offering empirical analysis of *Twombly* and *Iqbal*'s impact).
40 Professor Engstrom laments the "steep opportunity costs that arise from the unproductive diversion of scholarly capacity into time-consuming and resource-intensive empirical projects." Ibid., 1236. He notes that "[i]t is hard to imagine a better illustration of this than the tens of thousands of hours of research effort reflected in ... Twiqbal studies." Ibid. My major disagreement with this conclusion is the remarkable value that many of these studies added to the legal academy. When the *Twombly/Iqbal* cases were first issued, there was substantial confusion in this area as to their meaning and impact. These studies helped provide substantial guidance in this area, focusing light on the plausibility standard's impact on different areas of the law. The studies further began an impressive debate on this topic, and set the stage for additional, more refined analyses that would come in later years. In addition, such studies uncover irrational results in specific cases, as those discussed, which may have gone undetected without such analysis.
41 2008 WL 141574 (N.D. Ind. January 11, 2008).
42 *Urbanski*, 2008 WL 141574, at *9.
43 2008 WL 659503 (N.D. Tex. February 26, 2008).
44 *Williams*, 2008 WL 659503, at *1.
45 496 F.3d 773 (2007).
46 Joseph A. Seiner, "After *Iqbal*," *Wake Forest Law Review* 45 (2010): 179, 222–23.
47 Swierkiewicz v. Sorema N.A., 534 US 506, 512, 514–15 (2002).
48 *Twombly*, 550 US at 570.
49 David L. Noll, "The Indeterminacy of *Iqbal*," *Georgetown Law Journal* 99 (2010): 144.

50 al-Kidd v. Ashcroft, 580 F.3d 949 (9th Cir. 2009).

51 Fowler v. UPMC Shadyside, 578 F.3d 203, 211 (3d Cir. 2009).

52 See Joseph Seiner, "Plausibility Beyond the Complaint," *William & Mary Law Review* 53 (2012): 987.

53 See, e.g., Taddeo v. L.M. Berry and Co., 526 F. App'x 121, 122 (2d Cir. 2013) (quotation omitted) (explaining *McDonnell Douglas* framework for intentional discrimination); see also Nancy L. Zisk, "What Is Old Is New Again: Understanding *Gross* v. *FBL Financial Services, Inc.* and the Case Law That Has Saved Age Discrimination Law," *Loyola Law Review* 58 (2012): 799 ("It is not easy, and sometimes not even possible, to prove an employer's discriminatory intent, but McDonnell Douglas and its progeny give courts, as well as employees and employers, the framework they need to ferret out discrimination.").

54 Credit Suisse First Boston, LLC v. Intershop Commc'ns, 407 F. Supp. 2d 541, 546 (S.D.N.Y 2006) (internal quotation marks and bracket omitted).

55 See, e.g., United States v. Portions of Sale of Lakes Region Greyhound Park, 2008 WL 187598, at *1 n.2 (D.N.H. January 17, 2008); Safe Bed Techs. Co. v. KCI USA, Inc., 2003 WL 21183948, at *2 (N.D. Ill. May 20, 2003).

56 Compare, e.g., Hayden v. United States, No. 3:14-CV-1060-AC, 2015 WL 350665, at *2 (D. Or. January 26, 2015) ("[T]his court finds the principles set forth in *Twombly* and *Iqbal* are the appropriate standard to apply to a motion which challenges the factual sufficiency of a pleaded defense."); Constr. Indus. Laborers Pension Fund v. Explosive Contractors, Inc., No. 12-2624-EFM, 2013 WL 3984371, at *2 (D. Kan. August 1, 2013) ("This Court agrees with *Hayne* and those jurisdictions that have interpreted the *Twombly/Iqbal* standard as applicable to affirmative defenses."), with Mifflinburg Tel., Inc. v. Criswell, 80 F. Supp. 3d 566, 573 (M.D. Pa. 2015) ("[T]he plausibility standard applicable to pleading claims based on a 'showing' does not apply to affirmative defenses that a party must merely 'state.'"); Lockheed Martin Corp. v. United States, 973 F. Supp. 2d 591, 595 (D. Md. 2013) ("[T]he Court declines to hold that *Twombly* and *Iqbal* apply to affirmative defenses.").

57 See, e.g., Holdbrook v. Saia Motor Freight Line, LLC, 2010 WL 865380 (D. Colo. March 8, 2010); Ameristar Fence Prods. v. Phoenix Fence Co., 2010 WL 2803907 (D. Ariz. July 15, 2010); First Nat'l Ins. Co. of Am. v. Camps Servs., 2009 WL 22861 (E.D. Mich. January 5, 2009).

58 Francisco v. Verizon South, Inc., 2010 WL 2990159 (E.D. Va. 2010).

59 Palmer v. Oakland Farms, 2010 WL 2605179 (W.D. Va. 2010).

60 United States v. Quadrini, 2007 WL 4303213 (E.D. Mich. 2007).

61 Seiner, "After *Iqbal*," 222–23.

62 See generally Swierkiewicz v. Sorema N.A., 534 US 506, 510–11 (2002) (establishing that a Title VII plaintiff does not need to plead a *prima facie* case to survive a motion to dismiss).

63 See generally Bell Atlantic Corp. v. Twombly, 550 US 544 (2007).

64 Seiner, "The Trouble with *Twombly*," 1047.

65 Ibid.

66 See, e.g., US Postal Serv. Bd. of Governors v. Aikens, 460 US 711, 715 (1983) ("[T]he prima facie case method established in *McDonnell Douglas* was 'never intended to be rigid, mechanized, or ritualistic.'").

67 Bennett v. Schmidt, 153 F.3d 516, 518 (7th Cir. 1998).

68 Suja A. Thomas, "The New Summary Judgment Motion: The Motion to Dismiss Under *Iqbal* and *Twombly*," *Lewis and Clark Law Review* 14 (2010): 18.

69 Federal Rules of Civil Procedure 12(a)(1).

70 John H. Marks, "Smoke, Mirrors, and the Disappearance of "Vicarious" Liability: The Emergence of a Dubious Summary-Judgment Safe Harbor for Employers Whose Supervisory Personnel Commit Hostile Environment Workplace Harassment," *Houston Law Review* 38 (2002): 1419 ("Preventive measures typically consist of formalized anti-harassment policies and grievance procedures that include a harassment complaint mechanism.").

71 Nancy R. Mansfield and Joan T. A. Gabel, "An Analysis of the *Burlington* and *Faragher* Affirmative Defense: When Are Employers Liable?," *Labor Lawyer* 19 (2003): 124 ("District and circuit courts have generally found that the employer will prevail [on the second prong] if either (1) a reasonable person in the employee's position would have come forward earlier or to a designated manager in order to prevent the harassment from becoming more severe or (2) the employee fails entirely to report the harassment." (citations omitted)).

72 See Kendall W. Hannon, "Much Ado About *Twombly*? A Study of *Bell Atlantic Corp. v. Twombly* on 12(b)(6) Motion," *Notre Dame Law Review* 83 (2008): 1811–46.

73 In 2009, Senator Arlen Specter introduced the Notice and Pleading Restoration Act of 2009. The proposed bill would have reverted the standard for dismissing complaints under Rules 12(b)(6) or (e) back to that established in *Conley v. Gibson*, 355 US 41 (1957). The bill was read twice and referred to the Senate Committee on the Judiciary, but never took off. See Notice and Pleading Restoration Act of 2009, S. 1504, 111th Cong. (2009). In addition, Representative Jerrold Nadler introduced the Open Access to Courts Act of 2009 in the House. This bill would have amended 28 U.S.C. § 2078 to say, "(a) A court shall not dismiss a complaint under subdivision (b)(6), (c) or (e) of Rule 12 of the Federal Rules of Civil Procedure unless it appears beyond doubt that the plaintiff can prove no set of facts in support of the claim which would entitle the plaintiff to relief. A court shall not dismiss a complaint under one of those subdivisions on the basis of a determination by the judge that the factual contents of the complaint do not show the plaintiff's claim to be plausible or are insufficient to warrant a reasonable inference that the defendant is liable for the misconduct alleged." The bill was referred to the House Committee on the Judiciary and the Subcommittee on Courts and Competition Policy. While Subcommittee hearings took place in December 2009, no further action has yet been taken on this bill. See Open Access to Courts Act of 2009, H.R. 4115, 111th Cong (2009).

74 See Richard B. Stewart, "The Discontents of Legalism: Interest Group Relations in Administrative Regulation," *Wisconsin Law Review*, 1985, 662.

75 See Marc Galanter, "The Vanishing Trial: An Examination of Trials and Related Matters in Federal and State Courts," *Journal of Empirical Legal Studies* 1 (2004): 462–63, Table 1 (highlighting that civil trials were dropping from 1962, long before *Twombly* and *Iqbal*).

76 See Joe S. Cecil et al., "A Quarter-Century of Summary Judgment Practice in Six Federal District Courts," *Journal of Empirical Legal Studies* 4 (2007): 883 (showing that between 1975 and 2000, the percent of summary judgment motions granted in whole or in part and cases terminated by summary judgment nearly doubled).

77 See Honorable Mark W. Bennett, "From the 'No Spittin', No Cussin' and No Summary Judgment' Days of Employment Discrimination Litigation to the "Defendant's Summary Judgment Affirmed Without Comment" Days: One Judge's Four-Decade Perspective," *New York Law School Law Review* 57 (2013): 687–88 (noting that while Title VII was still "in its infancy," "summary judgment motions were filed less frequently").

78   477 US 242, 247–48 (1986).

79   477 US 317, 323 (1986).

80   475 US 574, 587 (1986).

81   See Patricia M. Wald, "Summary Judgment at Sixty," *Texas Law Review* 76 (1998): 1914–17 (exploring critical views of *Celotex* trilogy).

82   See Elizabeth M. Schneider, "The Changing Shape of Federal Civil Pretrial Practice: The Disparate Impact on Civil Rights and Employment Discrimination Cases," 158 *University of Pennsylvania Law Review* 158 (2010): 520. See generally Suja A. Thomas, *The Missing American Jury: Restoring the Fundamental Constitutional Role of the Criminal, Civil, and Grand Juries* (New York: Cambridge University Press, 2016).

83   Arthur R. Miller, "The Pretrial Rush to Judgment: Are the "Litigation Explosion," "Liability Crisis," and Efficiency Clichés Eroding Our Day in Court and Jury Trial Commitments?," *New York University Law Review* 78 (2003): 1041. See also Bennett, "From the 'No Spittin', No Cussin' and No Summary Judgment' Days," 690–91.

84   Kevin M. Clermont and Stewart J. Schwab, "How Employment Discrimination Plaintiffs Fare in Federal Court," *Journal of Empirical Legal Studies* 1 (2004): 438.

85   See Joseph Seiner, "The Failure of Punitive Damages in Employment Discrimination Cases: A Call for Change," *William and Mary Law Review* 50, no. 3 (2008): 735.

86   Ibid.

87   Bennett, "From the 'No Spittin', No Cussin' and No Summary Judgment' Days."

88   Ibid., 688.

89   See generally Theresa M. Beiner, "The Many Lanes Out of Court: Against Privatization of Employment Discrimination Disputes," *Maryland Law Review* 73 (2014): 838–39; John Bronsteen, "Against Summary Judgment," *George Washington Law Review* 75 (2007): 522–51; Brooke D. Coleman, "The Vanishing Plaintiff," *Seton Hall Law Review* 42 (2012): 502; Deborah Thompson Eisenberg, "Stopped at the Starting Gate: The Overuse of Summary Judgment in Equal Pay Cases," *New York Law School Law Review* 57 (2013): 816; Angela K. Herring, "Untangling the *Twombly-McDonnell* Knot: The Substantive Impact of Procedural Rules in Title VII Cases," *New York University Law Review* 86 (2011): 1084; Brian N. Lizotte, "Publish or Perish: The Electronic Availability of Summary Judgments by Eight District Courts," *Wisconsin Law Review*, 2007, 109–10; Ann C. McGinley, "Cognitive Illiberalism, Summary Judgment, and Title VII: An Examination of *Ricci v. DeStefano*," *New York Law School Law Review* 57 (2013): 866–67; Elizabeth M. Schneider and Honorable Nancy Gertner, "'Only Procedural': Thoughts on the Substantive Law Dimensions of Preliminary Procedural Decisions in Employment Discrimination Cases," *New York Law School Law Review* 57 (2013): 768–69; Elizabeth M. Schneider, "The Changing Shape of Federal Civil Pretrial Practice: The Disparate Impact on Civil Rights and Employment Discrimination Cases," *University of Pennsylvania Law Review* 158 (2010): 517; Elizabeth M. Schneider, "The Dangers of Summary Judgment: Gender and Federal Civil Litigation," *Rutgers Law Review* 59 (2007): 706–7; Stephen N. Subrin and Thomas O. Main, "The Fourth Era of American Civil Procedure," *University of Pennsylvania Law Review* 162 (2014): 1840–41.

90   Suja A. Thomas, "Why the Motion to Dismiss Is Now Unconstitutional," *Minnesota Law Review* 92 (2008): 1851–90.

91   Ricci v. DeStefano, 557 US 557 (2009).

92   Ibid., 562.

93   Ibid.

94 Ibid., 564.
95 Ibid., 566.
96 Ibid.
97 Ibid., 569.
98 Ibid., 588.
99 Ibid., 572.
100 Ibid., 573.
101 Ibid. (citations omitted).
102 Ibid., 560.
103 Ibid., 579 (emphasis added).
104 Ibid.
105 Ibid.
106 Ibid., 579.
107 Ibid., 584.
108 Ibid., 585.
109 Ibid.
110 Ibid., 589.
111 Ibid., 587–90.
112 Ibid., 592.
113 Ibid., 593.
114 Ibid.
115 Ibid., 594–96 (Scalia, J, concurring).
116 Ibid., 593.
117 Ibid.
118 Ibid., 596. Justice Alito, joined by Justices Scalia and Thomas, wrote a separate concurrence as well, addressing the dissent's concerns that "the Court's recitation of the facts leaves out important parts of the story." Ibid., 596–609 (Alito, J., concurring).
119 Ibid., 609 (Ginsburg, J., dissenting).
120 Ibid., 644 (quoting Griggs v. Duke Power Co., 401 US 424, 431 (1971)).
121 See Michael J. Zimmer, "*Ricci*'s 'Color-Blind' Standard in a Race Conscious Society: A Case of Unintended Consequences?," *Brigham Young University Law Review* (2010): 1257–1307.
122 Scholars have already questioned the validity of the statistical approach taken by the lower courts, however. See Joseph L. Gastwirth and Weiwen Miao, "Formal Statistical Analysis of the Data in Disparate Impact Cases Provides Sounder Inferences than the US Government's 'Four-Fifths' Rule: An Examination of the Statistical Evidence in *Ricci v. DeStefano*," *Law, Probability and Risk* 8 (2009): 173 (arguing that, under the framework used by the lower court, there is a 60 percent chance that even a perfectly fair test will be found to have a disparate impact).
123 Richard Primus, "The Future of Disparate Impact," *Michigan Law Review* 108 (2010): 1341.

3 CLASS ACTIONS, SYSTEMIC CLAIMS, AND ARBITRATION

1 Eve Tahmincioglu, "*Wal-Mart* Ruling Raises the Bar for Class Actions," *NBC News*, June 21, 2011, 7:59:35 AM, www.nbcnews.com/id/43468398/ns/business-careers/t/wal-mart-rulingraises-bar-class-actions (archived at http://perma.cc/H4KB-G5E3).

2   Andrew Longstreth, "*Wal-Mart* v. *Dukes* Shakes Up Employment Class Actions," *Reuters*, January 9, 2012, 7:19 PM, www.reuters.com/article/2012/01/10/us-walmart-study-idUSTRE 8090132 0120110 (archived at http://perma.cc/78VS-VEGL).

3   See Deborah R. Hensler, "Of Groups, Class Actions, and Social Change: Reflections on *From Medieval Group Litigation to the Modern Class Action*," *University of California at Los Angeles Law Review Discourse* 61 (2013): 126–34.

4   Federal Rules of Civil Procedure 23(b)(3).

5   See Kalee DiFazio, "CAFA's Impact on Forum Shopping and the Manipulation of the Civil Justice System," *Suffolk Journal of Trial and Appellate Advocacy* 17 (2012): 133; Richard Maloy, "Forum Shopping? What's Wrong with That?," *Quinnipiac Law Review* 24 (2005): 49 (noting that class-action suits have forced some courts to apply forum shopping principles).

6   431 US 324, 339 (1977).

7   See Gen. Tel. Co. of the Nw. v. EEOC, 446 US 318, 323 (1980).

8   Wal-Mart Stores, Inc. v. Dukes, 564 US 339, 342 (2011).

9   Ibid., 344–45.

10   Ibid.

11   Ibid., 352.

12   Ibid., 359–60 (quoting C.J. Kozinski, 603 F.3d. at 652) (dissenting).

13   Ibid., 368.

14   Ibid., 371.

15   Ibid., 374.

16   Ibid., 377.

17   Tristin K. Green, "The Future of Systemic Disparate Treatment Law," *Berkeley Journal of Employment and Labor Law* 32 (2011): 397.

18   Noah D. Zatz, "Introduction: Working Group on the Future of Systemic Disparate Treatment Law," *Berkeley Journal of Employment and Labor Law* 32 (2011): 387.

19   Michael Selmi, "Theorizing Systemic Disparate Treatment Law: After *Wal-Mart* v. *Dukes*," *Berkeley Journal of Employment and Labor Law* 32 (2011): 479.

20   See, e.g., Melissa Hart, "Civil Rights and Systemic Wrongs," *Berkeley Journal of Employment and Labor Law* 32 (2011): 457 ("Individual claims alone simply will not ensure – or even permit – full enforcement of federal civil rights laws."); Suzette M. Malveaux, "How Goliath Won: The Future Implications of *Dukes* v. *Wal-Mart*," *Northwestern University Law Review Colloquy* 106 (2011): 34, http://scholarlycommons.law.northwestern.edu/cgi/viewcontent .cgi?article=1054&context=nulr_online; George Rutherglen, "*Wal-Mart, AT&T Mobility*, and the Decline of the Deterrent Class Action," *Virginia Law Review in Brief* 98 (2012): 24.

21   563 US 333 (2011).

22   Ibid., 351.

23   Gen. Tel. Co. of the Nw. v. EEOC, 446 US 318, 323 (1980).

24   See generally EEOC v. United Road Towing, Inc., No. 10 C 6259, 2012 WL 1830099, at *3 (N.D. Ill. May 11, 2012) ("[T]he Court will not inquire into whether the EEOC's administrative investigation adequately supported the claims of the 17 claimants on behalf of whom the EEOC has brought suit.").

25   See EEOC's Opposition to Texas Roadhouse's Motion to Dismiss at 11 n.8, EEOC v. Tex. Roadhouse, Inc., No. 1:11-cv-11732-DJC (D. Mass. November 9, 2012); EEOC's Response in Opposition to Defendants' Motion to Dismiss First Amended Complaint at 12, EEOC v. Bass Pro Outdoor World, LLC, No. 11-CV-03425 (S.D. Tex. April 3, 2012).

26 Charles Alan Wright et al., *Federal Practice and Procedure*, vol. 18, 2nd ed. (Eagan, MN: Thomson West, 2002), § 4402 (internal quotation marks omitted).

27 Ibid.

28 Ibid.

29 See *American Jurisprudence*, vol. 47, *Judgments*, 2nd ed. (Eagan, MN: West, 2012): § 571.

30 See John Bernard Corr, "Supreme Court Doctrine in the Trenches: The Case of Collateral Estoppel," *William and Mary Law Review* 27 (1985): 41–42 (footnotes omitted) (citing Parklane Hosiery Co., Inc. v. Shore, 439 US 322, 332–33 (1979)).

31 See ibid., 41–42.

32 See Wright et al., *Federal Practice and Procedure*, § 2383.

33 Ibid. ("The district court is given broad discretion to decide whether consolidation under Rule 42(a) would be desirable and the district judge's decision inevitably is highly contextual").

34 See Federal Rules of Civil Procedure 42(a) (allowing consolidation for actions with common questions of law or fact).

35 Ibid.

36 See generally Wright et al., *Federal Practice and Procedure*, § 2383, 35 n.2.

37 Wal-Mart Stores, Inc. v. Dukes, 546 US 338, 341, 358 n.9, 359 (2011) (internal citation and quotation omitted).

38 Ibid., 342 (majority opinion).

39 See Developments in the Law, "The Paths of Civil Litigation," *Harvard Law Review* 113 (2000): 1810 (noting benefits to defendants of class-action litigation).

40 Federal Rules of Civil Procedure 23(c)(4). Prior to the 2007 amendments to the Federal Rules of Civil Procedure, issue class certification was authorized by Rule 23(c)(4)(A). See Federal Rules of Civil Procedure 23(c)(4)(A) (2006) (repealed 2007). In 2007, subparts (A) and (B) were removed, and the issue class provision was relabeled 23(c)(4); the change did not alter the Rule's substantive meaning. See Federal Rules of Civil Procedure 1, advisory committee's note to 2007 amendment ("Subdivisions have been rearranged within some rules to achieve greater clarity and simplicity"); ibid. 23, advisory committee's note to 2007 amendment ("The language of Rule 23 has been amended as part of the general restyling of the Civil Rules to make them more easily understood").

41 See ibid. (c)(4) (allowing the certification of specific issues in a case).

42 See Charles Alan Wright et al., *Federal Practice and Procedure*, vol. 7AA, 3rd ed. (Eagan, MN: Thomson West, 2005): § 1790 (quoting Jenkins v. United Gas Corp., 400 F.2d 28, 34 (5th Cir. 1968)).

43 See Note 40, Federal Rules of Civil Procedure 23(c)(4).

44 See Jonathan Fineman, "The Inevitable Demise of the Implied Employment Contract," *Berkeley Journal of Employment and Labor Law* 29 (2008): 353 (discussing an employer's "often informal" regulations and practices)

45 See Joseph A. Seiner, "The Failure of Punitive Damages in Employment Discrimination Cases: A Call for Change," *William and Mary Law Review* 50 (2008): 735–96.

46 See Exxon Shipping Co. v. Baker, 554 US 471, 2620–21 (2008) (discussing purposes of punitive relief); David G. Owen, "A Punitive Damages Overview: Functions, Problems and Reform," *Villanova Law Review* 39 (1994): 374–77 (discussing role of punitive damages); Jim Gash, "Solving the Multiple Punishments Problem: A Call for a National Punitive Damages Registry," *Northwestern University Law Review* 99 (2005): 1670 (same); Seiner, "Failure of Punitive Damages," 745–47 (same).

47 *Exxon Shipping Co.*, 554 US at 492; see generally Seiner, "Failure of Punitive Damages," 492 (discussing recent Supreme Court case law on punitive damages).

48 Cf. Nancy Levit, "Megacases, Diversity, and the Elusive Goal of Workplace Reform," *Boston College Law Review* 49 (2008): 372 ("Although the threats of large economic losses (from litigation defense costs and risks of damage awards) and adverse publicity can be the catalysts for settlement, those economic risks do not, on their own, seem to be sufficient factors to prompt significant restructuring of workplaces.").

49 See 42 U.S.C. § 1981a(b)(3).

50 See Hart, "Civil Rights and Systemic Wrongs."

51 Ibid., 474.

52 Ibid.

53 See Malveaux, "How Goliath Won."

54 Ibid.

55 Ibid., 52.

56 311 US 32 (1940).

57 Ibid. See Joshua A. Rosenthal, "The Case against Constitutionalized Commonality Standards for Collective Civil Litigation," *Yale Law and Policy Review* 32 (2013): 316 ("At the core of the constitutionalized commonality claim is an imagined form of the defendant's 'day in court' ideal.").

58 *Hansberry*, 311 US at 42.

59 490 US 755 (1989).

60 527 US 815 (1999).

61 Ibid., 846.

62 Rosenthal, "Case against Constitutionalized Commonality Standards," 314.

63 See Lubin v. Wackenhut, No. BC326 996 (L.A. Cty. Sup. Ct. August 1, 2012); Jacobsen v. Allstate Ins. Co., 310 P.3d 452 (2013); Duran v. US Bank Nat'l Ass'n, 137 Cal. Rptr. 3d 391 (Ct. App.), *petition for review granted*, 275 P.3d 1266 (Cal. 2012). See generally Rosenthal, "The Case against Constitutionalized Commonality Standards," 316 (discussing state court litigation over constitutionalizing commonality).

64 No. BC326 996 (L.A. Cty. Sup. Ct. August 1, 2012)

65 Ibid.

66 Lubin v. Wackenhut, No. BC326 996 (L.A. Cty. Sup. Ct. August 1, 2012), Chamber of Commerce Amicus Curiae Brief, JCCP4545, B244383 at 36.

67 Jacobsen v. Allstate Ins. Co., 310 P.3d 452 (2013).

68 Allstate Ins. Co. v. Jacobsen, No. 13–916 (petition for *certiorari*) (submitted March 2014), *cert. denied*, May 2014.

69 Ibid., 7 (quotation omitted) (citing *Wal-Mart*, 564 US at 347).

70 See generally Wal-Mart Stores, Inc. v. Dukes, 564 US 338 (2011).

71 *Wal-Mart*, 564 US at 342. See generally Suja A. Thomas, "How Atypical, Hard Cases Make Bad Law (See, e.g., the Lack of Judicial Restraint in *Wal-Mart, Twombly*, and *Ricci*)," *Wake Forest Law Review* 48 (2013): 989–1025 (discussing the highly unusual nature of the facts of the *Wal-Mart* case).

72 See generally *Wal-Mart*, 564 US 338.

73 Ibid., 353.

74 Ibid., 349 (quoting Dukes v. Wal-Mart Stores Inc., 603 F.3d 571, 652 (2009) (Kozinski, C. J., dissenting)).

75 Ibid.

76 Ibid., 350.
77 Ibid., 349.
78 See generally ibid.
79 Ibid.
80 See generally ibid.
81 Ibid.
82 Joseph A. Seiner, "Commonality and the Constitution: A Framework for Federal and State Court Class Actions," *Indiana Law Journal* 91 (2016): 455–91. In sum, to satisfy the Due Process Clause of the Constitution with regard to commonality, all complex litigation must have:

1. A uniform company policy or problem;
2. A policy effectuated by management-level employees;
3. Common harm;
4. Mutual questions shared by all plaintiffs;
5. Questions that are capable of resolution across the entire class.

4 RETALIATION: THE LAST SAFE HAVEN FOR PLAINTIFFS

1 See Joanna L. Grossman and Deborah L. Brake, "Revenge: The Supreme Court Narrows Protection against Workplace Retaliation in University of Texas Southwestern Medical Center v. Nassar," *Verdict Justia*, July 9, 2013, https://verdict.justia.com/2013/07/09/revenge-the-supreme-court-narrows-protection-against-workplace-retaliation-in-university-of-texas-southwestern-medical-center-v-nassar (noting that the Court is more concerned about protecting employers from lawsuits than it is about fully protecting employees from retaliation).
2 See Burlington N. & Santa Fe Ry. Co. v. White, 548 US 53, 54 (2006) (citing Robinson v. Shell Oil Co., 519 US 337, 346 (1997)) (noting that the primary purpose of anti-retaliation provisions is maintaining unfettered access to statutory remedial mechanisms).
3 See Haines City HMA, Inc. v. Carter, 948 So. 2d 904, 905 (Fla. Dist. Ct. App. 2007) (holding that the plaintiff was fired for filing a charge alleging gender and pregnancy discrimination); Smith v. Xerox Corp., 584 F. Supp. 2d 905, 906 (N.D. Tex. 2008), *aff'd*, 602 F.3d 320 (5th Cir. 2010) (noting that Xerox fired the plaintiff shortly after the plaintiff complained to the EEOC of age and gender discrimination).
4 See, e.g., Jamie Darin Prenkert et al., "Retaliatory Disclosure: When Identifying the Complainant Is an Adverse Action," *North Carolina Law Review* 91 (2013): 898 n.35. It is, however, difficult to gather concrete data on this issue, so the higher success rates suggested by several sources may be somewhat speculative. See, e.g., David Sherwin et al., "Experimental Evidence that Retaliation Claims Are Unlike Other Employment Discrimination Claims," *Seton Hall Law Review* 44 (2014): 486.
5 See EEOC, "EEOC Releases Fiscal Year 2015 Enforcement and Litigation Data," Press Release, February 11, 2016 (Retaliation: 44.5 percent of all charges filed in 2015, Race: 34.7 percent of all charges filed in 2015).
6 42 U.S.C. § 2003e-3(a).
7 Hamilton v. Geithner, 666 F.3d 1344, 1357 (D.C. Cir. 2012) (quoting Woodruff v. Peters, 482 F.3d 521, 529 (D.C. Cir. 2007)).
8 See Robinson v. Shell Oil Co., 519 US 337 (1997).

9 See Clark Cty. Sch. Dist. v. Breeden, 532 US 268 (2001) (asserting that no reasonable person could have believed that the single incident violated Title VII's standard); Spadola v. N.Y.C. Transit Auth., 242 F. Supp. 2d 284, 292 (S.D.N.Y. 2003) (holding that there was not sufficient evidence to establish that the plaintiff's belief was subjectively genuine or objectively reasonable).

10 Pettway v. Am. Cast Iron Pipe Co., 411 F.2d 998, 1007 (5th Cir. 1969) (holding a false and malicious letter to EEOC protected); Proulx v. Citibank, N.A., 659 F. Supp. 972, 979 (S.D.N.Y. 1987) (upholding protection for an employee who filed with an appropriate agency a Title VII discrimination claim, although it was false and malicious).

11 562 US 170, 171 (2011) (citation omitted).

12 Ibid., 178.

13 Compare McCoy v. City of Shreveport, 492 F.3d 551, 559 (5th Cir. 2007) (holding that for all Title VII claims, "[a]dverse employment actions include only ultimate employment decisions such as hiring, granting leave, discharging, promoting, or compensating" (citation omitted)), with Verges v. Shelby Cty. Sheriff's Office, 721 F. Supp. 2d 730, 739 (W.D. Tenn. 2010) (noting that an adverse employment action does not need to rise to the level of an ultimate employment decision to be actionable, the employer's conduct must create a "serious and material" change to the terms, conditions, or privileges of the employee's employment).

14 548 US 53 (2006).

15 350 F.3d 716 (2003).

16 Ibid., 723.

17 Burlington N. & Santa Fe Ry. Co. v. White, 548 US 53, 68 (2006).

18 Ibid.

19 Ibid.

20 Ibid., 70–71.

21 Ibid., 72.

22 Michael P. Spellman, "A Primer on Retaliation," *Trial Advocate Quarterly* 28, no. 4 (2009): 29 (noting that the Supreme Court's decision in *Burlington Northern* sent shock waves in the area of retaliation, and after the decision, the number of retaliation claims filed with EEOC greatly increased).

23 *Burlington Northern*, 548 US at 70–71 (2006).

24 See, e.g., Ledbetter v. Goodyear Tire & Rubber Co., 550 US 618 (2007), *overturned due to legislative action* (January 29, 2009); Price Waterhouse v. Hopkins, 490 US 228 (1989); Wards Cove Packing Co. v. Atonio, 490 US 642 (1989).

25 133 S. Ct. 2517 (2013).

26 Ibid., 2536.

27 See Gross v. FBL Fin. Serv. Inc., 557 US 167 (2009).

28 *Nassar*, 133 S. Ct. at 2534.

29 Ibid. (Ginsburg, J., dissenting).

30 Ibid., 2535.

31 Ibid., 2547.

32 Ibid.

33 Ibid.

34 Ibid.

35 532 US 268 (2001).

36 Ibid., 269.

37 Ibid.

38 Ibid., 271.

39 Ibid.

40 See Lawrence D. Rosenthal, "Reading Too Much into What the Court Doesn't Write: How Some Federal Courts Have Limited Title VII's Participation Clause's Protections After *Clark County School District v. Breeden,*" *Washington Law Review* 83 (2008): 345.

41 458 F.3d 332 (4th Cir. 2006); see Gwendolyn Leachman, "*Jordan v. Alternative Res. Corp.*: The Fourth Circuit Limits Protection from Retaliation for Employees Reporting a Hostile Work Environment," *Berkeley Journal of Employment and Labor Law* 28 (2007): 599.

42 *Jordan,* 458 F.3d at 336.

43 Ibid., 341.

44 See John M. Husband et al., "Trying Discrimination and Retaliation Claims in Tandem – How Jurors React," *Colorado Lawyer* 41 (2012): 46 (asserting that statistics reveal that retaliation lawsuits are more likely to prevail at trial and recover significant damages than typical discrimination claims).

45 See generally Max Messmer, "The Delicate Art of Reference Checking," *Business Credit* 101, no. 5 (May 1999): 40, www.questia.com/magazine/1G1-54711182/the-delicate-art-of-reference-checking (noting that 74 percent of Fortune 1000 companies have a policy limiting employee references to a confirmation of basic employment information); Markita D. Cooper, "Beyond Name, Rank, and Serial Number: 'No Comment' Job Reference Policies, Violent Employees and the Need for Disclosure-Shield Legislation," *Virginia Journal of Social Policy and Law* 5 (1998): 287–339.

5 STRIKING AT RELIEF

1 "Jurors Hit Exxon Mobil with $11.9-Billion Verdict," *Los Angeles Times,* November 15, 2003, http://articles.latimes.com/2003/nov/15/business/fi-newexxon15. The $11.8 billion punitive damage award involved a dispute with the state of Alabama over how gas royalties should have been calculated. See generally Exxon Mobil Corp. v. Ala. Dep't of Conservation & Natural Res., 986 So. 2d 1093 (Ala. 2007). The trial court reduced the jury's punitive damage award to $3.5 billion. Ibid., 1100. The Alabama Supreme Court subsequently eliminated all of the punitive damages in the case. Ibid., 1116–18.

2 David G. Owen, "A Punitive Damages Overview: Functions, Problems and Reform," *Villanova Law Review* 39 (1994): 370 (quoting Fay v. Parker, 53 N.H. 342, 382 (1872)).

3 Fay v. Parker, 53 N.H. 342, 382 (1872).

4 Owen, "Punitive Damages Overview," 377–78.

5 Anon., "An Economic Analysis of the Plaintiff's Windfall from Punitive Damage Litigation," *Harvard Law Review* 105 (1992): 1900 (quoting E. Donald Elliott, "Why Punitive Damages Don't Deter Corporate Misconduct Effectively," *Alabama Law Review* 40 (1989): 1055).

6 Linda L. Schlueter and Kenneth R. Redden, *Punitive Damages,* 4th ed. (Conklin, NY: LexisNexis Matthew Bender, 2000), 1: 1; Melvin M. Belli, Sr., "Punitive Damages: Their History, Their Use and Their Worth in Present-Day Society," *University of Missouri Kansas City Law Review* 49 (1980): 2.

7 See Justice Janie L. Shores, "A Suggestion for Limited Tort Reform: Allocation of Punitive Damage Awards to Eliminate Windfalls," *Alabama Law Review* 44 (1992): 64.

8 Schlueter and Redden, *Punitive Damages*, 1: 1.

9 Belli, "Punitive Damages," 3.

10 Ibid., 4.

11 See Mark A. Peterson, Syam Sarma, and Michael G. Shanley, *Punitive Damages, Empirical Findings* (Santa Monica, CA: RAND Corp., 1987), 1–2 (discussing the American history of punitive damages and setting forth the English decision of *Wilkes* v. *Wood*, Lofft 1, 98 Eng. Rep. 489 (K.B. 1763), which addressed punitive damages).

12 1 Bay. 6, 1784 WL 26 (S.C. Comm. Pl. 1784).

13 Coryell v. Colbaugh, 1 N.J.L. 77 (1791) (emphasis omitted).

14 See, e.g., Schlueter and Redden, *Punitive Damages*, 16 (discussing the history of punitive damages in the United States).

15 54 US 363 (1851).

16 *Woodworth*, 54 US at 371.

17 Schlueter and Redden, *Punitive Damages*, 16.

18 Owen, "Punitive Damages Overview," 369.

19 Shores, "Suggestion for Limited Tort Reform," 69. But see Stephen Daniels and Joanne Martin, *Historical Fiction: Punitive Damages, Change, and the Politics of Ideas* (Chicago: American Bar Foundation, 1996), 1–3 (discussing the legal debate over punitive damages and the argument for tort reform).

20 Am. Coll. of Trial Lawyers, "Report on Punitive Damages of the Committee on Special Problems in the Administration of Justice (1989)," 8, www.actl.com/library/report-punitive-damages-committee-special-problems-administration-justice; see generally Belli, "Punitive Damages," 4.

21 *Black's Law Dictionary*, 7th ed. (St. Paul, MN: West Group, 1999), 396.

22 Owen, "Punitive Damages Overview," 375.

23 See Jim Gash, "Solving the Multiple Punishments Problem: A Call for a National Punitive Damages Registry," *Northwestern University Law Review* 99 (2005): 1670.

24 See Steven Sneiderman, "The Future of Punitive Damages after *Browning-Ferris Industries* v. *Kelco Disposal*," *Ohio State Law Journal* 51 (1990): 1036 (quoting Oliver Wendell Holmes, *The Common Law* (Cambridge, MA: Harvard University Press, 1881), 4).

25 Ibid.

26 Lisa Litwiller, "From *Exxon* to *Engle*: The Futility of Assessing Punitive Damages as Against Corporate Entities," *Rutgers Law Review* 57 (2004): 324 (citing Pac. Mut. Life Ins. Co. v. Haslip, 499 US 1, 54 (1991) (O'Connor, J., dissenting)).

27 See, e.g., Owen, "Punitive Damages Overview," 377.

28 Leslie E. John, "Formulating Standards for Awards of Punitive Damages in the Borderland of Contract and Tort," *California Law Review* 74 (1986): 2053 (discussing the role of deterrence in punitive damage awards). See also Meredith Matheson Thoms, "Punitive Damages in Texas: Examining the Need for a Split–Recovery Statute," *St. Mary's Law Journal* 35 (2003): 216.

29 Owen, "Punitive Damages Overview," 374.

30 Ibid.

31 Owen, "Punitive Damages Overview," 380; see also Nathan C. Prater, "Punitive Damages in Alabama: A Proposal for Reform," *Cumberland Law Review* 26 (1995–96): 1030 (setting forth modern rationales for punitive damages including "inducement of private law enforcement").

32 See Anon., "Developments in the Law-Employment Discrimination and Title VII of the Civil Rights Act of 1964," *Harvard Law Review* 84 (1971): 1263.

33 See ibid.; Christine O. Merriman and Cora G. Yang, Note, "Employer Liability for Coworker Sexual Harassment Under Title VII," *New York University Review of Law and Social Change* 13 (1984–85): 112. See, e.g., Krista J. Schoenheider, "A Theory of Tort Liability for Sexual Harassment in the Workplace," *University of Pennsylvania Law Review* 134 (1986): 1462, 1475.

34 Lex K. Larson, *Civil Rights Act of 1991* (New York: Matthew Bender, 1992), 10.

35 Sharon T. Bradford, "Relief for Hostile Work Environment Discrimination: Restoring Title VII's Remedial Powers," *Yale Law Journal* 99 (1990): 1619.

36 H.R. REP. No. 102–40, pt.2, at 1. See, e.g., H.R. Rep. No. 102–40, pt.1, at 18 (1991).

37 H.R. REP. No. 102–40, pt.1, at 18.

38 Ibid., 70.

39 H.R. REP. No. 102–40, pt.1, at 1, 70.

40 Susan Schenkel-Savitt, "New and Improved Remedies for Intentional Discrimination and the Expanded Reach of Title VII and the Disabilities Acts," in *The Civil Rights Act of 1991: Its Impact on Employment Discrimination Litigation*, ed. Susan Ritz (New York: Practicing Law Institute, 1992), 219.

41 David A. Cathcart and Mark Snyderman, "The Civil Rights Act of 1991," *Labor Lawyer* 8, no. 4 (1992): 849–922.

42 Susan Ritz, "Introduction," in *The Civil Rights Act of 1991: Its Impact on Employment Discrimination Litigation*, ed. Susan Ritz (New York: Practicing Law Institute, 1992), 9.

43 42 U.S.C. § 1981a(b)(1) (2000).

44 See, e.g., Colleen P. Murphy, "Determining Compensation: The Tension Between Legislative Power and Jury Authority," *Texas Law Review* 74 (1995): 408.

45 527 US 526 (1999).

46 Ibid.

47 See generally ibid., 546.

48 See Jonathan C. Hancock and John B. Starnes, "Revisiting *Kolstad* v. *American Dental Association*: Reform of Punitive Damages Awards in Employment Discrimination Cases Since the Supreme Court Adopted the Standard of Malice or Reckless Indifference," *University of Memphis Law Review* 31 (2001): 658; Kim J. Askew, "Punitive Damages *Kolstad* v. *American Dental Association*," VPB0919 ALI-ABA (ALI-ABA Course of Study, September 19, 2000): 525, https://1.next.westlaw.com/Document/I7e80f0e1095211dc8e8a83d126d3a434/View/FullText.html?originationContext=typeAhead&transitionType=Default&contextData=(sc.Default).

49 See Anon., "The Supreme Court, 1998 Term, Leading Cases," *Harvard Law Review* 113 (1999): 359–60.

50 See ibid., 366 (quoting "High Court Ends Term with Important Rulings on ADA, Punitive Damages," *Pennsylvania Employment Law Letter* (Pittsburgh: Buchanan Ingersoll, 1999), 4).

51 Andrea Meryl Kirshenbaum, "*Kolstad* v. *American Dental Ass'n*: The Opportunity for Punitive Damages in Employment Discrimination Cases," *University of Pennsylvania Journal of Labor and Employment Law* 3 (2001): 645.

52 Tamara Schiffner, "Employment Law: The Employer Escape Chute from Punitive Liability Under *Kolstad* v. *American Dental Ass'n*," *Oklahoma Law Review* 54 (2001): 195–96.

53 Philip Morris USA v. Williams, 549 US 346, 349 (2007).

54 See generally ibid.

55 Ibid.

56 Kolstad v. Am. Dental Ass'n, 527 US 526, 538 (1999).

57 *Philip Morris*, 549 US at 357–58.

58 See generally ibid.

59 Exxon Shipping Co. v. Baker, 554 US 471 (2008).

60 See generally ibid.

61 Ibid., 501.

62 Ibid.

63 See generally ibid.

64 BMW of N. Am., Inc. v. Gore, 517 US 559, 568 (1996).

65 Ibid., 582–83.

66 State Farm Mut. Auto. Ins. Co. v. Campbell, 538 US 408 (2003).

67 Ibid., 425.

68 Exxon Shipping Co. v. Baker, 554 US 471, 502 (2008).

69 *Exxon*, 554 US at 501–02.

70 42 U.S.C. § 1981a(b)(3) (2006).

71 42 U.S.C. § 1981a(b)(3)(A)–(D).

72 Romano v. U-Haul Int'l, 233 F.3d 655, 673 (1st Cir. 2000).

73 Exxon Shipping Co. v. Baker, 554 US 471, 502 (2008); see also Abner v. Kan. City S. R. Co., 513 F.3d 154, 164 (5th Cir. 2008) ("Given that Congress has effectively set the tolerable proportion [for Title VII claims], the three-factor *Gore* analysis is relevant only if the statutory cap itself offends due process. It does not and, as we have found in punitive damages cases with accompanying nominal damages, a ratio–based inquiry becomes irrelevant.").

74 *Phillip Morris*, 549 US at 353–54.

75 *Romano*, 233 F.3d at 673.

76 EEOC v. Siouxland Oral Maxillofacial Surgery Assocs., 578 F.3d 921 (8th Cir. 2009).

77 Ibid. (internal quotation marks omitted).

78 Ibid., 924.

79 Ibid., 925.

80 Ibid., 927.

81 Ibid., 925.

82 466 F.3d 1156 (10th Cir. 2006). The damages provision of the ADA adopts the punitive damages standard set forth in Title VII. 42 U.S.C. § 1981a(a)(2). The author served as lead counsel in the *Heartway* case (as well as the *Stocks, Inc.* case, 228 F. App'x 429 (5th Cir. 2007), on behalf of the EEOC). The views expressed in this chapter are those of the author and do not represent the views of the EEOC or of the United States.

83 Ibid., 1168–71.

84 228 F. App'x 429 (5th Cir. 2007).

85 Ibid., 431–32. Interestingly, unlike the courts in *Siouxland* and *Heartway*, the Fifth Circuit refused to order a trial solely on the issue of punitive damages. Ibid., 432–33. Instead, the court left to the plaintiff "the choice of whether it wants a new trial on all issues, or wishes instead to retain its judgment [issued by the first jury]." Ibid., 433.

86 Canny v. Dr. Pepper/Seven-Up Bottling Grp., Inc., 439 F.3d 894, 905 (8th Cir. 2006).

87 Ibid., 905.

88 Ibid. (quoting Schlueter and Redden, *Punitive Damages*, § 4.4(B)(2)(a), at 181 (internal quotation marks omitted)).

89 Ibid.

90 Ibid. (quoting 2 James D. Ghiardi and John J. Kircher, *Punitive Damages: Law and Practice* (Deerfield, IL: Clark Boardman Callaghan, 1981 and 1996), 2:§ 24.05, 14 (1998) (internal quotation marks omitted)).

91 133 S. Ct. 2434 (2014).

92 The *Vance* case takes a limited approach as to the scope of who is a supervisor in work-place cases. Again, the court has used a "narrowed" technical approach to the statute, which limits the breadth of its reach for civil-rights litigants.

93 See Burlington Indus., Inc. v. Ellerth, 524 US 742, 759 (1998).

94 *Kolstad*, 527 US at 543 (citing *Restatement (Second) of Agency* § 217C (1957)).

95 Bruso v. United Airlines, Inc., 239 F.3d 848, 858 (7th Cir. 2001) (citing Passantino v. Johnson & Johnson Consumer Prods., Inc., 212 F.3d 493, 516 (9th Cir. 2000)).

96 Kolstad v. Am. Dental Ass'n, 527 US 526, 536–37 (1999).

97 See generally *Kolstad*, 527 US at 542–43 (quoting *Restatement (Second) of Agency* § 217C)).

98 Ibid., 544 (quoting *Restatement (Second) of Agency* § 230 cmt. B).

99 Ibid.

100 See Davey v. Lockheed Martin Corp., 301 F.3d 1204, 1209 & n.4 (citing Zimmermann v. Assocs. First Capital Corp., 251 F.3d 376, 385 (2d Cir. 2001); Romano v. U-Haul Int'l, 233 F.3d 655, 670 (1st Cir. 2000); Passantino v. Johnson & Johnson Consumer Prods., Inc., 212 F.3d 493, 516 (9th Cir. 2000); Deffenbaugh-Williams v. Wal-Mart Stores, Inc., 188 F.3d 278, 286 (5th Cir. 1999).

101 Federal Rules of Civil Procedures 50(a)–(b).

102 See, e.g., EEOC v. Stocks, Inc., 228 F. App'x 429, 432–33 (5th Cir. 2007) (holding that district court erred in failing to give punitive damages instruction and stating that "[a] future jury's decision to award punitive damages will be tied to the same evidence of intent as will be the liability decision, and the factual dispute surrounding the events leading to [the victim's] suspension will be central to the decision that [the defendant] retaliated in reckless indifference to her rights. By our remand, we leave to the [plaintiff] the choice of whether it wants a new trial on all issues, or wishes instead to retain its judgment [without punitive damages].").

103 See 42 U.S.C. § 1981a(b)(3) (2006).

104 42 U.S.C. § 2000e-2(a) (2006).

105 42 U.S.C. § 1981 (2006).

106 524 US 775 (1998).

107 524 US 742 (1998).

108 Burlington N. & Santa Fe Ry. Co. v. White, 548 US 53 (2006).

109 See Richard B. Stewart, "The Discontents of Legalism: Interest Group Relations in Administrative Regulation," *Wisconsin Law Review*, 1985, 662 ("The more certain the law – the less the variance of expected outcomes – the more likely the parties will predict the same outcome from litigation, and the less likely that litigation will occur because of differences in predicted outcomes.").

6 THE ON-DEMAND ECONOMY EXAMPLE

1 "Q&A: Robots, Uber and the Role of Government," *Financial Times*, June 25, 2015, www.ft.com/cms/s/0/ed5ec9c4-1b37-11e5-8201-cbdb03d71480.html#axzz3trC6MmtG.

2 See, e.g., "Defining 'Employee' in the Gig Economy," *New York Times*, July 18, 2015, www.nytimes.com/2015/07/19/opinion/sunday/defining-employee-in-the-gig-economy.html; Kathleen Hennessey, "The 'Gig Economy' Gets the Campaign Treatment," *Los Angeles Times*, July 13, 2015, 3:39 PM, www.latimes.com/nation/politics/la-na-gig-economy-20150713-story.html; Gabe Miano, "How Freelancers Can Thrive in 2015's Gig Economy," *Forbes*,

November 18, 2014, 10:12 AM, www.forbes.com/sites/groupthink/2014/11/18/how-freelancers-can-thrive-in-2015s-gig-economy/2/; Sara Ashley O'Brien, "The Uber Effect: Instacart Shifts Away from Contract Workers," *CNN Money*, June 22, 2015, 9:17 PM ET, http://money.cnn .com/2015/06/22/technology/instacart-employee-option/; Luke O'Neil, "Surviving the Gig Economy," *Boston Globe*, August 31, 2014, www.bostonglobe.com/opinion/2014/08/30/ surviving-gig-economy/kNnzDGxgu7nvju8JhdAKVN/story.html; Aimee Picchi, "One Startup Reconsiders the Merits of the 'Gig Economy,'" *CBS MoneyWatch*, June 23, 2015, 4:54 PM, www.cbsnews.com/news/one-startup-reconsiders-the-merits-of-the-gig-economy/; Tom Risen, "Hillary Clinton Boosts Workers, Blasts Uber," *US News & World Report*, July 13, 2015, 5:32 PM, www.usnews.com/news/articles/2015/07/13/hillary-clinton-boosts-workers-blasts-uber; Erik Sherman, "How the US Just Knee-Capped the 'Gig Economy,'" *Inc.com*, July 17, 2015, www.inc.com/erik-sherman/did-the-feds-just-knee-cap-the-gig-economy.html; James Surowiecki, "Gigs with Benefits," *New Yorker*, July 6 and 13, 2015, www.newyorker .com/magazine/2015/07/06/gigs-with-benefits; Mark R. Warner, "Asking Tough Questions about the Gig Economy," *Washington Post*, June 18, 2015, www.washingtonpost.com/ opinions/asking-tough-questions-about-the-gig-economy/2015/06/18/b43f2d0a-1461-11e5-9ddc-e3353542100c_story.html.

3　Cotter v. Lyft, Inc., 60 F. Supp. 3d 1067, 1070 (N.D. Cal. 2015) (order denying summary judgment); O'Connor v. Uber Techs., Inc., 82 F. Supp. 3d 1133, 1135–38 (N.D. Cal. 2015) (order denying summary judgment).

4　See, e.g., *O'Connor*, 82 F. Supp. 3d at 1137–38 (stating that "Uber bills itself as a 'technology company,' not a 'transportation company'").

5　*Cotter*, 60 F. Supp. 3d at 1081 (order denying summary judgment).

6　29 U.S.C. § 203(e)(1) (2012).

7　Ibid., § 203(g) (internal quotation marks omitted).

8　Antenor v. D & S Farms, 88 F.3d 925, 929 n.5 (11th Cir. 1996).

9　See Sec'y of Labor v. Lauritzen, 835 F.2d 1529, 1534–35 (7th Cir. 1987).

10　Bartels v. Birmingham, 332 US 126, 130 (1947), *superseded by statute*, Act of June 14, 1948, ch. 468, § 2(a), 62 Stat. 438, 438.

11　82 F. Supp. 3d 1133 (N.D. Cal. 2015) (order denying summary judgment).

12　Ibid., 1136 (internal quotation marks omitted).

13　Ibid., 1137, 1150–51.

14　See, e.g., Cal. Lab. Code § 2750.5 (2016).

15　*O'Connor*, 82 F. Supp. 3d at 1139 (citing S.G. Borello & Sons, Inc. v. Dep't of Indus. Relations (*Borello*), 769 P.2d 399, 404 (Cal. 1989) (en banc)).

16　Ibid., 1140–45 (internal quotation marks omitted). The holding, correct in our view, was significant because California law creates a presumption of employment once an individual establishes that he or she has performed work for the principal. Ibid., 1138. Thus, the court required Uber to rebut the presumption that its drivers were employees. Ibid., 1145.

17　60 F. Supp. 3d 1067 (N.D. Cal. 2015) (order denying summary judgment).

18　Ibid., 1072–73.

19　Ibid., 1072 (internal quotation marks omitted).

20　Ibid., 1069.

21　Ibid., 1070.

22　Sec'y of Labor v. Lauritzen, 835 F.2d 1529, 1539 (7th Cir. 1987) (Easterbrook, J., concurring).

23 See, e.g., Goldberg v. Whitaker House Coop., 366 US 28, 32–33 (1961) (assessing the economic reality of a cooperative).

24 *About Us*, DOORDASH, www.doordash.com/about/ (last visited January 27, 2016); *About Us*, GRUBHUB, http://about.grubhub.com/about-us/what-is-grubhub/default.aspx (last visited January 27, 2016).

25 Tan v. GrubHub, Inc., 2015 WL 5673027 (Super. Ct. Cal. 2015).

26 Ibid. at para. 9.

27 *Tan*, 2015 WL 5673027, at para. 10; see also Scott Holland, "Drivers Deliver Class Action Saying GrubHub Needs to Treat Them as Employees, Not Contractors," *Cook CountyRecord*, July 11, 2016, http://cockcountyrecord.com/stories/510955592-drivers-deliver-class-action-saying-grubhub-needs-to-treat-them-as-employees-not-contractors ("Drivers Earn a Flat Fee for Each Delivery Plus Tips").

28 Tan v. GrubHub, Inc., 2015 WL 5673027 para. 10 (Super. Ct. Cal. 2015).

29 Ibid. at para. 12; see also Tan v. Grubhub, 3:15-cv-05128 (Cal. N. Dist. Ct. 2015), www.pacermonitor.com/public/case/9899619/Tan_v_Grubhub,_Inc.

30 Kissner v. DoorDash, Inc., 2015 WL 5673036 (Cal. Super. Ct. 2015).

31 *What Is Instacart?*, INSTACART, www.instacart.com/help/section/200758544#204426950. See also Farhad Manjoo, "Grocery Deliveries in Sharing Economy," *New York Times*, May 21, 2014, www.nytimes.com/2014/05/22/technology/personaltech/online-grocery-start-up-takes-page-from-sharing-services.html?_r=0.

32 Instacart, "What Is Instacart?"; Manjoo, "Grocery Deliveries."

33 See Brian Solomon, "America's Most Promising Company: Instacart, The $2 Billion Grocery Delivery App," *Forbes*, January 21, 2015, www.forbes.com/sites/briansolomon/2015/01/21/americas-most-promising-company-instacart-the-2-billion-grocery-delivery-app/#5e4092544858.

34 See Moton v. Maplebear Inc., No. 1:15-cv-08879 (S.D.N.Y. Nov. 10, 2015); Bynum v. Maplebear Inc., No. 1:15-cv-06263 (E.D.N.Y. Oct. 30, 2015); Cobarruviaz v. Maplebear, Inc., No. 3:15-cv-00697-EMC (N.D. Cal. Feb. 13, 2015); Sumerlin v. Maplebear, Inc., No. BC 603030 (Cal. Super. Ct. Dec. 2, 2015).

35 See Complaint, Cobarruviaz v. Maplebear, Inc., No. 3:15-cv-00697-EMC (N.D. Cal. February 13, 2015).

36 See ibid.

37 See ibid. at para. 41, 42.

38 See ibid. at para. 42.

39 See ibid. at para. 53.

40 See Complaint, para. 45, Cobarruviaz v. Maplebear, Inc., No. 3:15-cv-00697-EMC (N.D. Cal. February 13, 2015).

41 See ibid. at para. 64.

42 See ibid. at para. 47.

43 See Memorandum and Order, Bynum v. Maplebear Inc., No. 1:15-cv-06263 (E.D.N.Y. Oct. 30, 2015); Order Granting Defendant's Motion to Compel Arbitration, Cobarruviaz v. Maplebear, Inc., No. 3:15-cv-00697-EMC (N.D. Cal. February 13, 2015).

44 *About Amazon Prime Now*, AMAZON, www.amazon.com/gp/help/customer/display.html?nodeId=201687630.

45 Truong v. Amazon.com, Inc., 2015 WL 6501019 (Cal. Super. Ct. 2015).

46 Ibid. at para. 1.

47 Ibid. at para. 18 and 25.

48 See ibid.

49 Ibid. at para. 20.

50 Ibid. at para. 21.

51 Ibid. at para. 23.

52 *About Us*, YELP, www.yelp.com/about (last visited September 9, 2016).

53 See ibid.

54 Ibid. ("Every business owner (or manager) can setup a free account to post photos and message their customers."); Complaint against Defendant Yelp Inc., Lily Jeung et al. v. Yelp Inc., 3:15-CV-02228 (August 8, 2014), 2015 WL 4776424; see also Lydia O'Connor, "Yelp Reviewers File Class-Action Lawsuit Claiming They Are Unpaid Writers," *Huffington Post*, October 13, 2013, www.huffingtonpost.com/2013/10/30/yelp-lawsuit-_n_4179663.html.

55 *See* Jeung v. Yelp, Inc., 2015 WL 4776424 (N.D. Cal. 2015).

56 Ibid.

57 Ibid.

58 *About Handy*, HANDY, www.handy.com/about (last visited January 27, 2016).

59 Zenelaj v. Handybook, 82 F. Supp.3d 968, 975 (N.D. Cal. 2015).

60 Ibid.

61 Zenelaj v. Handybook, 82 F. Supp.3d 968 (N.D. Cal. 2015); see also Maya Kosoff, "Two Workers Are Suing a Cleaning Startup Called Handy over Alleged Labor Violations," *BusinessInsider*, November 12, 2014, www.businessinsider.com/handy-cleaning-lawsuit-2014-11.

62 Zenelaj v. Handybook, 82 F. Supp.3d 968 (N.D. Cal. 2015).

63 *About Postmates*, POSTMATES, https://about.postmates.com/ (last visited September 21, 2016).

64 See Singer v. Postmates, Inc., No. 4:15-cv-01284-KAW (N.D. Cal. March 19, 2015); Peppler v. Postmates, Inc., No. 2015-CA-006560 B (D.C. Super. Ct. August 25, 2015); Marable v. Postmates, Inc., No. BC 589 052 (Cal. Super. Ct. July 23, 2015). See also Katy Steinmetz, "Homejoy, Postmates, and Try Caviar Sued over Labor Practices," *Time*, March 19, 2015, http://time.com/3751745/postmates-homejoy-try-caviar-lawsuits/.

65 See Collective and Class Action Complaint and Jury Demand, Singer v. Postmates, Inc., No. 4:15-cv-01284-KAW (N.D. Cal. March 19, 2015).

66 Ibid.at para. 17.

67 See ibid. at para. 19.

68 Jessica Karmasek, "Boston Plaintiffs Attorney Targets Startup Companies in Class Actions," *Legal Newsline*, May 27, 2016, http://legalnewsline.com/stories/510743555-boston-plaintiffs-attorney-targets-startup-companies-in-class-actions.

69 *About Us*, CROWDFLOWER, www.crowdflower.com (last visited January 27, 2015).

70 *Success Stories*, CROWDFLOWER, https:// success.crowdflower.com/ hc/ en- us/ articles/ 201856129- Platform- Overview (last visited September 9, 2016) ("When users log in to CrowdFlower and create a new job, the first option that appears is to load data into the job.").

71 See ibid.

72 Otey v. CrowdFlower, Inc., 2014 WL 1477630, at *1 (N.D. Cal. 2014).

73 Ibid. at *2.

74 *Crowdsourcing Supplier Settles Class Action Lawsuit*, STAFFING INDUSTRY ANALYSTS, July 8, 2015, www.staffingindustry.com/Research-Publications/Publications/CWS-3.0/July-2015/July-8-2015/Crowdsourcing-supplier-settles-class-action-lawsuit.

75 See Lora Kolodny, "Homejoy Raises $38M for House Cleaning on Demand," *Wall Street Journal: Venture Capital Dispatch*, December 5, 2013, 9:00 AM, http://blogs.wsj.com/venturecapital/2013/12/05/homejoy-raises-38m-for-house-cleaning-on-demand/.

76 See Kolodny, "Homejoy Raise $38M"; Kia Kokalitcheva, "Home Cleaning Startup Homejoy Bites the Dust – Literally," *Fortune*, July 17, 2015, 3:05 PM, http:// fortune.com/ 2015/ 07/ 17/ homejoy- closing- cleaning- google/ .

77 See Kolodny, "Homejoy Raise $38M."

78 See Iglesias v. Homejoy, Inc., No. 3:15-cv-c1286 (N.D. Cal. March 19, 2015); Ventura v. Homejoy, Inc., No. CGC-15-544750 (Cal. Super. Ct. March 16, 2015); Zenelaj v. Homejoy, Inc., No. CGC-15-544599 (Cal. Super. Ct. March 9, 2015); Malveaux-Smith v. Homejoy, Inc., No. 37-2015-00005070-CU-OE-CTL (Cal. Super. Ct. February 13, 2015).

79 See ibid.

80 Collective and Class Action Complaint and Jury Demand, Iglesias v. Homejoy, Inc., No. 3:15-cv-01286 (N.D. Cal. March 19, 2015).

81 Class Action Complaint for Damages, para. 43, Ventura v. Homejoy, Inc., No. CGC-15-544750 (Cal. Super. Ct. March 16, 2015).

82 Ibid.

83 See ibid. at para. 37.

84 See ibid. at para. 44.

85 Class Action Complaint for Damages, para. 35, Ventura v. Homejoy, Inc., No. CGC-15-544750 (Cal. Super. Ct. March 16, 2015).

86 See ibid. at para. 39.

87 Ibid. at para. 40.

88 See Kokalitcheva, *supra* note 77; Ellen Huet, "Homejoy Shuts Down, Citing Worker Misclassification Lawsuits," *Forbes*, July 17, 2015, 2:58 PM, www.forbes.com/sites/ellenhuet/ 2015/07/17/cleaning-startup-homejoy-shuts-down-citing-wor ker-misclassification-lawsuits/ #1006dcb87780.

89 See Brian Solomon, "Washio, the On-Demand Laundry Startup, Washes Out," *Forbes*, August 30, 2016, 3:16 PM, www.forbes.com/sites/briansolomon/2016/08/30/washio-the-on-demand-laundry-startup-washes-out/#97aa85a68361

90 Taranto v. Washio, Inc., No. CGC-15-546584 (Cal. Super. Ct. June 29, 2015). See Biz Carson, "The Lawyer Fighting for Uber and Lyft Employees Is Taking the Fight to Four More Companies," *Business Insider*, July 1, 2015, 5:18 PM, www.businessinsider .com/postmates-shyp-and-washio-hit-with-legal-action-from-contractors -2015–7. See also Bennett v. Washio, Inc., No. BC603067 (L.A. Super. Ct. December 8, 2015) (a separate case brought against Washio but not discussed here).

91 Class Action Complaint and Jury Demand, para. 11, Taranto v. Washio, Inc., No. CGC-15-546584 (Cal. Super. Ct. June 29, 2015).

92 Ibid. at para. 11, 12.

93 Ibid. at para. 14.

94 See Solomon, *supra* note 90; Shan Li, "On-Demand Laundry Start-Up Washio Shuts Down," *Los Angeles Times*, August 30, 2016, 4:10 PM, www.latimes.com/business/la-fi-washio-startup-20160830-snap-story.html.

95 See Tan v. GrubHub, Inc., 2015 WL 5673027 (Super. Ct. Cal. 2015).

96 See Truong v. Amazon.com, Inc., 2015 WL 6501019 (Cal. Super. Ct. 2015).

97 See Jeung v. Yelp, Inc., 2015 WL 4776424 (N.D. Cal. 2015).

98 Cf. Estate of Suskovich v. Anthem Health Plans of Va., Inc., 553 F.3d 559 (7th Cir. 2009) (merely setting work schedule is not sufficient to support finding that person is employee rather than independent contractor, nor is the fact that person is required to be at given place at given time or assigned project work sufficient to support employer-employee relationship). See, e.g., Nationwide Mut. Ins. Co. v. Darden, 503 US 318, 323 (1992) (determining that "hired party's discretion over when and how long to work" is a consideration in whether someone is an employee).

7 THE SOLUTION

1 *Scent of a Woman* (Universal City, CA: Universal Films, 1992).
2 McReynolds v. Merrill Lynch, Pierce, Fenner & Smith, Inc., 672 F.3d 482 (7th Cir. 2012), *cert. denied*, 133 S. Ct. 338.
3 133 S. Ct. 2517 (2013).
4 532 US 268 (2001).
5 See Notice Pleading Restoration Act of 2009, S. 1504, 111th Cong. (2009) (introduced by Arlen Specter); Open Access to Courts Act of 2009, H.R. 4115, 111th Cong. (2009).
6 133 S. Ct. at 2534 (Ginsburg, J., dissenting).
7 527 US 471 (1999).